BATAAN SURVIVOR

The American Military Experience Series
John C. McManus, Series Editor

The books in this series portray and analyze the experience of Americans in military service during war and peacetime from the onset of the twentieth century to the present. The series emphasizes the profound impact wars have had on nearly every aspect of recent American history and considers the significant effects of modern conflict on combatants and noncombatants alike. Titles in the series include accounts of battles, campaigns, and wars; unit histories; biographical and autobiographical narratives; investigations of technology and warfare; studies of the social and economic consequences of war; and in general, the best recent scholarship on Americans in the modern armed forces. The books in the series are written and designed for a diverse audience that encompasses nonspecialists as well as expert readers.

BATAAN SURVIVOR

A POW'S Account of Japanese Captivity in World War II

David L. Hardee

Edited by Frank A. Blazich, Jr.

UNIVERSITY OF MISSOURI PRESS
Columbia

University of Missouri Press, Columbia, Missouri 65211
Printed and bound in the United States of America First printing, 2016.
First paperback printing, 2026.

Paperback ISBN: 978-0-8262-2369-2
Library of Congress Catalog Number: 2016937789

™This paper meets the requirements of the
American National Standard for Permanence of Paper
for Printed Library Materials, Z39.48, 1984.

Typefaces: Frutiger and Minion

Contents

Editor's Preface

In many respects, this current work is only available due to a series of coincidences and instances of good fortune, not the least of which being Colonel Hardee's survival. I stumbled on his memoir in the course of my doctoral studies. While researching the civil defense history of North Carolina in the fall of 2009, I happened upon a small item in the November–December 1969 North Carolina Civil Defense Agency newsletter, mentioning the passing of the colonel. Two sentences about Hardee's life caught my eye: "His distinguished military career lasted from World War I to 1949, when he retired with twenty decorations, including the Distinguished Service Cross and Bronze Star. He was a survivor of the Battle of Bataan, the infamous Death March and three years as a prisoner of war."

Thus began my journey back to the dark days of World War II. After an initial internet query proved disappointing, a reference in the footnotes of Duane Heisinger's *Father Found* pointed to a copy of the Hardee memoir located at the U.S. Military Academy Library. Out of sheer curiosity, I hunted through the collections of the various state and university libraries in North Carolina, but I could not turn up a copy of the memoir. It was through working with two fellow graduate students, Geoff Earnhart and Will Waddell, that I finally got my hands on Hardee's text. Geoff obtained the memoir for me to transcribe, and Will proofed my typing.

Locating Hardee's family initially proved challenging. After finding Hardee's 1969 obituary on microfilm archives, I located his son-in-law, Dr. Lee Remmers, who had married Hardee's eldest daughter, Elizabeth, at INSEAD graduate business school in Fontainebleau, France. I emailed Dr. Remmers on April 9, 2012, coincidentally, the seventieth anniversary of Bataan's surrender.

In his reply, he acknowledged awareness of the manuscript but noted the amount of editing required had thwarted previous publishing attempts. Elizabeth Frances Hardee Remmers had passed away in 1979, but Dr. Remmers put me in touch with his late wife's sister, Mary Hardee Stutz.

From my first phone call in April 2012 to the present, I have had the greatest pleasure in working with "Miss Mary" to bring her father's story to press. My first visit in June 2012 was an absolute treat as we spoke at length about her father's service. With her permission, I drove home that evening transporting the personal papers and artifacts her father had carried throughout the war in the Philippines and oversaw their donation to the State Archives of North Carolina and the North Carolina Museum of History, respectively. Through a contact in the U.S. Army Awards and Decorations Branch, I assisted Miss Mary in submitting paperwork for a review of her father's military service record. This effort resulted in his retroactively receiving the Prisoner of War Medal, a second Purple Heart for gas exposure in World War I, and other additions to his service decorations. Tragically, Miss Mary passed away on October 11, 2016 while the memoir was being typeset, but she went to the Lord knowing her father's story would be told at last.

In presenting this memoir, every effort has been made to retain Hardee's original text and structure. Using a blend of primary and secondary sources—especially other prisoner memoirs—I have attempted to provide for Hardee's story a thorough contextual underpinning. I intentionally placed an emphasis on using published memoirs and other scholarly works to make this story as accessible as possible to both general readers and scholars.

As is often the case with an early draft, names and geographical locations were frequently misspelled in the original manuscript, and where I could confirm the appropriate names, these have been amended. In the interest of consistency, terminology and abbreviations have been standardized throughout the text. Other vestiges of the memoir's origins as a seemingly spoken text, such as paragraphs composed of one or two sentences or idiosyncratic punctuation or spelling, have given way to complete paragraphs and regularized punctuation and spelling. In rare instances, subtle editing has provided clarity for inexplicable word choice or sentence structure. Fortunately, little of Hardee's writing required modification.

Readers may take issue with the decision to retain the period language, notably Hardee's references to the Japanese as "Japs." Hardee's animosity and racist descriptions of his captors are the products of his experiences during the conflict, and he rarely shares such attitudes toward Filipinos or other cultures in his writing; therefore, I have chosen to leave them as written by Hardee.

Hardee's story would not now be in the light of day without the time, energy, and support of countless people. I wish to express my gratitude to my former colleagues at the Ohio State University—Major Geoff Earnhart, for obtaining a copy of the memoir from West Point's library, and Dr. William Waddell, for assisting in the location of source material, proofing the manuscript, and assisting in the editing process. Without their work and good counsel, this project would never have advanced beyond an internet search.

In addition, no book comes together without the assistance of the family. From the Hardee family, I wish to thank Dr. Lee Remmers for sharing memories of his father-in-law. Most of all, I am indebted to Mrs. Mary Hardee Stutz, who opened up her home and warmly welcomed me, generously giving her time to provide invaluable insight into her father and clarification of facts about points in his life.

My own family has supported me throughout this project. My older sister, Joan, assisted with editing oversight on the text and notes, and my brother-in-law, Brian, always had a good word when I hit a wall. My father died unexpectedly before this book's publication. A keen historian in his own right, he took a great interest in Hardee's story and made editorial suggestions after reviewing the manuscript. My mother listened to my research quandaries, supported trips to the archives, and could always be depended upon for an encouraging hug and a supportive chat.

In the course of my work, I crossed paths with a number of archivists, historians, researchers, colleagues, and friends who have all contributed to the final product. Dr. Robert Doyle, Mr. Kenrick Simpson, Dr. Joe Porter, Dr. John McManus, Ms. Sara Davis, Mr. Clair Willcox, Ms. Diann Benti, Ms. Kim Andersen, Mr. Phil Zubiate, Mrs. Mary P. Johnson, and Mr. Wesley Injerd helped with research, literary, or technical questions. To the friends from graduate school and federal service with whom I have shared this memoir I express my deepest appreciation for keeping my spirits up and faith strong. Notably, a gracious thank-you to Dr. James Bartholomew, the late Dr. John "Joe" Guilmartin, Dr. Peter Mansoor, Mr. Zack Fry, Major Shauna Hann, Mr. Tom Reilly, and Mrs. Sharon Reilly. Finally, a hearty salute to Colonel Hardee for saving his part of the past, thus granting me the privilege of sharing his story with you.

Acronyms

AA	Anti-aircraft
C.O.	Commanding officer
Dapecol	Davao Penal Colony
FEAF	Far East Air Force
G-1	General headquarters staff officer, personnel
G-2	General headquarters staff officer, intelligence
G-3	General headquarters staff officer, operations
G-4	General headquarters staff officer, supply
G.I.	"Government Issue," expression to refer to an American soldier
LUBSEC	Luzon Base Section
MP	Military Police
PA	Philippine Army
PBY	Patrol bomber (Consolidated Aircraft)
P.I.	Philippine Islands
POW	Prisoner of War
PS	Philippine Scouts
QM	Quartermaster
R.H.I.P.	"Rank has its privileges"
S-1	Executive headquarters staff officer, personnel
S-2	Executive headquarters staff officer, intelligence
S-3	Executive headquarters staff officer, operations
S-4	Executive headquarters staff officer, supply
S.O.Q.	Sick Officers' Quarters
USAFFE	United States Army Forces in the Far East
USFIP	United States Forces in the Philippines
WPO-3	War Plan Orange, No. 3

Editor's Introduction

Few conflicts completely transformed modern society like World War II. Countless men and women around the globe were caught up in the conflagration, and millions lost their lives. The proliferation of literature by historians who examine practically every facet of World War II shows no sign of abating, but fewer firsthand accounts are published as the years go by and remaining participants pass away. Personal memoirs and collected interviews allow readers to "hear the voices" of the men and women who experienced the twentieth century's worst catastrophe. In the memoir that follows this introduction, the distinctive voice of Colonel David Lyddall Hardee comes through strong and clear.

Hardee was born on September 16, 1890, to Dr. Parrott Rastus Hardee and Roberta Buford Bacon Hardee. The land on which the Hardees' home was built is now part of the Camp Butner Military Reservation in Granville County, North Carolina. The Hardees belonged to the emerging white-collar middle class, and they reared their children—seven boys and a girl—in a culture permeated by respect for education, faith, and work. Hardee graduated from Stem High School in 1909, and from Trinity College in 1913. His first job was with the Atlantic Coast Realty Company, but he soon moved on to become public relations officer for the Wachovia Bank and Trust Company of Winston-Salem, a job he kept for three years. On January 29, 1918, Hardee enlisted in the army, joining Company H, 61st Infantry, 5th Division. He shipped out with the 61st Infantry to France on April 1, 1918, and joined the 28th Infantry, 1st Infantry Division on September 1.[1]

While overseas, he rose through the ranks from private to corporal to sergeant. After completing a sixty-day officer candidate training school at

Sergeant David L. Hardee, late summer 1918, prior to receiving his commission in France. **Source: Mary Hardee Stutz.**

Langres, France, Hardee received his commission as a second lieutenant on September 25. As a member of the 3d Battalion, 28th Infantry, Hardee participated in defensive operations in the Anould Sub-Sector, Montdidier-Noyon, and St. Die Sectors, as well as in offensive actions in the Meuse-Argonne and Maison-Sedan. He proved to be an able and competent infantry officer, receiving three Silver Stars for valor and a Purple Heart for gas exposure. Promotion followed gallantry, and Hardee rose to first lieutenant on October 25, 1918. Following the Armistice, he served in the army of occupation in Germany at the Coblenz Bridgehead.[2]

When Hardee returned home in September 1919, he decided to remain in the army, and he spent the next several years moving from post to post. He was first stationed with the 28th Infantry at Camp Zachary Taylor in Kentucky then transferred to North Carolina where he served as a recruiting officer for the First Division in 1920. For his work there, he received a commendation from division commander Major General Charles P. Summerall. After graduating from the Infantry School Basic Course at Fort Benning, Georgia, in 1922, Hardee was stationed at Fort Ontario and Plattsburg, New York. That same year, on October 5, in Salisbury, North Carolina, he married Elizabeth Neely Harry of Charlotte. In 1924, Hardee became the first infantry officer and nonaviator to graduate from the Air Corps Tactical School, Langley Field, Virginia, and was sent to Fort Sam Houston, Texas, then finally returned to Fort Benning, where he became an instructor at the Infantry School.[3]

As a member of the 24th Infantry, Hardee taught the tactics of defense of infantry against aircraft. Hardee's instruction was the first of its kind for ground service schools and a model for future course development. While Hardee was stationed at Fort Benning, his first daughter, Elizabeth Frances, was born (May 18, 1927). During this time Hardee also authored several short articles in the *Infantry Journal* regarding infantry defense against air attack and the relationship between aviation and the infantry.[4]

On September 12, 1929, Hardee and his family moved to the Philippines where he served with the 31st Infantry in the Cuartel de España in Manila. His second daughter, Mary Lucille, was born on December 18, 1931, in Sternberg General Hospital, Manila. From February to July 1932, Hardee and the 31st Infantry deployed to Shanghai to support the 4th Marine Regiment in defense of the international settlement. For his Shanghai service, the commandant of the Marine Corps awarded Hardee the Yangtze Service Medal in 1935. On July

30, 1932, he returned to the United States and served with the 12th Infantry at Fort Howard, Maryland, until 1934. After Hardee's promotion to captain on October 1, 1934, the army ordered him to Winston-Salem where he served as instructor of organized reserves for the 322nd Infantry until August 1938. Thereafter, he moved to Oak Ridge, North Carolina, to assume the position of professor of military science and tactics at the private Oak Ridge Military Institute, where he was promoted to major on July 1, 1940.[5]

Last prewar family portrait, October 1941 (clockwise, starting at left): Elizabeth H. Hardee, David L. Hardee, Elizabeth F. Hardee, Mary L. Hardee. **Source: Mary Hardee Stutz.**

Following President Franklin D. Roosevelt's declaration of an unlimited national emergency in 1941, the army ordered Hardee to Camp Wheeler, Georgia, where he trained new recruits in the fundamentals of infantry tactics. On September 15, the army promoted him to lieutenant colonel, and a week later he was advised that General Douglas MacArthur had selected him, along with hundreds of other infantry officers, to sail to Manila to assist in the organization and training of ten new Filipino divisions. Hardee arrived in the Philippines once more on November 20, 1941.[6]

In December 1941, the men and women in the Philippines could not have anticipated the years of struggle that lay ahead. Although General MacArthur had taken command of American and Filipino forces in July 1941 and developed plans to prepare the archipelago's defenses, Japanese attacks in December 1941 swiftly destroyed his air and naval assets, driving his army into the Bataan Peninsula. His forces were determined to hold out as long as possible, preferably until a relief force could arrive from Hawaii or Australia. Once hostilities commenced, Hardee found himself initially attached to the headquarters, United States Army Forces in the Far East (USAFFE). For the first weeks of the war he handled a series of administrative tasks for General MacArthur's chief of staff, but on January 26, 1942, USAFFE assigned him as executive officer of the Provisional Air Corps Regiment under the command of Colonel Irvin E. Doane. The makeshift regiment consisted of grounded airmen from the destroyed Far East Air Force.[7]

One of the "Battling Bastards of Bataan," Hardee would remain on the front lines seventy-three consecutive days as American and Filipino forces fought to hold the Bataan Peninsula against the Imperial Japanese Army. Promised relief never came, and in February 1942, President Roosevelt ordered General MacArthur to leave the command for Australia. Outmanned, outgunned, and unsupplied, the Americans and Filipinos were overwhelmed by the Japanese and forced to surrender on April 9, 1942. It remains the largest surrender in American history. Taken prisoner the following day, Hardee would spend the next thirty-four months in Japanese captivity.[8]

The vanquished forces in the Philippines faced an aftermath of death and misery unprecedented in the American military experience. Approximately 78,100 prisoners, including 11,796 Americans, had surrendered on Bataan, and 25,580 Americans would be captured in the Philippines by mid-1942; 10,650 of them would die in captivity. The infamous Death March claimed the lives of

600 to 650 Americans and approximately 10,000 Filipinos. Those who made it to the prisons faced a deadly triad of disease, malnutrition, and physical abuse, and approximately 4,100 Americans would die at Camps O'Donnell and Cabanatuan by the end of 1942. Thousands more would perish at sea when the U.S. Navy attacked and sank the unmarked Japanese prison "hellships."[9]

The Japanese were caught unprepared and had little in the way of provision for so many prisoners. The Japanese had provided humane, courteous treatment to prisoners in the Russo-Japanese War and World War I in accordance with Bushidō tradition, but the xenophobic nationalism of the 1930s as well as revisions to the Japanese Field Service Code in 1940 had excised the elements of humanity from Bushidō and codified capture as disgrace. The altered view of POWs coupled with an emphasis on obedience and self-discipline, often enforced by physical abuse, increased the likelihood that Japanese soldiers would view and treat prisoners as releases for their own frustrations and sadistic impulses.

For Hardee and his compatriots in Japanese captivity, the 1929 *Convention Relative to the Treatment of Prisoners of War* signed in Geneva proved a hollow document. The Japanese government had signed the document but never ratified the convention at home. On January 29, 1942, in response to American and Allied inquiries, the Japanese government announced that it would observe the convention *mutatis mutandis* (with necessary modifications) relative to the treatment of prisoners, observing the convention when not in conflict with Japanese policies and regulations. With international law absent in the Pacific, the prisoner accounts that emerged described Japanese atrocities, torture, and depravity. The POW accounts mirrored the testimony later given at war crime tribunals in Asia, in which Japanese prison camp guards and officers were held responsible for the crimes. These accounts, in some cases from escaped prisoners, shocked and angered those in America.[10]

Narratives of the Philippine POW experience first emerged in 1944. Several prisoners who successfully escaped from the Davao Penal Colony on Mindanao brought the first news of the Death March and atrocities to America's military and civilians. After the Japanese surrender in September 1945, additional chronicles by former Japanese POWs corroborated and added to these stories. Some prisoners had kept wartime diaries, which they published. Hardee wrote his account immediately following his liberation, although it remained private.[11]

As the second half of the twentieth century unfolded, other prisoners published accounts of their experiences. Three tiers of literature connected to the

Philippine POWs have emerged: decades of memoirs by participants often written years after the events they describe; journalistic histories incorporating oral histories or postwar testimonies; and previously unpublished or "lost" memoirs. Scholarly histories discussing the POW experience under the Japanese have drawn upon such prisoner accounts to craft a strong corpus of literature about what befell MacArthur's surrendered forces.[12]

Following his liberation on February 4, 1945, in Manila, Hardee began to rebuild his body and career. Promotion came swiftly, and he was made a colonel on February 23, 1945. Physical recovery came more slowly, as he had to regain seventy pounds he had lost as a POW. For the third and final time in his military career, he returned to the United States, traveling aboard the SS *Cape Meares* from April to May 1945.

During the voyage, he drafted the 195-page account of his war experiences and time as a prisoner of war. The memoir was initially distributed only to family and friends. This candid account, filled with vivid detail of events still fresh in his mind, described the grim realities facing the American and Filipino forces on Bataan, the utter depravity of some of their Japanese guards, and the complex relationship between the American POWs and their Japanese captors. His unabashed commentary about interprisoner relations and the dynamics of collaboration and resistance offers insights into the battle for survival under the worst of conditions. While Hardee's animosity toward and disdain for the Japanese and their actions is strongly expressed in the account, he grudgingly acknowledges the humanity of some of his captors. Hardee also meticulously singles out a number of men for their courage and devotion to their comrades and country. Regrettably, the majority of men Hardee recognized perished in the final months of the war aboard Japanese hellships sunk by American submarines or aircraft.[13]

Hardee's recollections are invaluable. They provide a remarkable window into the actions and events that ultimately claimed the lives of so many individuals. As a previously "lost" memoir, his story conforms to the framework of other American POW accounts, with a narrative arc exhibiting major responses to captivity—namely resistance, survival, assimilation, and lamentation. Hardee bore witness to the death of countless friends and comrades. In these pages, he voices emotions that range from gratitude to disgust, from grief to adulation, when he describes those who shared his deplorable circumstances.[14]

Hardee was one of the few lieutenant colonels with both headquarters and regimental level experience in the Philippines to survive and document his time as a POW. He is the highest ranking member of the Provisional Air Corps Regiment to document the impromptu unit's fight on Bataan. Unlike memoirs written decades after the wars they recall, when details became hazy and the writer's perspective altered by time, Hardee's is stark and fresh, a voice straight from 1945 unaffected by the writings of other prisoners or scholars. The immediacy of his recollections of the atrocities and close connections to notable events and celebrated commanders of the Philippines campaign make the memoir an especially powerful and useful account of the battle, the Death March, and the subsequent imprisonment.

Upon his return to the United States on May 12, 1945, Hardee took time to further recover from his ordeal. During his convalescent leave at the Walter Reed General Hospital in July 1945, doctors treated a debilitating hernia he had suffered while at the Davao Penal Colony. With the war in Europe over and all resources devoted to defeating Japan, Hardee gave several public talks in North Carolina about his experience. Following the Japanese surrender, he provided sworn affidavits to army investigators on potential Japanese war crimes. He revised his manuscript in apparent hopes of publication. He continued his revisions into the early 1960s, occasionally rewriting portions, adding additional material, and reorganizing it for publication. In July 1946, he provided a copy to the War Claims Committee, Liberated Military Personnel (Japan), an organization created by liberated army officers to pursue monetary compensation for maltreatment and for next-of-kin of deceased POWs. Hardee, however, requested the return of the manuscript upon settlement of the former POW claims. As to his reason for sharing his story, Hardee wrote on the cover: "I believe it would help our cause if this could be published in book or Sunday newspaper form. Have had no such success to date. If you have good connections or ideas in this respect please advise me."[15]

Returning to active military service in July 1946, he served the remainder of his time in the army as an instructor and adviser in the adjutant general's office for the North Carolina National Guard. He retired on December 31, 1949, after more than thirty-one years of service spanning two world wars and one police action, and his decorations included the Distinguished Service Cross, four Silver Stars, the Bronze Star, two Purple Hearts, and numerous campaign medals. In 1950, Hardee founded the ready-mix Hardee Concrete Company in Durham and served as the organization's president to 1953. After selling the company in 1954, he became the civil defense director for Raleigh and Wake

County, a position he held until July 1961. From 1957 to 1958, Hardee also served as the national commander for the Army and Navy Legion of Valor. Hardee died in Raleigh on November 23, 1969 at the age of seventy-nine.[16]

Colonel David L. Hardee, September 16, 1890–November 23, 1969. **Source: Mary Hardee Stutz.**

Foreword

This book was originally written to give the families of those who did not return a truthful and as near an accurate picture as possible of the conditions under which their loved ones spent their last days; to serve as a reminder to those who returned and to remind the American people of the humiliation, suffering, and despair symbolized by the names Bataan, Corregidor, the Death March, Jap prison camps, and hellships.

It is intended as a reminder and a warning to all, that our children and children's children will be the victims of similar or worst experiences if we forget and lapse again into the vicious circle of wistful thinking, pacifism, and unpreparedness. The enemies of America can wish for nothing better than to have our people fall back into these old ruts and become unprepared to defend our rights and ideals on land, sea, and in the air. If we forget and fail to secure our homes, Bladensburg, Bull Run, and Bataan will be repeated with ever-recurring violence, for we may never again have allies to fight while we prepare. Our ports, production plants, cities and homes may be the first targets when the War God talks again.[1]

This book has been written out of a desire not to talk of the cruel starvation and unpardonable atrocities of the Jap prison camps. It was first prepared for the sole consumption of members of the family and close personal friends who have insisted that it be expanded and published. It is published because the manuscripts are too bulky and worn to continue loaning to friends, and to the families of my companions who did not return, and to those who value the information and may preserve it in book form.

To General and Mrs. Charles E. Kilbourne, U.S. Army, retired, I am due the inspiration for putting this work together for publication. It was Mrs.

Kilbourne who insisted that she would like to see a story accounting for the great volume of American prisoners of war who did not accompany General Wainwright and the small group of generals and colonels that accompanied him to Formosa, Japan, and Manchuria. No one is competent to write the whole story, for no one person saw it and no one person knows all of it, but here is an outline of the main events that took about nine out of ten of the lives of the American prisoners of war that were left behind by the Japs.[2]

Acknowledgement is made to a British lady who sailed with me on the *Cape Meares* from Manila to San Francisco. This lady, whose name I am unable to recall, typed the first manuscripts as an expression of appreciation for what America meant and had done for her. She had suffered under the Japs for over three years in the Jap internment camps in and near Manila.

DAVID L. HARDEE
Raleigh, North Carolina

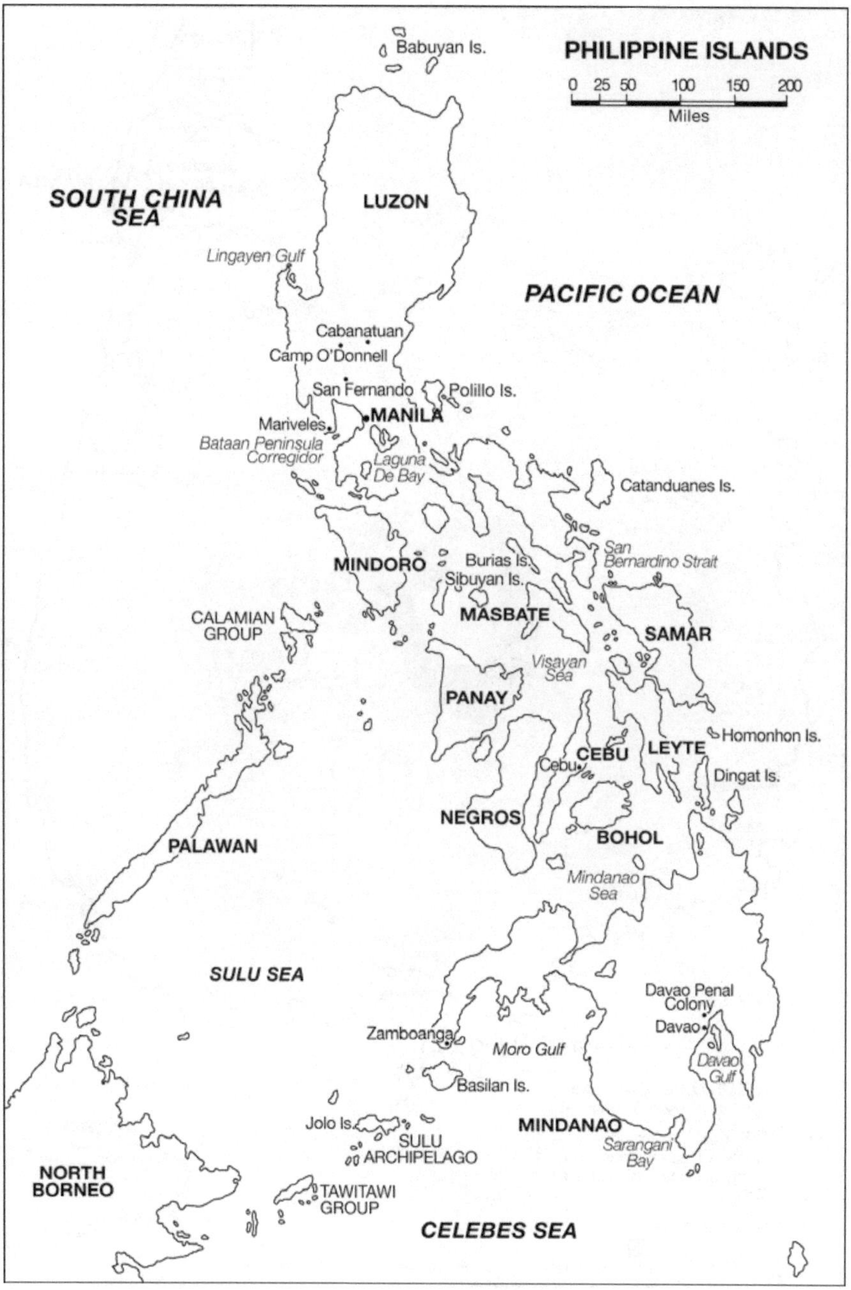

Map of the Philippines, with the prison camps of Colonel Hardee marked.

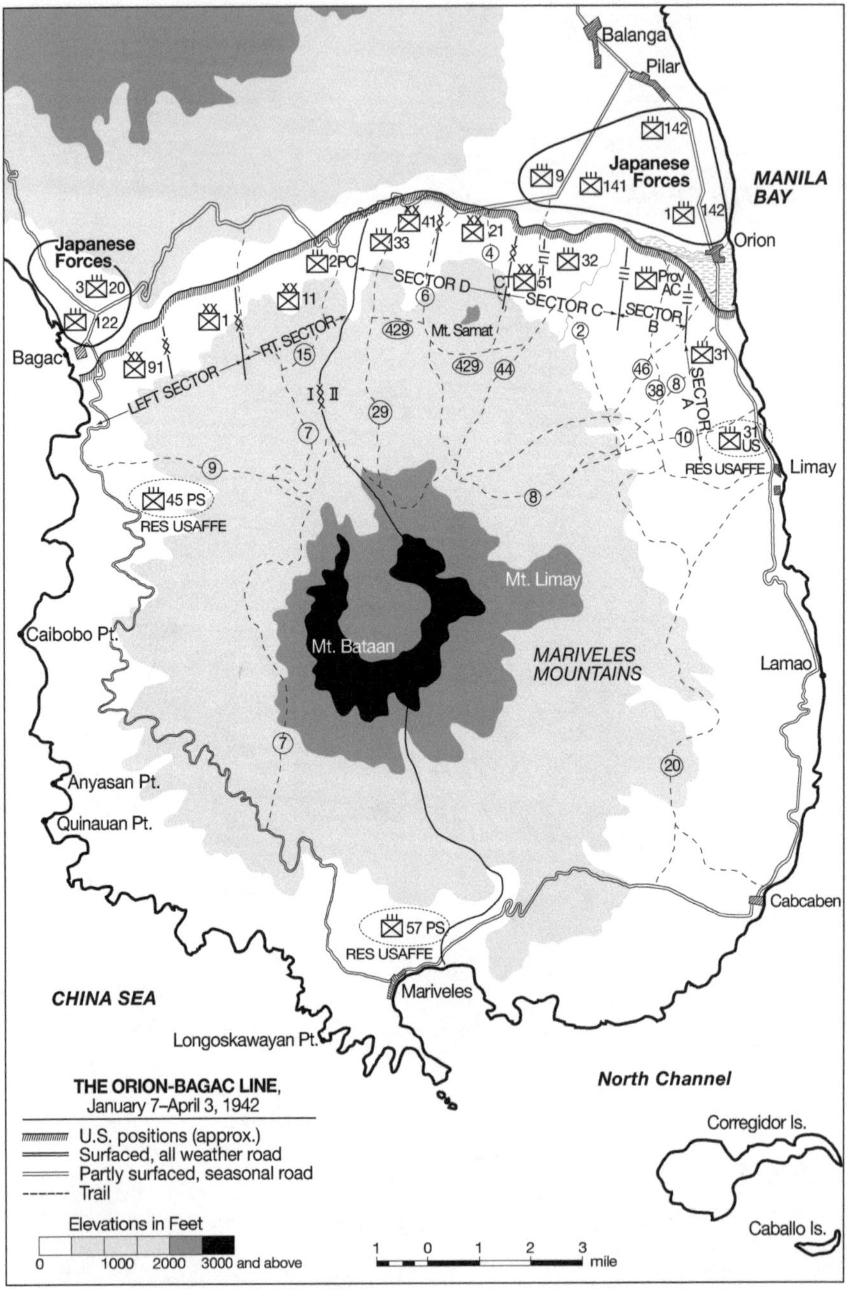

The Orion-Bagac Line where Hardee served with the Provisional Air Corps Regiment, seen on the right in Sector B. Source: Map modified from original developed by U.S. Army Center of Military History (CMH).

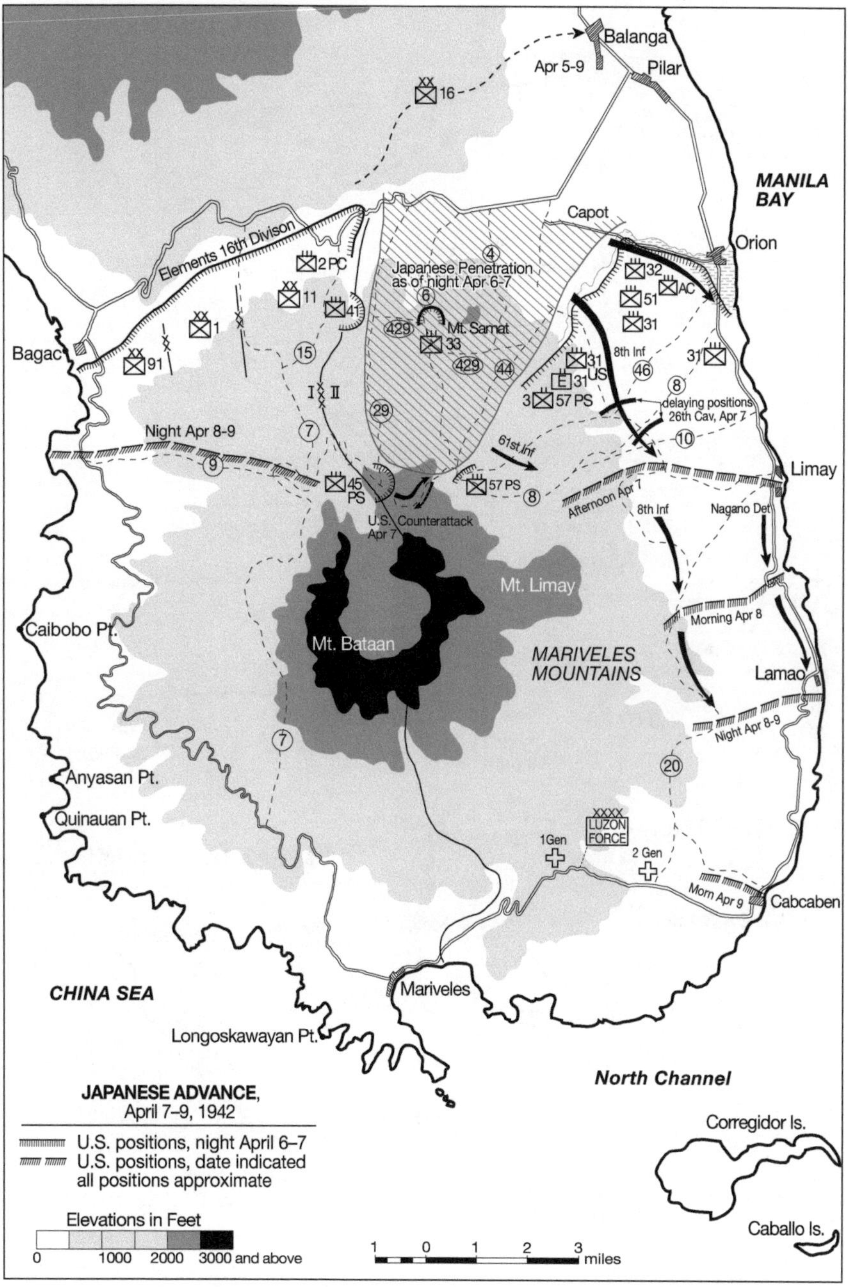

The Japanese advance on Bataan, which collapsed the Orion-Bagac line and forced the American surrender. By April 9, Hardee ended up west of Cabcaben. Source: Map modified from original developed by CMH.

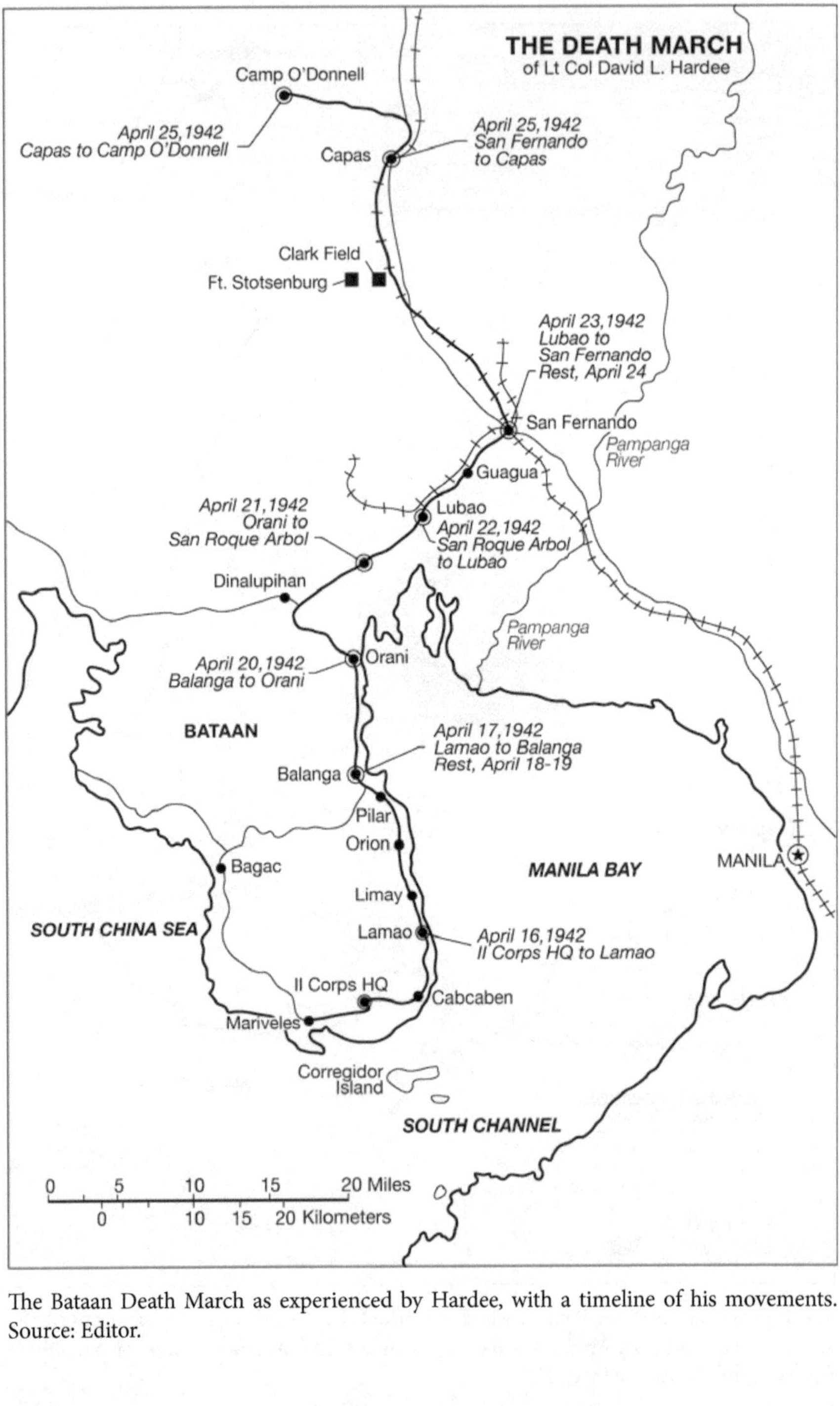

The Bataan Death March as experienced by Hardee, with a timeline of his movements. Source: Editor.

BATAAN SURVIVOR

To the nine out of ten of my comrades who fell in Bataan and Corregidor, whose bodies marked the route of the Death March, whose silent forms lie unshrouded in uncoffined graves at O'Donnell, Cabanatuan, Davao, Bilibid, and wherever Filo-American prisoners of the Japs worked as slaves; to the thousands that went down in Jap hellships; and to those who died in Formosa, Manchuria, and Japan while awaiting liberation by our forces; this work is dedicated.

Section I
Fighting on Bataan

> Don't worry about me. What is to be will be. I have faith that I will be with you and the children again. Be of good cheer, strong and courageous. Get your affection off me, so your grieving will not scare the children's lives. Take life tranquilly, look at the big pictures, forget the little details that amount to tiny little in the end.
>
> **—David L. Hardee to Elizabeth Hardee, February 18, 1942**

In July 1941, as the military situation in the Far East grew increasingly tense, the War Department recalled Major General Douglas MacArthur to active duty and placed him in command of the newly established U.S. Army Forces in the Far East (USAFFE). The order establishing the USAFFE and recalling MacArthur included provision for sending 425 U.S. Army Reserve officers to the Philippines to assist in training and mobilization of ten reserve divisions of the Philippine Army. Each division would be assigned forty American officers and twenty noncommissioned officers, either American or Filipino, as instructors. On September 24, 1941, Lieutenant Colonel David L. Hardee received orders assigning him to help mobilize and train one of these ten reserve divisions.

Hardee had barely settled in Manila before the Japanese launched simultaneous attacks on American military forces in Hawaii and the Philippines on December 7–8. At Pearl Harbor, the United States Pacific Fleet sustained heavy losses. On the island of Luzon, Japanese air attacks caught the bulk of the Far East Air Force (FEAF) on the ground at Clark Field north of Manila and destroyed half of the American aircraft, effectively eliminating FEAF. Ensuing air attacks on American and Filipino military installations destroyed additional aircraft and supplies. On December 10, the first Japanese forces landed on northern Luzon, and two days later an additional force landed in the south.

Initially rejecting as defeatist a prewar plan to withdraw to the Bataan Peninsula and the island of Corregidor, MacArthur chose instead to counter the Japanese at the invasion beaches. He dispersed his forces and relocated supply dumps nearer the sites of the landings. But the destruction of the FEAF and the swift advance of Japanese forces in North Luzon following the landing of the Japanese 14th Army at Lingayen Gulf forced MacArthur to withdraw his forces into Bataan. Approximately 80,000 American and Filipino troops together with 26,000 civilians then moved haphazardly into the malaria-plagued peninsula, and vast stores of supplies were destroyed to prevent capture.

During the first weeks of the war, Hardee served as a staff officer for the Bataan echelon of the USAFFE. In January 1942, he organized the command

American troops huddled in a trench on Bataan. Shrapnel from Japanese bombers and artillery proved a constant threat for the forces along the Orion-Bagac Line. **Source: National Archives and Records Administration (NARA).**

post for the USAFFE on Bataan. He witnessed firsthand the rapid dwindling of supplies while hearing reports of the fighting intended to blunt the Japanese invasion. After the establishment of the Orion-Bagac defensive line on the peninsula in the fourth week of January, Hardee became executive officer for the Provisional Air Corps Regiment, now an impromptu infantry unit composed of the airmen without aircraft from the Far East Air Force.

For 73 days Hardee and his regiment, occupying the extreme right flank of the defensive line, found themselves at the front of the fighting as the situation on Bataan began to worsen. President Franklin D. Roosevelt in a February fireside chat acknowledged that no help would arrive for the beleaguered defenders. General MacArthur, commanding from the island of Corregidor, fled under presidential order on March 11 to Australia, and Lieutenant General Jonathan M. Wainwright assumed command of U.S. forces in the Philippines with Major General Edward P. King Jr. commanding the Luzon force. By late March, morale was ebbing among the American and Filipino forces, which were subject to disease and hunger as supplies ran low.

The final Japanese attack on Bataan commenced on Good Friday, April 3, 1942. Approximately 150 Japanese artillery pieces shelled the Orion-Bagac Line for five hours, and enemy aircraft dropped over sixty tons of bombs on American and Filipino positions. Following the bombardment, the Japanese infantry and armor swiftly pushed through the defensive positions, seizing Mount Samat on Easter Sunday. General King attempted to counterattack, but the Japanese overcame all resistance and continued to sweep forward. Overwhelmed by enemy forces, Hardee's Provisional Air Corps Regiment joined other units in falling back south along the coastal road.

From April 7 to 9, American and Filipino forces fought a series of delaying actions even as organized units all but disintegrated. After failing to hold a defensive line on April 8, General King decided around midnight to seek a surrender to preserve the lives of the remaining men under his command. King did not notify General Wainwright of his intentions so as to spare his superior the responsibility for contradicting MacArthur's explicit orders not to surrender.

On the morning of April 9, King and his aides met with a representative of the Japanese 14th Army headquarters near Lamao. King requested an armistice and permission for American and Filipino troops to march out of Bataan under their own officers while the wounded were carried out by motor

Hands tied behind their backs (left to right) Private First Class Samuel Stenzler, Private First Class Frank Spear, and Captain James M. Gallagher listen to a Japanese soldier during a stop on the Death March, April 1942. Gallagher would die shortly after this photo was taken. **Source: NARA.**

transport. He offered to deliver his men wherever the Japanese commander desired and asked for assurances the prisoners of war would be treated in accordance with the Geneva Convention. The Japanese ignored King's requests, but the American general agreed to an unconditional surrender of his Luzon forces at midday on April 9, 1942.

The surrender and movement of the Filipino and American forces north to prison became infamously known as the Bataan Death March. Having badly miscalculated the number of prisoners they would be required to evacuate, the Japanese were unprepared, and their operations proved a muddled, confused mess. Weakened by disease and starvation and exhausted by battle, prisoners died of exposure or from abuse at the hands of the Japanese guards. Water and food proved almost nonexistent along the way, and Hardee witnessed countless acts of murder and sadistic cruelty by the Japanese guards toward Filipino

American and Filipino forces stream out of Bataan to prison in Camp O'Donnell. An estimated 600–650 Americans and 5,000–10,000 Filipinos would die along the way. **Source: NARA.**

civilians who attempted to help the vanquished. After ten days of marching and movement by rail, Hardee arrived at Camp O'Donnell on April 25, 1942, where a new battle for survival would begin.

CHAPTER 1

The War Is On

A colonel of anti-aircraft artillery was shaking me violently by the shoulder.

"Wake up! Wake up! You work at General MacArthur's headquarters, don't you? They have been on the alert and working since 3:00 a.m. The war is on."

"Don't try to kid me," I drawled, rubbing my eyes, "that won't come until next April."

He held the early edition of the *Manila Bulletin* before me as I sat up in bed. "I'm not trying to kid you."

"HONULULU BOMBED" the boxcar headlines flared.

I was shocked and dazed.

I called Lieutenant Wermuth, later to be called the "One Man Army of Bataan," who was sleeping in the next room and began dressing. As I dressed, rushed through breakfast and hurried to headquarters, my mind surged with a summary of recent events.[1]

First my thoughts rushed back overseas to my wife and two daughters, mother, brothers and their families, the group of the dearest ones in the world who had bid me good bye at the station in Raleigh, North Carolina on October 24, 1941 as I began my long and second journey to Manila.

My thoughts seemed to dwell on my youngest daughter Mary, now nine, who was born at Sternberg General Hospital when we were living in this very house. This was just a couple of months before I grabbed my field equipment and took off with the 31st Infantry to help the marines protect American life and property in the beleaguered international city of Shanghai. The Japs, yes, it was always the Japs, fomenting and stirring up trouble in the Orient.[2]

A year previous (1931), I had traveled a good deal in China and Japan, visited their home land while they were invading Manchuria and trying to close the door we had long before declared and were not trying by peaceful means to keep open.[3]

Their designs were so well known, our lack of preparedness so vivid, and our weakness and general plans for the defense of the Philippines so familiar to me that I said to my wife, Elizabeth, on the drive to the station: "You know, dear, I have never missed being in the thick of it. If war breaks, it will break in the Orient first, and you can prepare to have communications broken for at least two years. I have made my allotments to the family for a period of three years."

The guess was not far astray.

Reminiscences of my recent temporary promotion to lieutenant colonel, immediately followed by secret orders to Manila from Camp Wheeler, Georgia, passed in a quick panorama through my mind. The fact that General MacArthur was training ten Philippine divisions and needed help brought fond recollections of the hurried trip my old friend, Colonel Louis Hutson, and I had made from Macon, Georgia across the continent to San Francisco where we were to join others assigned to this undertaking.[4]

The voyage of the *President Coolidge* was without incident. The great luxury liner of the Pacific, new queen of the President Line, formerly the Dollar Line, left Pier 45, San Francisco at noon, November 1, 1941, and docked at Pier 7, Manila, on November 20, 1941. My stateroom, while not luxurious, contained two iron beds with good inner spring mattresses and a couch similarly equipped; a comfortably sized room with private bath accommodating three officers. The entire boat had been leased for the trip and carried only military personnel and equipment. One brigadier general, Maxon S. Lough; three colonels, Bradford G. Chynoweth, Charles L. Steel, and Joseph P. Vachon; 46 lieutenant colonels; about ten majors; over 200 junior officers; and about 2,000 enlisted men constituted the human cargo. The materials varied from small QM supply items to complete rolling photographic laboratories.[5]

We were just passing under the Golden Gate Bridge when two of my former reserve officers approached me saying there were a couple of nurses aboard who wanted to know me. I turned around on the deck and met Miss Evelyn B. Whitlow from Leasburg, North Carolina and Nancy J. Gillahan from Danville, Tennessee. Colonel Hutson and I had been looking for them ever since we left Chattanooga as Louis had heard they were leaving Chattanooga at the same time we left. They, however, had been routed through Texas instead of Chicago.[6]

They were pleasant young ladies, and asked me to look after them as I would daughters. I assumed the responsibility that proved a pleasant one. Lieutenant Colonel Irving Compton joined us and the dinner gong sounded. We arranged so us four would be seated together for meals for the voyage. They made our meal hours very pleasant. The menus were elaborate with many dishes and entrées to choose from and we had many a joke initiating them, and more often ourselves to new dishes and old ones under new names.[7]

The officer personnel being few, we were taken care of at two sittings in the tourist dining room with first class meals and service, while the enlisted men ate from their mess kits in the large first class dining room. The fare was sumptuous, rating with any fine hotel anywhere. The trip was pleasant except for the many homesick officers aboard. Most of them had not been away from their families, and many were just parting with their loved ones for the first time since either marriage or World War I. My four month separation while at Camp Wheeler provided a great help to me in this respect, and I remained on the whole as cheerful as usual. Coming events cast their shadows and all felt that we were going into war and many aboard would never see their native land and loved ones again. None of us felt that we would have a good time for two years at the very pleasant task of training the Philippine Army.

The stay at Honolulu was short and pleasant. We arrived and went ashore about 8:30 or 9:00 a.m. and sailed about 4:00 p.m. the same day. I took an auto trip about half-way around the island of Oahu with three other officers, stopping for lunch at the Post Exchange lunch room at Schofield Barracks.[8]

When we cleared the harbor we were closely followed by the army transport *Hugh L. Scott* also loaded with troops and war materials. An escort composed of the cruiser USS *Louisville* and two sub chasers accompanied us. This also brought a calm realization that trouble was rampant in the world and that we might not be long at peace. The *Scott* went into the harbor at Guam to unload some cargo. The *Coolidge* lay out to sea and we were not allowed an opportunity to see the island. I had seen it before, having visited relatives there in 1929. The wait was short, from breakfast until 3:00 p.m., and then we were on our way again.[9]

To the sea-worn traveler the San Bernardino Straits is a welcome sight with its blue waters and its green shores glistening in a tropical sunshine. It looked particularly beautiful as we looked upon the shore of Luzon and of many small islands in the Sibuyan Sea in which we cruised for the best part of a day. We were soon to be fighting over these hills and deep jungles.

The *Coolidge* docked at Pier 7, known as the Million Dollar Pier, the largest one in the world, at 10:00 a.m. on November 20. General MacArthur had recently taken over the entire use of the pier for military purposes and it was a beehive of activity. Everyone was in a bustle with thousands of people and cars all moving to and fro, but few military personnel were apparent. All were at their posts, and all at work. There were no brass bands, no fanfare of welcoming music. The old transport holiday had gone with the wind.[10]

Soon I spotted Lucy, my sister, Mrs. Carl E. Olsen of Manila, and the children Roberta and Esten, coming along the second-story balcony of the pier and the hellos and throwing of kisses began.

"Where is Carl?" I asked.

"Playing golf, but he will be here by the time you get ashore."

"Why is he playing golf this time of day?"

"It's a holiday."

"What holiday?"

"Thanksgiving, and I have a big turkey dinner for you tonight."

After the customary drinks and greetings of old friends at the Army and Navy Club, we drove out to Lucy's home for lunch, and then P.O., their driver, carried me to Fort McKinley where we were quartered for a few days awaiting our assignments and getting over our sea legs. P.O. returned for me in the V12 Lincoln-Zephyr about 4:00 p.m. after I had gotten unpacked and settled for the night. The Thanksgiving dinner was very enjoyable; the guests included about a dozen people, some of whom were old acquaintances of the American colony.[11]

Next day I visited the headquarters of the United States Army Forces in the Far East (USAFFE) to call on General MacArthur. I asked his aide to tell the general I had just arrived on the *Coolidge* and had a couple of messages from people in Congress, one from his first cousin, and that I would like about five minutes of his time to deliver them.

"The general is a very important man and is very busy. He cannot see you," was his quick protective retort.

"I expected you to say that. Please get up and go tell him what I have just said." This was not a bold adventure for I had known the aide for a number of years.

He came back saying that there had been a break in the general's appointments and he would see me in ten minutes. General MacArthur was extremely courteous and congenial, leaving his desk and sitting beside me on a large office settee. I conveyed the messages of Senator Robert R. Reynolds, my senator from North Carolina, who was the number two man on the Senate Military Affairs Committee, and of an old friend and former comrade in arms, Representative Charles I. Faddis of the House Committee on Military Affairs. Both messages were to the effect that whatever came they had perfect confidence and would back his judgments and actions.[12]

He told me the War Department had some 30 to 40 B-17 bombers on the way, and when they arrived Formosa would be in our laps. They never arrived and how different was the story. We then talked of his first cousin Elizabeth Hardy Jones, who was preparing a book on the Hardy-Hardee family that would include both of us. This struck another responsive chord.[13]

"When this comes out we will be so proud of ourselves, we won't know who we are."

I did not want to take up too much time so I excused myself and retired. He was not only congenial but folksy, much different from the way I had pictured him when I first saw him at Fort McKinley, Philippines in 1930 taking a final review when he was leaving as Philippine Department commander to take the position as Chief of Staff of the U.S. Army. Then I adjudged him to be stern and aloof. All of my personal contacts proved him to be the opposite.

At his headquarters I found many old friends who gathered around to greet me: Paul Stivers, Lewis Beebe, Dick Marshall, Charles Willoughby, LeGrande Diller and others with whom I had served at Benning and elsewhere. I was told by Colonel Stivers, the G-1 personnel officer, to inform the officers at McKinley that assignments would not be out for a few days and to do all necessary shopping in Manila, as many would go to the provinces and to distant islands.[14]

About four days after arrival, I was ordered to report to Colonel Stivers at USAFFE, bringing all my baggage. The headquarters were located at No. 1 Victoria, the enlarged set of quarters formerly occupied by Colonel Gasser and other commanders of the 31st Infantry. Upon arrival at USAFFE, I was told that many projects would be opened when the next convoy came in. It was due about December 17th, in about two weeks. These projects did not materialize on account of the outbreak of hostilities on December 8, 1941.[15]

I was given several jobs to occupy my time pending this new project assignment. The first was to assign office space to the sections as the headquarters building was expanded to include the Santa Lucia Barracks next door. My quarters were in the old Spanish quarters in the Cuartel de Espana facing on the General Luna. We had a number of officers in each set of quarters, and each ran a separate mess with good Filipino servants.[16]

The first war assignment was a directive from Colonel Richard J. Marshall, then deputy chief of staff, to form a headquarters detachment and procure everything needed to take the headquarters into the field. This meant to organize a headquarters detachment, train it, and break in the officers to serve as headquarters commandants of the advanced and rear sections of the command post.

I called for two officers to serve in these positions. Lieutenants Short and Weil reported during the day. I gave them a list of material and personnel they were to procure and they set to the task at once. The first things organized and set up were a motor pool and a kitchen section, and all officers were issued bedding rolls, arms, and equipment.[17]

I shall not soon forget the engineer detachment that came in from Fort McKinley to join us: swarthy, rugged Philippine Scouts of many years service, tanned by the tropical sun, handy with bolos, infantry weapons, camouflage, and tools. These were the men to dig in and set up our command posts, as well as conceal and protect them. All did good work, accomplished things quickly, and we soon had USAFFE ready to load on wheels and roll on into the field.[18]

Colonels Charles L. Steel and Irvin E. Doane of the 31st Infantry (U.S.) were living in bachelor quarters in the large wooden field officer sets on the General Luna. They soon learned that I was attached to the 31st Infantry (U.S.) for assignment to quarters and invited me to come and live with them. Their mess had been in operation for some time with excellent servants. Both these officers were in the field most of the time and they wanted the house with the servants kept intact.[19]

Here I lived in a room with my old friend, Colonel Warren J. Clear, who had been doing military intelligence work in India and Burma. He was en route to the United States, after completing a long period of fine work in observation in those countries. He had been caught in Manila at the outbreak of the war while awaiting the arrival of some final documents from India. He had observed and had a great deal of first-hand information on the Japanese fighting methods and we became constant companions in off-duty hours, later taking Colonels Francis Wilson and Roy Hilton into the house with us.[20]

Baguio and Clark Field were first hit by the Jap bombers and we felt that Manila was next on their list. We prepared foxholes in the Luneta adjacent to our quarters. They were the first prepared in the beautiful parks of the city. Many others were prepared after the first bombings and the parks resembled plowed fields before our forces evacuated the city.[21]

I still have a mental picture of Clear and myself when the air raid sirens first warned of the approach of hostile airplanes. It was around noon and we abandoned our well-spread luncheon table, and after warning the servants to do likewise, sought the open park of the Luneta where we could observe the approach of the planes and take cover if necessary.

Upon reaching the center of the Luneta we looked for the approaching enemy planes; the first, but by no means the last, I was to see in the war. We spotted three formations of 24 each, all heavy bombers, glistening in the sun at from about 25 to 27,000 feet altitude. As they approached from the north, our anti-aircraft artillery that had just taken position in the sunken gardens outside the walled city opened fire. It was the first "fireworks" I saw in the war and the first rounds the men of the battalion had ever fired in action. With their short fuses they could not reach the altitude of the hostile formations. We felt helpless. But practice was to make perfect, and in a short time afterwards they were exploding their shells in the midst of and breaking hostile formations, and taking their toll of the enemy.[22]

At the approach of the enemy formation Filipinos who had sought the open spaces of the Luneta in the thousands continued to run to and fro and cluster in large groups under the trees, thus presenting the enemy with the best possible targets. Colonel Clear and I yelled ourselves hoarse trying to get them to scatter out, throw themselves flat on the ground and lie still, but they did not understand as they were to later. Experience is a hard school, and we humans too often have to learn the hard way. We took cover in our shallow foxholes, but the planes went on directly over us and unloaded their deadly cargo on the Cavite Naval Base installations and Nichols Field. Several dog fights were in evidence as our depleted fighters challenged the bombers and their accompanying fighters.[23]

Before the fight ceased, one of the enemy strafers turned our way and one of their .50 caliber machine gun bullets struck Clear on the back of his hand. Fortunately it was spent and did little more than burn, bruise, break the skin and draw blood. It was the first wound I knew of in the city of Manila, at least the first for military personnel. However, this was only the beginning, as the Japs laid on the city and its environs steadily each day, usually striking around noon.

I recall that a few days later I attempted to have Lieutenant Nancy Gillahan and Lieutenant Evelyn Whitlow, two nurses who had come with us on the *Coolidge*, join us for lunch, but we had to grab our lunch in our hands and eat it while running to the air raid shelters. Clear accompanied me to Corregidor upon our withdrawal and was ordered out by submarine with the G-2 material he had obtained in Indochina, Thailand, British Malaya, and the East Indies, much of it on bombing objectives and all in code.[24]

The first field reconnaissance was made with Colonel William P. Morse. We were to make recommendations for the location of the command post in Bataan. Going and returning via San Fernando, our day's search carried us as far as Cabcaben. We had little knowledge of the plans of operation except what we knew of the developing tactical situation and our geographical observations. We keenly observed the high hog-back ridges of the Zambales Mountains running down the center of the Bataan Peninsula and terminating in the towering Mariveles, land of many clouds. We observed understandably the abrupt coasts and short plains between the water and the mountains, and noted the great general defensive assets of the terrain against a force coming from the north as the Japs were then doing.[25]

"Dave, it looks like the Orange Plan to me," said Bill, a merry twinkle in his deep gray eyes. The "Orange Plan" in prewar army lingo meant the plan for action against Japanese attack.

"How should I know? I have never sat in the councils of the mighty. Might be the Pink, Green, or Yellow, but to me it looks like hell and Maria."[26]

I was then given the temporary work of keeping the notes and calls for General Richard K. Sutherland, chief of staff. At the end of two days he stated that my experience was needed elsewhere. Next morning, I was relieved by an officer from Nichols Field who had recently arrived and had not been assigned to an airplane. I was assigned to the G-1 section and helped to organize the Awards and Decorations Department. The first general order awarding Distinguished Service Crosses, Silver Stars, and Purple Hearts was issued the next day. It was my pleasure to help Captain George A. Muzzey, a former professor of education at Temple University, put together out of submitted statements, the citation order for Captain Colin P. Kelly that seemed to electrify the people at home. After the first order was published, this work was turned over to Captain Muzzey.[27]

The next task was to make a reconnaissance of all available places in Manila not in military use that would serve as a headquarters for the rapidly growing

USAFFE. I took three days, looked over about 25 places and reported the University of Santo Tomas and De La Salle University as first and second choices. The general staff decided on De La Salle, and I began to have the building prepared for the move.

CHAPTER 2

The Billion Dollar Christmas Tree

The tactical situation was changing very rapidly and the Japanese advance was faster than anticipated. Colonel Stivers called for me about 5:30 p.m. and gave me confidential instructions to proceed that night to Corregidor and prepare to move the command post there. I returned next afternoon and reported and was then on the night duty shift. The next morning, December 24, 1941, I was put in charge of the details of the move. It was a busy day with the heavy bombing of Manila's port area interrupting us for an hour at noon. There were no hits on the *Don Esteban*, the vessel on which our personnel would go. The QM laundry, utilities, and parts of the sales commissary were hit, water mains were broken, and fires were started in the area.[1]

The raid began in this fashion. The air raid sirens sounded at high noon. You could set your watch by their appearance. We had opened an air raid shelter in one of the long-closed gun emplacements in the old Spanish wall on which the headquarters building has long since been erected. The staff and helpers moved to the shelter while General MacArthur continued to sit at his desk. I observed him since I was the last to leave.

"Come on general, let's go."

"You go ahead Hardee. The Jap planes are 90 seconds away. I will be there in plenty of time."

I moved on to the shelter and heard soft foot steps behind me. As I turned to close the gate he was behind me to help. Then things went "columity lum." They were bombing the port area, about a thousand yards away. So I will say in all fairness he was the only man among the quick and the dead that ever drove me to cover.[2]

I shall never forget that Christmas Eve and the move to Corregidor. The scene would have been picturesque had it not been so ghastly and our plight so desperate. The sky was lighted for miles by burning supplies of gasoline and oil from Fort McKinley, Nichols Field, Pandacan, and other strategic points. The flames licked the sky and lighted Manila Bay. Many explosions rent the air. Sternberg General Hospital where my younger daughter was born in 1931 was ablaze. The whole thing looked like a billion dollar Christmas tree. My friend, Colonel Hugh J. Casey, with his crew of assistants, was doing a good job in destroying most of the things adjudged to be of value to the invading army. Although Manila had been declared an open city that did not mean we were giving the enemy everything.[3]

The *Don Esteban*, one of our six or seven thousand ton inter-island boats, carried the headquarters baggage and personnel. It left Pier 7 about 7:30 p.m. and arrived at Corregidor about midnight. There were no Christmas carols. A group in the boat lounge tried to sing "Noel" while we were sailing the bay but their efforts died in their throats.

We were met at the pier at Corregidor by General George F. Moore and his staff with all the motors and men to transfer everything to the Malinta Tunnel before daylight when we would be out of sight of the Jap's observation of our activities. The passengers assembled on the porch of the wharf landing; General MacArthur and his staff heading the parade. Here they congregated in some confusion. His chief of staff, General Sutherland gave me a hard look and made some cryptic remarks, for which he later made amends.

"Hardee," he said, "this is a hell of a mess."

"Just hold your horses a minute, general." I waved the first car around. General and Mrs. MacArthur got in.

"Malinta Tunnel," I said to the driver.[4]

The second car carried Colonel and Mrs. Carl Seals, our adjutant general, whose wife was left in Manila when evacuation was ordered for all dependants. She suffered from arthritis so badly that her husband had to put her on the toilet at nights and she was permitted to stay with him. After I had seen these couples off in cars for the Malinta Tunnel, I asked General Sutherland to load his staff and headquarters personnel for the tunnel and turned to other duties. The stevedores were rapidly unloading the *Don Esteban* and were throwing tightly baled bundles on a narrow dock. They were bouncing and it appeared that some of them might bounce off in the water on the opposite side of the dock. A military policeman was patrolling the pier. He was dressed in white pistol belt, white gloves, and helmet. He appeared not to know that the war was on.[5]

I cautioned him, speaking for General MacArthur, with special instructions to be particularly careful about the property being unloaded, and if any of the packages bounced into the water to have them fished out and recovered. I explained that we had to move the Philippine Treasury with us and that some of the bundles contained as much as ten million pesos (five million dollars in our currency).

He looked at me with the saddest expression I have seen on the face of any person.

"Ten million pesos," he exclaimed, "God almighty I would give it all for four and a half acres in West Virginia."[6]

All of us felt about that low. By daylight the personnel and baggage had been transferred from the docks out of immediate danger to the Malinta Tunnel where headquarters was located and work in the offices began.

I spent the next few days helping to get headquarters settled and acting as coordinator between our headquarters and the harbor defense headquarters, settling many minor matters. We forgot it was Christmas. The only one to wish me a Merry Christmas was President Quezon who lived in the tunnel close by. Conditions in the tunnel were crowded and constantly getting more so. As laterals of ammunition and supplies were consumed, additional troop and headquarters activities occupied the added tunnel space. The conditions in the naval tunnel where torpedoes and submarine materials were kept were no better. Everyone in USAFFE slept on double decker beds and mine was about four feet from General MacArthur's desk. The heavy bombing of Corregidor had not yet begun and many officers still slept in their quarters.[7]

The troops in Northern Luzon were constantly on the retreat towards Bataan, and Colonel Arnold J. Funk and I were sent over to Bataan to make a reconnaissance for an advanced command post; this would, in a measure, relieve the congestion in the tunnel. We went over to Cabcaben on about December 29, spent the night at the engineers dump (Little Baguio) and there had the last eggs for breakfast I was to eat for over three years.[8]

Little Baguio was rightly named. Baguio in the mountain province is the summer capital of the Philippines and Little Baguio was the capital of our operations in Bataan. It was on the east coast, several miles from the shore line and in a large wood on the road from Cabcaben to Mariveles. The ordnance and engineer depots had already been constructed as a pre-war plan, and had this work included the quartermaster installations with part of the stock from Manila placed there the stand in Bataan would have been more effective;

another example of our lack of funds and unpreparedness. It would later become Hospital No. 1 and sheltered 3,000 patients.[9]

A two-day reconnaissance showed a veritable beehive of activity and much unnecessary traffic congested the main arteries. Hundreds of tons of supplies had been hauled in from Manila and elsewhere and dumped along the sides of the main roads. It was all we could do to get our supplies into Bataan. They could be stored later. The stupid Japs, had they used several squadrons for a couple of days strafing these roads, wrecking our motor vehicles and burning our supplies, they could have ruined us. Instead, they spent most of their air strength bombing almost vacant airfields.

Upon return to Corregidor, Colonel Funk and I made some recommendations that resulted in the motors being pooled which saved much useless traffic. Our recommendations for an advanced command post were for Signal Hill or adjacent to the ordnance area. We laid the advantages and disadvantages before the high command. They chose Signal Hill, and I was detailed to go back two days later, take the necessary permanent enlisted detail and the advance echelon commandant, and get the place ready for occupancy.[10]

The heavy bombing of Corregidor had begun and some 50 to 75 had been killed and wounded before we left. The bombing seemed especially heavy the first day we were in Bataan but we learned from those who came over from "the Rock" (Corregidor) later that it was no more than usual. It was being outside that made it seem more intense. We slept in the woods the first night, and looked for a stream that should have been within a 100 yards of the camp site. We had recommended the camp site be half-way up the hill. The air corps had a real camp near the top of the hill by a very cool, clear mountain stream. I had forebodings about this air corps rest camp and the advance command post being located close together so I had gotten General MacArthur's authority to move them out, if necessary.

We found no stream half way down the hill where we expected to locate our camp. The stream disappeared in the ground a hundred yards below the air corps camp, so I had to move them out, and put the advance command post where they had been located. At the end of the second day we got our kitchen set up, our water pipes and bath in, and the telephone line in with one telephone—no switchboard layout yet in prospect. I called General Marshall, the deputy chief of staff, to tell him we would be ready for them to move over day after tomorrow. They were so crowded in the tunnel that I could not hold him off that long. I met the group at Mariveles the next morning at daylight. It took several days to get the place established and dug in. Then the problem of supply began to get hard. We were placed on half rations and two meals a day on January 5, 1942.[11]

About the middle of the month, the Japs made a small landing at Agloloma Bay and at Mariveles. We soon had them under control and eventually cleared them out, but this landing demonstrated the weakness of the command post position that Colonel Funk had pointed out.[12]

Around January 25 while at Corregidor looking after supplies, the chief of staff, General Sutherland, called me in and gave me orders to make a reconnaissance and move the command post again. This resulted in moving the post to the ordnance area close to Little Baguio, where it remained until the surrender. For a number of days in January, the G-2 and G-3 sections of the advanced command post were worried almost constantly about the 57th Infantry (PS). They were not holding, the Japs were always infiltrating into their lines, and on more than one occasion they had lost either part or all of a battalion sector of the front line and at times were driven back on the battalion support or regimental reserve lines.[13]

One morning I found Colonel Arnold Funk, who had been chief of the G-3 section, packing up his bedding roll and I could see that he was not pleased. He had orders from "the Rock" to take command of the 57th Infantry. He had considered it a letdown but had been told if he got the regiment going that he would get his star out of it. Funk disappeared from our midst and next morning I overheard a telephone conversation to the effect that Colonel Funk had ordered one battalion of the 57th Infantry to counter attack supported by the fire of another battalion.[14]

The counter attack was successful, the lines were restored, and a few days afterwards General MacArthur and the chief of staff, General Sutherland, visited us. The latter was jubilant over the success of the regiment since he had sent Funk to command it. During my visit to Corregidor on the 25th, when I was given a directive by the chief of staff to move the advance command post, I was told that General Sutherland was much elated because he had made radio recommendations for general officers one night and the next afternoon the confirmation had been received, and that Colonel Funk was among them. This was received on the afternoon I was leaving Corregidor.[15]

I made a day's hurried reconnaissance without finding a suitable command post location. I carried a major of engineers assigned to the Philippine Scouts with me. He had spent two years in Bataan and had put in most of our army installations. I was amazed that he did not recognize what we wanted as he knew Bataan to the very inch. Water and suitable cover were the main points to be sought for in the area given me. The department engineer had informed me that he could furnish 500 yards of pipe line. As I lay in bed that night thinking over places visited during the day, I tried to reason out the location of the dam and pipe line that supplied Little Baguio and connected them with a location that otherwise answered all requirements.

Next morning, I ordered a car after early breakfast and went to the spot. A little scouting located the dam and the main pipe line, also the place where the splice could be made, and the 500 yards of pipe determined the location of the kitchen and shower baths for the new set up. It all worked out exactly and with the engineers doing some road work it would make an ideal location.

I had already enjoyed the pleasure of taking the eagle off Dick Marshall and pinning on his first star. He was deputy chief of staff and in charge of the advance command group. I laid my plans before him that night, which he approved. Early the next morning I started the headquarters commandant of the advance echelon off with the first load, giving him a mission to do en route. It was moving day. All non-essentials were to be moved on the first day and the Signal Corps were to wire in the switchboard. The second day was to finish the move whether the engineers had laid the water lines or not. Water could be hauled for cooking purposes for a few days.

I had prepared my bedding roll, packed my things, and was ready to go to the new location to meet the engineers and signal men to show them what the layout would be. At about 7:30 a.m., I was called over to the place of the G-1 and given a copy of an order. This assigned Colonel Irvin E. Doane to command the Provisional Air Corps Regiment and assigned me as executive officer. The regiment was in sub-sector B, just south of Orion. The entire Filo-American forces had just fallen back from the Abucay-Mauban line to the Orion-Bagac line, and were out of contact with the enemy.[16]

I expected the enemy to make contact during the day and to attack at daylight the following morning. I could think of nothing worse than to be caught under such circumstances and not be familiar with the personnel and the location of our regimental front lines. So this meant I had to get the command post moved, shifted to someone else, and report through II Corps to the regiment and inspect the front lines before night. As about forty miles of traveling on dusty crowded roads, with several interviews and conferences involved, it looked like an impossible day's task. The solution was to telephone the rear echelon headquarters commandant at Corregidor to come to Bataan at once prepared to help us for two or three days and to meet me at the new location at 12:30 p.m. The inspector then accompanied me to take over my work.

At about 12:30 to 1:00 p.m., the two headquarters commandants, the signal officer, and the engineer officer assembled at the new location and in company with the inspector I showed them on the ground, during about one hour's walking, where each function of the command post was to be located. This of course was subject to such improvements as they saw fit to make as the plan was developed.

I then turned over the responsibility for the move and the making of these installations to the inspector, Colonel Hill, and departed for II Corps in the car I had taken in the morning. In the defense of Bataan the Northern Luzon Forces under General Wainwright had become the I Philippine Army Corps and defended the western half of the Bataan peninsula, while the Southern Luzon Forces under General Parker had been designated the II Philippine Army Corps and defended the eastern (Manila Bay) sector. Upon arrival at II Corps at about 4:00 p.m., I dismissed the car to go back home and was carried in a jeep to my regimental headquarters by the regimental liaison officer at the corps headquarters.[17]

At II Corps, I found Colonel Funk serving as chief of staff. I told him he was already a general, but he pretended not to believe me. But the next time I saw him the news had reached him and he had discarded the eagles for the star of a brigadier. The reason for my assignment to the regiment was the great scarcity of field officers of infantry experience. They were relieving and replacing all staff officers of infantry experience and sending them to handle the battalions and regiments at the front.

CHAPTER 3

Many Pilots and No Airplanes

The Provisional Air Corps Regiment was a particularly difficult assignment. This was fully appreciated by General MacArthur, and his chief of staff General Sutherland, for both have spoken of it when I saw them after almost three years as a prisoner of war. They and the corps commander, Major General George M. Parker, were well satisfied with the work of Colonel Doane and me.

The regiment had been put together by Colonel Harrison H.C. Richards, who as an air corps officer was experienced in air rather than infantry operations and tactics. It was composed of ten squadrons of air corps troops who had lost their airplanes and were forced to finish the war fighting as infantry. We had almost 2,000 men organized into two battalions of five squadrons each, without the headquarters and service companies so necessary to proper infantry operations. We had to improvise these as best we could from personnel and materials available. The men and officers, however, were up against hard propositions and we found them ready, able, and willing. It was a pity to take all the good pilots, bombardiers, aerial gunners, and mechanics of many years' training, at a time when the American army was so short of these technicians, and not be able to use them to the fullest of their special skills, but such is the fate of war, particularly when a force is trapped like we were and had to make the best of it.[1]

It was about 5:00 p.m. when I reached our headquarters. Colonel Doane had arrived about two hours earlier, relieving Colonel Richards who had gone back to Signal Hill to take care of a rest camp. Colonel Doane had maneuvered several times in the area and knew the terrain well. His former regiment, the 31st Infantry (U.S.), had organized our regimental position. He had paid a visit to the front lines, and I felt it not so necessary to go over them that day. We went to supper after which I prepared my bunk for the night and soon darkness came on. One of the disadvantages of the entire war, including prison camp life, was the lack of lights at night and the density of mosquitoes that forced one to bed under his mosquito bar (netting) a little after dark and up at daylight. This made the time in bed entirely too long in the tropical 12 hour day and 12 hour night.

Around daylight there was a great deal of small arms fire and I expected a general attack but it did not come. The same happened each morning for some time. Unseasoned troops usually get nervous and do a good deal of shooting to boost up their courage just before daylight. After breakfast I looked over our front lines and spent a good deal of time there every day. The main line of resistance ran along the edge of the woods for 2,400 yards where a knoll or small hill ended and the rice paddies of the San Vicente Valley began. These rice paddies were very level and open and made an ideal field of fire.

The engineer battalion in our support was beginning to open and close the dams on the San Vincente River and flood the rice paddies so hostile tanks could not cross them. The men were digging in and deepening foxholes and preparing machine gun, AA, and mortar emplacements, as well as increasing the barbed wire entanglement barricades. Our tank defense was just beginning; not more than a dozen of the several thousand rice paddies had been soaked and the roads leading into our lines were wide open to hostile tanks. So for the first few nights we had the artillery commander send us some 75mm pieces on self-propelled mounts to strengthen our tank defenses. In a few days, a large number of rice paddies were flooded and softening up and the engineers had blown large holes in the road, filling them with water, so this was no longer necessary.[2]

On the second morning there was a great deal of firing on our left flank. I sent Captain Mark Wohlfeld with a patrol to contact the battalion on our left and find out what it was about. He found a good many Filipinos shooting at each other and at Japanese snipers whom they ran out of the trees. This practice of shooting at each other in the dark hours of the early morning is not uncommon among unseasoned troops. I got a Silver Star decoration for Captain Wohfeldt for his gallantry in leading this patrol. He was a brave soldier and was fond of patrol work. Next morning there again was heavy firing at the same place, so on my daily inspection of our front line I visited the battalion commander on our left. This time the Japs had come down in considerable numbers, and he had three or four dead ones lying out in the front of his lines to show for his day's work besides a couple of Jap wristwatches and a pocket watch he had garnered for souvenirs.[3]

Things settled down in the sector and we had about sixty or more days of relative calm so far as ground activities were concerned. The Japs had pulled out their main forces moving them on towards Singapore and the Dutch East Indies. They left only a holding force behind and we used the time in heavy night patrolling and completing our defenses. The front line foxholes had to be consolidated into continuous trenches, machine guns had to be sighted, dead spaces covered with rifle fire and grenade pits, and a thousand and one little details attended to which make up an infantryman's work. Colonel Doane and I kept the men on the job, and when General Hugh J. Casey, chief engineer for USAFFE came through on an inspection of all Bataan front lines, he cited our regiment for the progress made. We received at all times 100 percent support from all higher commanders. On one occasion, General Jonathan M. Wainwright came to see us and approved our policies.[4]

The visit of General Wainwright came about in an unusual way. A young air officer whom I had known at Langley Field, Virginia some years before, now an air corps lieutenant colonel, paid us a visit. His proposition was that air aid was coming from Australia, and that our pilots, now commanding companies and platoons operating as infantry, were too weak due to slim rations to handle the new high-powered planes.

His plan was to take them back to air corps headquarters and feed them up so they would be strong enough to operate these planes that he had been assured would soon be in. Colonel Doane and I listened carefully to his proposition. I excused myself to go to the rear. Doane followed, and we discussed what to tell him. Our decision was to give them all the pilots they wanted upon written orders from II Corps or higher authority. The young officer went back to his car walking on dust and air. He had won his victory.

I called II Corps and asked for General Parker. He was not available but his G-1, Colonel Ovid O. "Zero" Wilson, was on the phone. I explained the situation and insisted that every time he took a pilot from us that he replace him with an officer of equal rank. Next morning about 1:00 a.m. the phone rang. It was Zero wanting Colonel Doane, who was out in the front lines.[5]

"Get him quick. Generals Parker and Wainwright are on the way to your command post."

A runner soon located Doane and he came in; meantime the two generals arrived. I very cordially offered to conduct for them a thorough inspection of our front lines. No, they did not want that, but sat for a pair of minutes to await the arrival of Colonel Doane who told them briefly of the situation. General Wainwright was complimentary of our work. He had just seen a report of General Casey on our front line progress.

Colonel Doane detailed our situation and the plan to take our pilots from us and from front line duty.

"Tell them to show me an airplane and I will give them all the pilots they need, but in the meantime they will stay here and do what you and Hardee tell them to do," was General Wainwright's quick decision. This was the last we ever heard of the matter. It has always been my experience that higher commanders in time of war, whether they knew you personally or not, were so glad to have subordinates who could do the work that they gave them their unqualified support.

When the front areas were nearing completion, I turned my attention to the regimental reserve line. Little could be done here except clear out a path through the jungle, and thin a field of fire. If the field of fire were cleared it would be too obvious to aviation. Trail 38 ran through about the middle of our sector from rear to front. There were no lateral trails to connect us with our neighbors on the right and left. On the left we opened a foot path to mark the reserve line, digging foxholes where old paths and trails intercepted. This in the final crisis was extremely useful for the C.O. 32nd Infantry (PA), Colonel Johnson, who with part of his forces used it to reach our command post. On the right a truck trail was opened for the delivery of supplies and to relieve traffic on Trail 38. This was planned and used by our regiment to retreat to the main north-south road. So the reserve line played a vital part in the final crisis.[6]

The enemy had complete air superiority during this period. Our air strength consisted of from four to six pursuit planes on Bataan airfield. These were not released as fighters but had to be held by the high command for reconnaissance purposes. When we were in Shanghai in 1932 and the Japs were mercilessly bombing the helpless Chinese army in the Chapei district of the city, they came over so regularly at 9:30 a.m. and 2:00 p.m. that you could set your watch by them. I used to thank God in all sincerity that I was a soldier of one of the largest and richest countries on earth and they could never do that to me. But here we were in Bataan, about 15,000 Americans and some 70,000 Filipinos and in the same plight and taking the same merciless twice-a-day bombings except they were hammering us with more planes. Eighteen dive bombers, except when the engines were being overhauled in nine of them, visited us twice daily. The heavy bombers varied in number from 27 to about 75, but did most of their work against the rear areas and Corregidor.[7]

The hot season was on. All roads, trails, and paths were shoe-top deep in dust. We moved our regimental command post about three hundred yards to the rear to get better cover, to get on the reverse slope of a small hill, and to get away from the dust on Trail 38 that ran by the first command post.

By the middle of February we were beginning to lose considerable weight and to feel the pinch of a lack of food. On January 5, we had been put on two meals per day and on half rations. Many relics of garrison days brought from Manila, Stotsenburg, and Nichols Field began to disappear from the table. Then bread and meat began to appear less and less on the menu. About March 1, the meat was reduced to four ounces per day per man. This was a very tasty Australian combination of ham and mutton. In a few more days bread and meat disappeared entirely and it was largely rice, soup, and a cup of coffee or tea. I was to go without a good meat meal for more than three years.[8]

I tried for some weeks of this decreased diet to keep strong by keeping up the usual inspection and training tours daily, but soon realized this was only consuming what little energy and fat there was left, and I had best conserve it by taking as little exercise as possible consistent with sound sleeping at night. This policy I followed for the next three years and believe I owe my life to it. I did not weigh in Bataan but must have gone done from 190 to about 140 pounds.

The ground situation underwent a gradual change. Our patrols, cooperating with the patrols of the 31st Infantry (PA), commanded by my old friend Colonel John W. Irwin, soon found that the enemy held no definite front line, but were largely withdrawing their troops except for a few sentry squads in the daytime to rear areas. They were holding a front line at night by a series of roving patrols that would occupy alternate positions each night. A mountain range terminating in the Mariveles Mountains rose like a hog's back through the center of the Bataan Peninsula. Our front line ran through Mount Samat in the center of this range. The enemy were constantly concentrating their troops and artillery in the mountain opposite Mount Samat. This sector was about 4,000 yards to our left and was held by Filipino troops under a Filipino general, Mateo Capinpin, whom we had known at Fort McKinley some years before.[9]

It did not take Colonel Doane and me long to estimate that when the attack did come it would come right on top of this mountain range and be directed headlong on Mount Samat. We did not miss our guess. We had our front well-defended with every kind of automatic weapon the air corps men could tear out of wrecked planes. Our 2,400 yards contained over 75 machine guns, and with our excellent field of fire, entanglements and tank barricades, we longed to see them give us a frontal attack. But no such luck![10]

On March 11, 1942, General MacArthur and his group left Corregidor for Australia. Lieutenant Colonel Allen L. Stowell, the signal officer for II Philippine Corps, paid Colonel Doane and I a visit on the morning of March 12 and told us of the departure and the calling of General Wainwright from Bataan to Corregidor to take over the command. We talked it over at some length and decided it would be best not to give the information to the regiment until it was broadcast. Morale was low and getting lower as the prospect of any help by sea or air ever reaching us was dwindling. Many rumors of help coming circulated and we never put any damper upon them for each one seemed to boost morale. Those of us who knew the set up felt that help could not reach us, but to talk of it only added to despair.[11]

Our first intimation that help could not reach us came late in January when President Roosevelt said in a fireside chat to the nation that some places would have to be sacrificed and others immediately strengthened. The Philippines would be redeemed. We knew his words had been well chosen. Redemption could come only after its loss. After General MacArthur and his staff reached Australia we talked of their going freely to our officers. After the first few days of radio announcements concerning the organization of forces in Australia, I realized fully that it would take at least two years for our forces to fight back and that help of no sort would reach Bataan.[12]

The Japs were holding us in a small area with a small force. We did not have the air support, the supplies or the trained troops to drive out of it, though a combat force of two good divisions could have accomplished splendid temporary results. We were no more than self-supporting prisoners of war, and anytime the enemy chose to do so, he could bring in several good combat divisions and close us out. Just when he would do this was the imponderable. To keep up morale and encourage troops to fight under these conditions was the most difficult task I have faced in my army service. It is a lot easier to fight on the winning side.

Not only food, but medicine began to get scarce. Quinine for prevention of malaria had to be discontinued. All of it was necessary for treatment of actual cases instead of preventative use, but quinine for treatment held out through the days of Bataan. Wherever food is scarce, a black market arises. Local carabao, rice raised locally, canned goods, tobacco, and liquors brought from Manila in bancas (small boats) and sold at exorbitant prices were the black market items. The natives who ran the bancas usually landed at Orion, and since they supplied Americans the Japs would punish them if caught or would turn their machine guns on their bancas if seen.[13]

Our orders were to turn over all seized food to the quartermaster to be distributed to the troops. Of course, a great deal would have to be seized to make an issue of one cigar or cake of brown sugar per man. The result was that the troops on the front line would seize and turn in food to the quartermaster to distribute to all and only a small portion would get back to the front line troops. This made the order hard to enforce. Usually when a group of men killed a carabao they dressed it for their company mess and said nothing about it.[14]

During our quiet period at the front, I received a note from Colonel Louis Hutson stating that he had been badly wounded. I went to the rear for a day to see him and also talked a few minutes with the two nurses who came with us on the *Coolidge*. Louis was in bad condition. I found him on the operating table taking a blood transfusion and the doctors held little hope for him but everyone was doing what they could to help and encourage him. I was uneasy about the nurses as I could well foresee the fall of Bataan. Lieutenant Nancy Gillahan got through to Australia from Corregidor and back home in 1942, while Lieutenant Evelyn Whitlow was interned at Santo Tomas and returned home a few weeks after the American forces liberated the internees at Manila. Both were promoted upon return home. I found these young ladies sticking by Louis faithfully, just as the heroic women of Bataan did for all our sick and wounded. Braving untold hardships, unspeakable embarrassments, and frequently under hostile bombings these "Angels of Bataan" earned the admiration and gratitude of the Bataan forces such as have never been earned before in our history.

I shall never forget Easter Sunday and Monday 1942. The Japs laid days of preparation fire on Mount Samat with every available gun. The artillery was firing most of the day and night laying successive concentrations on a 2,400 yard front and through the depth of a division area. It was a very heavy concentration and it seemed impossible that anything could live through it. It far exceeded any preparation fire I had seen in the Meuse-Argonne in 1918.

They had concentrated and dug in their artillery pieces in the mountain facing Mount Samat and had concealed them on reverse slopes where our artillery could not reach them. Their artillery was supported by 18 dive bombers and 48 heavy bombers that worked all day against the sector, carried numerous loads of bombs from nearby fields, and swarmed over Mount Samat like so many buzzards.

After two days of this heavy preparation the Japanese infantry moved into the sector. They found little resistance as the Filipinos had been thoroughly blasted out. Flesh and blood has its limitations and these untrained, poorly equipped, and half-starved men, their ranks always thinning, were forced and blasted out. The Filipinos were not to be blamed for this condition. It has never been different throughout history. Recruits were pitted against seasoned veterans of five years fighting in China. Bladensburg and Bull Run were being repeated. The war was young; Gettysburg and Yorktown were yet to come.[15]

On Tuesday, after two days of preparation by the artillery and the airplanes, the Japanese infantry moved into the Mount Samat sector and the same artillery and air preparation was begun in the sector adjacent to and in our direction. After two days similar preparation in the sector next to ours, the Jap infantry moved in and by this time had penetrated the Mount Samat sector to a depth of from two to four miles.

It appeared that we were on the list for the next two days of artillery and airplane bombardment. We dreaded it tremendously. Only one or two things saved us. The enemy had penetrated on our left flank so deeply that he could attack us from the flank without artillery support; besides, his artillery as located was not best suited to support their infantry while coming in on our left flank. The San Vincente River was also a factor. It ran through our sector from south to north, paralleling our regimental boundary and just inside the other fellow's sector. When it reached the front line it turned east and ran parallel to it, thus furnishing water to flood the rice paddies in our front.[16]

On the night of April 6 we had information from II Philippine Corps that General Bluemel had formed a line on the east bank of the San Vincente River and would protect our left flank. I went to bed reasonably satisfied, but fully expecting the artillery to come down on us early next morning. When daylight came we went to breakfast as usual. No artillery. The airplanes opened up on us about 8:30 a.m. and shelling of our rear areas began. Small arms fire on our left began and continued intermittently. At 9:00 a.m., the commanders of two battalions on our immediate left reported to our headquarters. Both had the same story, they had lost their battalions. Lack of food and equipment, continuous bombing and shelling, hunger, despair, and constant attrition since December 8th had caused their thinning ranks to be cut to pieces under a heavy Japanese assault. This left our flank to the west (left flank) entirely unprotected.[17]

Before these battalion commanders had finished their stories, their regimental commander, Colonel Johnson of the 32nd Infantry (PA), came into the command post accompanied by two or three staff officers. Two of his battalions had been cut to pieces as aforementioned. His other battalion has been separated from him on the other side of the San Vincente, and presumably was fighting under his division commander, General Bluemel. We tried for the next two days to get in touch with General Bluemel without success. Colonel Johnson attached himself to us with permission of the corps commander.[18]

The enemy were penetrating our left flank just in the rear of our main line of resistance. They also were coming at us on the left in the vicinity of our regimental reserve line, and were attacking from the left flank in the vicinity of our kitchens some two miles in our rear and along Trail 38. We had withdrawn our outpost line of resistance earlier in the morning with the hopes that some of the enemy might come under fire of our well-defended front line, but no such luck. We were now in the act of withdrawing our front left battalion and facing them towards the west along Trail 38 and a carabao trail to prevent the Japs from cutting us into pieces.[19]

Colonel Doane reached the corps commander on the telephone. He gave permission to withdraw everything to the regimental reserve line. I took a car and truck, had the records and part of the radio equipment loaded on, and ventured down Trail 38 to our regimental reserve line where I turned left on the truck trail that had been opened and established the command post on a stream where our supporting engineers had been bivouacked. Colonel Doane followed within a half hour. We had no sooner established there with our front line along the regimental reserve line than it became obvious that we would soon have to take another position further to the rear. It was about 11:00 a.m. and the next likely defense line appeared to be along the Damulog Trail.

Neither the high command nor anyone else could conceive of the battle lasting after our Orion-Bagac line had been overrun, so no plans beyond this line had been made. It was the duty of every regimental or higher commander to fight his way back as best he could and do everything possible to preserve the combat effectiveness of his unit. I took the command car with its driver, Corporal Edward Gerken, and went in search of a command post site located in the rear of the Pandan Trail. As we went down the trail we found some of our units, not understanding their position in the line, and marching to the rear. As soon as they were oriented, turned around, and started towards their position, we were attacked by three dive bombers. We escaped their fire by running the car under some trees that overhung the trail a hundred or so yards ahead.[20]

The command post location was soon spotted on the trail near the Pandan River. By two o'clock we had the troops stretched along the Pandan Trail and the command post moved to the new location. I had sent a message (radio Morse code) to the corps commander via our signal officer, Lieutenant Damon "Rocky" Gause, stating that we could hold this position until midnight. The trail across the Pandan River in the direction we were headed towards the rear wound up a long steep hill, and while I was writing the radio message the Japs were using the most effective shrapnel barrage on this hill and trail that I had ever seen. It completely obstructed all traffic, and threw a piece of shrapnel onto the folding table where I was writing the message.

"You had better get in this shell proof until this is over," said "Rocky," who was one of the pluckiest young officers we had. I kept on writing and the barrage lifted.

This was the last message sent to Corps from the regiment, and the last time I saw Lieutenant Gause, our signal officer. He was a rugged individual, a good pursuit pilot, and had laid plans that as soon as the surrender came to get a *banca*, stock it, and take off for Australia. He had invited me to join him. I told him one in a thousand would get through and be the hero of the day. I had confidence that he would get through. I declined to join him on account of age and physical condition. He got through, communicated with loved ones, wrote a book of his experiences and was later killed in a test flight from an airfield in England during 1944. Upon arrival in the states he communicated with my family, the letter reaching them on Thanksgiving Day 1942—a real Thanksgiving Day for them as the official telegram from the War Department reached home just before Christmas 1942 giving the first official news that I was a prisoner of war.[21]

We had been moving towards the southeast. Our withdrawal had not been straight to the rear of our position but had been towards the rear of the front lines occupied by Colonel Jack Irwin's 31st Infantry (PA). They had been hit very lightly so far, but had conformed to our movements and occupied a position on our right flank. Their command post was close to ours. Captain Marion R. Lawton, one of his officers from Garnet, South Carolina, opened a bottle of good Scotch whiskey and passed it around. It was his last bottle and the first whiskey I had seen in over two months and the last I was to see for a long time.[22]

In a few minutes information was received that Japanese tanks had come down the main east road and assaulted and broken through Colonel Irwin's front on our right. As the trail we must use or take to the jungle still led diagonally across the rear of Irwin's regiment, it was time for us to move again if we were to avoid being cut off. There was no time to reconnoiter for a command post. We loaded up and started out into a new Hudson car that had about 1,200 miles on the speedometer. It had been used by our regimental surgeon, Major Charles H. Morehouse, before he was called to Corregidor to go to Australia with General MacArthur.[23]

The car was built very close to the ground, and had already been used badly by rocks and stumps that it could not straddle. Lieutenant George W. Kane, the S-1, had the records in it, and Lieutenant Bert Schwarz, the S-3, was the driver. We crossed the Pandan River where some Filipinos lay who had been killed during the morning's rain of shrapnel. We also passed a couple of army vehicles and a large commercial bus that had likewise been wrecked. As we went up the shelf-like road that wound up the hill that separated the Pandan River from Damulog Trail, a rock appeared in the center of the road. Lieutenant Schwarz chose to avoid it by going around on the soft embankment side of the newly made road. The left side of the car sank in the soft dirt.[24]

Six dive bombers dived on us without firing. We took cover in the woods ahead. The car left the road blocked. It was soon obvious that the bombers were out of ammunition or were waiting for more remunerative targets. A traffic jam on the hill would be what they were looking for, and this would occur shortly with our wrecked car stopping the road. The planes kept circling and diving, but not expending any ammunition. I took the detail back to the car. Taking out our musette bags and the regimental records while abandoning our bedding rolls and typewriters, we rolled the car over the embankment and watched it roll over several times until it was completely wrecked.

When we arrived at the Damulog Trail, sentries were put out to guard against surprise, and the troops rested while Colonel Doane and I went about four miles down the main road to a radio station where Colonel Jack Irwin was to meet us. Irwin was there and had contacted II Corps who had him standing by for a reply. The reply came about dark and directed his regiment to take a position along the main road near Limay, some ten to 20 kilometers south and to our rear. "Doane's regiment to conform," read the radio. We sent back for the senior battalion commander to march the regiment to Limay.

Daylight found us about a kilometer south of Limay and on the road on the south bank of the Alangan River. We were to go in the woods here and take position facing north in the woods on a hill that overlooked the Alangan Valley, but we were about an hour late in arriving. Daylight broke with us still on and alongside the road, and the Japanese observation planes came over and spotted us. Colonel Irwin's 31st Infantry (PA) occupied the road from the first 1,000 yards to the west where we joined him and occupied the next 1,000 yards. The men set in to organize their line for defense.

By 8:30 a.m., 18 dive bombers began to pour their bombs down on the 1,000 yard front occupied by Irwin's regiment, and kept up the fire all day. Jack had been very proud of his regiment up to this time and with cause. It was the only Philippine Army regiment with the Corps that was still intact, as the others had been badly mauled and cut to pieces. The bombing was heavy and almost continuous. Many men were killed and even more severely wounded so that when the attack came at 6:00 p.m. they were unable to put up a stiff enough resistance to hold off the assaulting Japs.[25]

CHAPTER 4

The Last Days in Bataan

I had established the regimental command post about five or six hundred yards in the rear of the front lines in an abandoned tank park where there were some Nips' shacks. I was completely exhausted, not having rested for over 30 hours. I took about a three-hour sleep while the front line under the senior battalion commander was being occupied. Upon awakening, I ate my first can of C-rations, meat and vegetable stew. I had carried the can in my musette bag for some days in anticipation of such an emergency. I also had a can of the dry rations, hard biscuits and chocolate, to go with it.[1]

I then went on an inspection of the front lines, beginning on our right where we joined Colonel Irwin's regiment. I saw at once the situation had already been made hopeless by the merciless bombings that had been poured on his regiment. A flight of dive bombers caught us when we were at the edge of his sector. It was about 3:30 p.m. We lay flat on the ground by a clump of bamboo and they dropped their bombs within fifty feet. The bombs fell in the ravine and scattered fragments and debris in the bamboo over our heads. Again we had saved ourselves by falling on our bellies when the planes attacked.[2]

The front line had an excellent command of the valley and the opposite hills. About 5:00 p.m. when I was finishing the inspection, I could see a few Jap infantrymen coming towards our lines on the opposite hills, some four to five hundred yards away. I had arrived at our command post but a few minutes when we began to hear brisk small arms firing. I had just finished telling Colonel Doane of the situation on our right, and how Colonel Irwin could not possibly have enough of his men left to hold the road against a hostile sortie when Lieutenant Colonel Maverick called from the front line on the "walkie talkie," the only piece of signal equipment we had left. A general attack was on.

Its spearhead followed the north and south road. The enemy was meeting little resistance there. Our right flank was unprotected. We had no reserves.[3]

"Withdraw and assemble the troops on Cabcaben," was Colonel Doane's brief reply.

Cabcaben was some six or more kilometers to the rear and the last possible position we could defend before the enemy would be in our hospital area, and even then the fire of their rifles would carry into the tents where our sick and wounded lay. We had in mind to gather the command and form a line facing the north at the far side of the air strip and astride the road. We took off in our command car with the staff in it accompanied by another car.

The Japs had blocked our egress into the main road, so we followed the trail towards the hills in the opposite direction for a few hundred yards. It was a broad, well-used trail, and appeared to lead on to our destination or join others that would, but it soon came to naught and we were forced to abandon our transportation. I left all behind but a field bag and a small black handbag and we started out on foot. I carried the field bag and the orderlies carried the black handbag. Its transportation was useless as I was never to see it again. The field bag and part of its contents went with me to the end of prison life.

The foot paths lead through the foot hills and it took us about six hours to make the trip. Colonel Doane was weak from his previous sickness, and I made efforts to slow the pace down to a reasonable rate of march and keep the group together. The younger men, however, got ahead, took separate trails, and soon about half of the personnel were separated from us. About 9:00 p.m., we reached the area of the artillery ammunition dumps and were hurried through because they were being prepared for demolition. Here Lieutenant Taylor, our artillery liaison officer, disappeared from our column never to be heard from again. He had been planning to take to the hills and not surrender. He could see the inevitable, and no doubt the preparation for the destruction of the ammunition dumps was enough evidence.[4]

In the dump area we came into the main truck trails now crowded with transportation and got a ride for our personnel. We were loaded on two trucks, Colonel Doane and I in the leading one. After going about a mile the trucks came to a fork in the trail and took the wrong fork that lead out to some artillery positions and ceased. The long convoy came to a halt and had to back up about 300 yards to get back on the right trail. I got out and went back on foot to direct this backing up. When I had finished I found that the truck I had been riding on had not backed up all the way but had cut across from one trail to the other, and had gone on and left me high and dry. This had separated me from Colonel Doane and that part of the command post personnel who were with him.

The main trail we were on led into the main road near Little Baguio, about two miles south of Cabcaben. I picked up a ride to the junction of this trail and a point where a trail led by the airfield to Cabcaben. From this point I walked to Cabcaben, a distance of about two miles, arriving there at midnight. The first thing I spotted was an armored car radio communication section located on the side of the road at the top of a knoll overlooking the Cabcaben airfield. I inquired here for Colonel Doane and party, and then went on an hour's search for them. My search being unsuccessful, I returned to the radio car about 1:00 a.m. It was at the point at which our regiment should pass in the next hour. I made inquiries as to the location of the front line, and even learned that General Bluemel whom we had been trying to get in touch with for two days had fought his way back to the main road and joined our forces. He had formed a line of defense along the Lamao River, and had stopped our regiment and used them in the line. This position was four or five kilometers north of Cabcaben and where the river crossed the main north and south road.[5]

I turned away from the radio car to attempt to find and assemble as many of our command post personnel as possible, and then get in touch with our battalion commanders. Most of this appeared to be impossible until daylight. The regimental surgeon, Major Lentz, and his men were in the unfinished house across the road but I did not know it at the time. While I was on the radio car getting off some messages one of the most violent earthquakes I have ever experienced occurred. As I turned away to leave the radio car, two young staff officers from the 200th Regiment (Anti-aircraft) approached the car asking about the location of the front lines and of the Provisional Air Corps Regiment. The operator referred them to me.[6]

As the conversation progressed, it developed that their regiment had been ordered by General King to relieve us of our front line duties. I began to go over the situation with them and they asked if I would not get in the jeep and go back to their headquarters, about a kilometer in the rear, and confer with their regimental commander, Colonel Sage. I accepted the invitation and they were to return me at the end of the conference. Colonel Sage was a big fellow, about six feet, six inches tall, a newspaper man from Deming, New Mexico. I went over the situation with him and we arranged for the relief to take place at daylight. It was about 1:30 a.m. His men were physically exhausted, having served their anti-aircraft guns continuously for the last 48 hours. Some of the batteries had undergone as many as 20 dive bomber attacks.[7]

I commented on sending one exhausted regiment to relieve another exhausted unit of front line duty.

Colonel Sage looked me straight in the eyes and remarked in his slow, solemn way, "Did you know, colonel, that yours and my regiment are all that General King has left on the east side of Bataan?"

"Yes," I replied, "I knew it, but I had not realized it."

For one by one I had heard of or seen the Philippine regiments cut to pieces. The 31st Infantry (U.S.) had also been thrown in against the Japs a day or two before without success. So everything east of Mount Samat except these two regiments, and possibly the 31st Infantry (U.S.) had about lost its combat integrity. The 200th being an anti-aircraft regiment, it was not armed with machine guns (.30 caliber) or mortars but only rifles and bayonets.

"I do not discount the courage and ability of your men," I told Colonel Sage, "but it is useless under present conditions to send them out to stop the Jap army with rifles and bayonets. You may hold them back on your limited front for a few hours but the hills and mountains are full of them and they will come by every path and trail and be in your rear in large numbers by noon today, and will kill our sick, wounded and non-combatants."

I had a perfect horror of our sick and wounded being helplessly killed in bed and our nurses being ravished and finally massacred, those brave and devoted women who had labored so faithfully and sacrificed so much for our wounded. They had already been evacuated to Corregidor but I had been too busy fighting to know it.[8]

"Yes, you are right," replied Colonel Sage. "There is only one answer, and that is something no good American likes to speak of. I am going now to a conference with General King. Do I have your permission to quote you?"

"By all means," I replied, and added "General King has known me for many years and I believe he will rely on my judgment."[9]

Upon return to the radio car at Cabcaben, I talked with the lieutenant in charge and arranged that the MP sentry was to stop all members of the Provisional Air Corps Regiment that were passing to the rear and call me. I lay down on the road bank along by the radio car to catch a few winks of sleep as I could do nothing until daylight or until the approach of the 200th Coast Artillery (AA).

Just as I was preparing my resting place with a shelter half and blanket borrowed from the MP, the earth shook with a tremendous explosion and about two miles away a great pattern of smoke and sparks were shot in the air like an erupting volcano. Our largest ammunition dump had been demolished. It was followed by a number of smaller scattered explosions from other and smaller dumps.[10]

I had hardly fallen asleep when I was awoken by the lieutenant in charge of the radio car to volunteer the information that Colonel Williams and Major Hurt from General King's headquarters had gone forward in a jeep at 3:30 a.m. with a flag of truce. Of course this cancelled all plans for the relief of the regiment by the 200th Coast Artillery (AA). It would be best for me to go back to the II Corps, report the operations, and locate Colonel Doane. As both were to the rear there was no hurry so I went back to sleep and slept until about a half-hour before daylight. Upon awakening, I learned that Major Hurt had returned to bring General King and his staff to the Japanese commander, they having held Colonel Williams as a token of our good intentions. They were later to hold all our high commanders as hostages until their unreasonable demands were met.[11]

I walked about a kilometer to the headquarters of a battalion of the 24th Field Artillery (PS) who had been in our support for the entire Bataan operation. I wanted to borrow a car, but before they loaned it to me they insisted that I go down to the officers' mess and eat breakfast. On this point I needed no insistence, as everything was finished and the mess officer was trying to serve the best of what food was left before the Japs came. He had real coffee with sugar and canned milk, hot cakes with butter and jam, and some dried beef fried in fat. After breakfast, I took the car and looked along the road in the edge of the adjacent woods to see if I could locate Colonel Doane and the command post personnel, but without success. I was uneasy about him, and was afraid that under the strain another heart attack had caught him.

News of the surrender had not reached the Japanese airdrome so the first bombing mission caught the driver and me alongside the MP vehicle park. We parked the car and took cover in the woods. I crouched down at the base of a big tree and was protected laterally by its high projecting roots but had no overhead cover. The bombs were falling close around and collapsed my eardrums and I suppose would have burst them but I had my mouth open. A small fragment of bomb seemed to come out of the top of the tree and struck me in the thin hair of my upper forehead, breaking the skin and causing some bleeding. When the bombing ceased I passed an aid station. A Filipino doctor disinfected the wound and covered it with collodion or new skin. I put my hat back on and slept in it for a day or so. A few days later when I rested enough to shave and looked in the mirror the new skin was shedding. I removed it and the wound cured without leaving a scar.[12]

At the II Corps motor pool, I dismissed the driver to carry the car back to its home pool as everyone had hopes of riding out of Bataan in our own transportation. On the way to the general's tent I met Colonel Doane. He had the same thing in mind. At the general's tent we found General George M. Parker, the corps commander, and Colonel Charles L. Steel, the chief of staff. We told them the simple story of our last two days' operations. They listened with deep interest, seemed satisfied that we had done our best, and expressed their appreciation of our efforts and gratification that we had both come through it with our lives.[13]

We were followed by the regimental commanders of the two regiments of Philippine Army troops that had served on our immediate right and left flank. They both had the same story differing only in time and place as to when and where their organizations had been cut to pieces and lacked the battle cohesion to maintain their combat integrity. They were much chagrined but not to blame, and neither were the Filipinos, but our general lack of preparation lay at the roots of the cause. The Filipino Scouts of the 45th, 57th, and other infantry regiments made excellent soldiers. Colonel Irwin told me that prior to Pearl Harbor, some of his men had a few weeks' good training in but for the regiment as a whole they averaged having fired the rifle less than two shots per man. Many of them were never fully equipped. The lack of such a single item as a steel helmet is very detrimental to morale. They had never been assembled in a cantonment as these were not quite completed when the war began.[14]

Colonel Steel sent these two regimental commanders to the casual camp, and it was the last time I was ever to see Colonel Irwin. Colonel Steel asked Colonel Doane and me to wait for him at his tent. We enjoyed his hospitality by finding something to lay our heads upon, laying down in front of the tent and going fast asleep. When he came he said we had best stay with him as we were both too exhausted to go further. He later gave us both staff assignments so that in case we rode to our destination the Japs would not have any reason to question it.

We then went to breakfast. It was my second breakfast now at about 10:00 a.m. but I needed no urging as I had eaten the first around 7:00 a.m. They had good coffee, toast, ham, bacon, and giblets fried together. I never realized until then that bacon had so much strength, nor did I realize that it was the last I was to taste for about 34 months. It soon became evident that if the Japs found us that day they would hardly move us out so we prepared to spend the night.

Lieutenant Colonel Compton was the headquarters commandant and he and I went over to USAFFE where General King's staff had lived and had marched out hurriedly. I equipped myself with a bedding roll, mattress, blankets, sheets, mosquito bar, and all the clothes and sundry items needed. Compton had earlier in the day taken one of our trucks with a pass from a Japanese officer and had drawn from our rations dump four days of rations for our headquarters and that of the Philippine Department.

The Japs had discovered the department and had taken them out leaving the precious C-rations behind. We took the truck and brought these to our II Corps kitchen that gave us about 8 days of C-rations on hand, a thing that saved mine and no doubt a number of other lives. Here we saw our first evidence of Jap wastage and looting. The dry C-ration can consists of biscuits, soluble coffee, lump sugar, and a square of chocolate. Some Jap soldiers had opened several hundred cans, taken the chocolate and sugar and scattered the remainder of the contents and partly trampled them under foot.

My old friend Colonel Abraham Garfinkle, Philippine Scouts, had a large tent fly pitched under a large, thick group of trees near the kitchen. He invited me to share his lot so we set up a bunk and I lay on it and slept most of the remainder of the day. Colonel Doane had a bunk close by and beyond him a few yards was Colonel Compton. By special arrangement with the Japanese and through the courtesy of Colonel Sato, the Japanese area commander, we were all with the exception of Major General Parker permitted to remain in our II Corps command post site almost unmolested for seven days. During this seven day period, we had two good, big meals of C-rations daily. This permitted us to strengthen and rest up for the Death March that was to follow, or otherwise I do not believe either Colonel Doane or I could have made it; another of the many times that a kindly Providence has provided that our lives be saved.[15]

Just after dark on the first night a group of corps staff officers were sitting around our bivouac, Colonel Doane and I were lying down and I was about half roused up and entered into conversation with them. Doane and I had been too tired to say anything previously. Someone asked me a question, and

I told them in about five minutes recitation our fighting experiences from the beginning to the arrival at II Corps.

Everyone was deathly quiet while I was talking. When I finished, no one said a word for the next five or ten minutes. I fell back to sleep and the silence was still unbroken. The next morning, I asked Colonel Garfinkle what the trouble was, as there had been no questions, no comment and no discussions. I had judged my remarks to have gone flat or fallen on empty ears. He replied that it was quite the opposite. That our experiences had been so bitter and so vividly stated that no one could speak. After I finished all sat in silence and one by one drifted off to bed.

Jap looters began on the first afternoon to work through our camp, "shaking down" everyone they met for money, jewelry, and watches. I escaped the first day but early on the morning of the second day I hid my watch—a government issue—in my field bag and walked up towards the motor pool. The first Jap I met took my money, some ten pesos out of my watch pocket, but did not find my pocket book in my hip pocket. When I came back to my bunk he had gone through my baggage and taken my watch. Those who resisted were beaten badly.[16]

We sent a staff officer to Colonel Sato to protest our treatment. In my 34 months as a prisoner I knew of only four decent Japs—Colonel Sato was one of them. He came personally to apologize to General Parker, had some of the money and watches restored, and placed guards from his regiment in our area to prevent further looting. He also told us that the road was very crowded with troops going one way and prisoners the other and we could prepare to stay in our present position for some days. This suited us exactly, but we did not know how well it suited us, for it meant we were to miss the worst part of the Death March. There was nothing to do but keep house, eat, sleep, and rest for the next six days, and these were the things we needed most.

The corps staff industriously set about to close up their records and bury them. They were working on a citation order as the corps commander could award Purple Hearts and Silver Stars. Lieutenant Colonel Dennis "Dinty" Moore, the G-2 officer, came around and said the general had directed that Colonel Doane and I turn in to the G-1 section the necessary data for a Silver Star for each of us. We were not much interested as both of us were well supplied with Silver Stars from World War I, but decided a half loaf was better than none.[17]

I located a lead pencil and some writing paper and wrote up for each of us a Silver Star for one of our minor experiences. Then we thought of the embarrassing position Colonel Steel was in. He had gone through most of the war to date as commanding officer of the 31st Infantry (U.S.), and was more deserving than we, but being chief of staff he could not mention it. Colonel Doane had been his executive officer in the 31st, so he related an incident while I wrote it up. We finished the recommendation with all but his serial number. Soon Colonel Steel came in sight and I called to him for his serial number. He came over, sat down on Colonel Doane's bunk and talked to us for some time, and I got him started on his experiences with the 31st Infantry (U.S.).

During the day, orders were issued awarding Doane and I an oak leaf cluster each to be worn on our basic Silver Star decorations, and a basic Silver Star with oak leaf cluster to Colonel Steel. Incidentally, I carried these and several paragraphs more of this order through the entire debacle, and closed the chapter by sending them to the War Department or to the next of kin of surviving parties concerned.

CHAPTER 5

The Death March

On April 16 it became our time to move out. We were informed by the Japanese to be ready at our motor pool to begin the march at 1:00 p.m. We did not have enough trucks and cars for all to ride. We loaded our baggage, kitchen section, and rations (about three days) on the trucks, carried our field bags, and formed a column of about seventy to march. Colonel Steel, who was our chief of staff of the corps, was in charge. General Parker, our corps commander, had been taken from us some days earlier. To be in charge or command was only a phantom title. The Japs were running the show. Colonel Steel, Doane, and a Japanese officer rode in a command car. The remainder of us marched and carried our field bags. Due to Colonel Compton's and O.O. Wilson's foresight, we were each equipped with two days' worth of C-rations, another life saver. Lootings of our men began by Jap soldiers before our column started, but once in motion the sentries were a protection.

The first to speak to me was Colonel Pat Callahan, a long time Philippine scout officer.

"Well Dave, you told your classes at Fort Benning some years ago what the airplane would do in the next war. We did not believe you when you gave the order of attack: sea lanes, airfields, port areas, storage, supply lanes, and lastly combat troops. We thought the infantry all-important, but it happened just like you predicted."[1]

Then looting and shakedowns began, again. They were constantly repeated, throughout the march, and afterwards.

"Be that as it may, I hope that God is with us for the Devil is behind us," I replied as we watched a fellow prisoner being beaten and robbed, but once our column was in motion much of this looting by apparently stray soldiers stopped.

We expected to march to Cabcaben, a distance of about eight to ten kilometers. The march began about 2:00 p.m., near Kilometer Post 189. From this point on, dead bodies, wrecked transportation, and the debris and stench of the battlefield were with us. The first horrible sight was the body of a Filipino who had been killed in the middle of the road and all types of heavy Jap artillery pieces were crushing his body to nothingness on the paved road. They were striving with all might and man to get in good range of Corregidor, the last stand of the Americans and Filipinos in their conquest pathway. At one place where we halted for a rest, about 2,000 steel helmets, flattened by transportation, lay on the ground close by. This was the bivouac area of the 200th Coast Artillery (AA) and the men had surrendered and discarded their helmets here.[2]

At Cabcaben there was no shift in sentries to take us over, so Colonel Steel and the Jap officer agreed that we could march on to Lamao. It was little more than mid-afternoon and the overall distance was not more than twelve to fourteen miles. We marched on, arrived at our camp site, and made down for the night, eating our supper of C-rations before dark, with nothing furnished by the Japs. It had been an easy day's march, and our transportation so far was with us. Some tension was added to the situation at dark because of looting and the Jap sergeant made us sleep in a small space.

Next morning we took our cold breakfast of C-rations and it was replaced from our kitchen before we began the march, for none could foresee when we would lose our transportation. So far our hike had been normal, the hardships negligible. We were on the road by 7:30 a.m. with a new bunch of sentries that were not so kind and not so considerate when it came to giving rest periods. We got rests about every two and a half or three hours during the day.

Colonel Garfinkle lagged behind the column; we heard a shot and felt very uneasy about him, but when the column halted for the next rest he caught up before we resumed the march. All the morning we were losing our transportation and we had to stop several times and unload a truck or two and pile up the others or discard the baggage to give the trucks to the Japs. On the hill before we got to Limay they took our kitchen truck. Goodbye to eats and rations. About 10:30 a.m. when we crossed the stream going into Limay, they halted us, had our drivers pull the remaining trucks alongside the column and made us unload them at one of their MP control posts. They told us to take what we could carry, the rest was to remain behind.

Their excuse was that they needed the trucks and we realized that was the last we were to see of our personal baggage. Each prisoner had his canteen, mess equipment, and the contents of his field bag or blanket roll if he cared to carry one over his shoulder. This was the first flagrant violation of international law, but we were to experience many more. About noon, we passed through our old front lines where Colonel Irwin's regiment had defended for some 75 days before the general attack. Colonel Irwin, a large heavy-set man, faded away on the march and his fate was never definitely determined.

In the southern edge of Orion we were marched through a building on the side of the road and the enlisted men who possessed blanket rolls had their blankets taken from them. We learned later that the enlisted men in the Japanese army were not entitled to a blanket while serving in the tropics. They were good in observing international law when it worked in their favor. We passed an artesian well in the center of the town about 1:00 p.m. and were permitted to fill our canteens, the first water of the day. On the north side of the town we were marched into an open field opposite a Japanese guardhouse. Here we were lined up and spread out all our possessions for inspection and a "shake down." Pocket knives, mess kit knives, razors, razor blades, watches, jewelry, medicines, sometimes money and anything else that a Jap fancied was taken away.[3]

A former warrant officer of the U.S. Army, now serving in his reserve grade of major, stood beside me. His false teeth were irritating his gums and he made the mistake of placing them in his open mess kit. The dentist had ornamented them by placing a little gold on the eye teeth, probably worth forty to fifty cents. When the Jap sentry saw this bit of gold his eyes began to shine. He grabbed the teeth, and when Major Moore protested he whacked him over the head with the handle of a gold club, took the teeth and went his way leaving Moore to gum his food until his life was finally taken on one of the hellships bound for Japan near the end of the war.[4]

There was a commotion in the ranks near me when Captain Spigler of the air corps warning service and a Technical Sergeant Lee were taken out of the ranks. The Japs took them up to a sentry post by the roadside, tied their hands and feet and began yelling at them and beating them with sticks and planks that made a tremendous amount of noise. We had been advised on the day of the surrender to dispose of anything we had of Japanese use or make. These men had Japanese yen in their pocket books and hidden on their persons. The

Japs seemed to think that the only source of their having it must have been to take it off the dead. Neither were front line soldiers and they must have procured it from others for souvenirs or for contemplated use in prison camp. The Japs were not using yen in the islands but were using invasion pesos. The beatings continued for some time; they stopped for a while and resumed spasmodically for a period of about two hours.

Our inspection was over and we were ready to resume the march. We were held up by the burning of a truck of ammunition about a hundred or more yards on the road we were to march out on. They caused us to lie down while the exploding shells sent fragments over our heads and into the town beyond. No one was hurt. About two hours before sundown we were formed up and marched out. Captain Spigler and Sergeant Lee were tied up and still being beaten occasionally when we left. I was later told by a sergeant of the 31st Infantry (U.S.) who came in as we left that they continued this until about sundown, when they were untied and marched by a squad of Japs to some straw stacks about a hundred yards from the road. Here they were told to run for their lives and were shot down in cold blood for attempting to escape. At any rate, they were never heard of again.[5]

The new guard that marched us out of Orion seemed irritated by the delay caused by the burning truck of ammunition and greatly increased the rate of march to make up for the lost time. It was excessively hot and if one lagged in the column they beat him across the back with a riding crop or the handle of a golf club that the sentries carried in addition to their weapons. Colonel Louis R. Dougherty, a very fine old artillery officer, about 62 years old, who marched beside me, was struck over the head twice rather severely with a stick. It made our blood boil but he took it like a good soldier, remarking humorously that it didn't hurt because he had just put a wet towel in his cap. I was struck across the back of the shoulders with a riding crop but not severely. Lieutenant Colonel "Dinty" Moore who had been on staff work at II Corps was having a hard time. He had fallen about 50 yards or more behind the column and we could hear the sentry hollering and beating him on the back with a stick. He came through okay but he had his anxious moments; so did we all.[6]

After about an hour and a half of hard marching in the hot sun, and with all of us wet with sweat from head to foot, we reached the ruins of the town of Pilar. Here we were given a halt and allowed to fill our canteens. It was about two kilometers from this place to a camp site just south of the Balanga River bridge in the southern edge of the town of the same name. We made it to this camp site and were halted for the night, arriving without further incident just before dark. Here we were joined by Colonels Steel and Doane. They had ridden to Orion where the command car had been taken away from them. They had been "shaken down" and marched from Orion to the camp site earlier in the evening. We were given no supper and had not been fed by the Japs since we left our II Corps headquarters. Our C-rations had come in good, but were less and less in evidence in the loads we were carrying on our backs.

The camp site at Balanga was a particularly dirty, dreary, and desolate spot—a sandy, sparsely shaded piece of ground between the road and a curve in the river. A large clump of bamboo shaded our group. At night we slept under it and in the day we moved around in its shade as the sun moved. The Japs observed few sanitary methods as we knew them. Here, in all the Death March camping spots, and prison camps we were frequently reminded of this and little regard was shown for cleanliness. Cattle and fresh human excrement were everywhere, and should you clean it off the ground and throw it in a sparsely located straddle trench the odor would still be on the ground where you had to lay, using only your field bag for a pillow. We realized this condition at Balanga and in many places afterwards.

We stayed there two full days and three nights. We were bringing up the tail end of the Death March and they were waiting for prisoners to clear the roads and camps ahead of us. During these days we were to have more of Japanese barbarity. On the first day we were issued one meal of uncooked rice and they knew that most of us had no means of cooking. On the second day we were issued one meal of cooked rice, and another for breakfast on the third morning just before the day's march began. Including the Filipinos there were about a thousand or more in the Balanga camp, with few Americans besides the seventy in our II Corps group.

This camp site was a place in the bend of the river before we reached the town which was also full of prisoners waiting their turn to continue the march. It was a small town, the capital of Bataan province, with a large Catholic cathedral in the center of the town with the customary statue of Rizal, the Filipino hero in the front yard. Our camp site was particularly filthy. Its filth had been increased by the lack of sanitation and the smell of bloating and unburied bodies. The longer we remained there the greater it was to our advantage for the roads and camps ahead were clearing of the great jam of prisoners. The captors were not so irate, smaller groups were easier to handle, and roadside rests could be arranged more frequently.[7]

A small group can be halted, allowed to rest or refill canteens, and be put back on the march easily and in a few minutes but to do so to a continuous column is another matter. I do not condone, however, the fact that they had continuous columns and failed to give the periodic rest halts that are customary in all civilized countries and which they must give to their own troops.

Each morning when the Filipinos got up and moved about they left a considerable number of sick and dead lying around on the ground. The Japanese sentries gathered a detail of Filipinos and Americans to dig graves down by the river bank, gather up the dead, and bury them. Lieutenant Colonel W. Hinton Drummond of the medical corps, who had been our II Corps surgeon and who slept by me under the bamboo clump, was put on this burial detail the second morning we were at the Balanga camp site. Drummond was honest, conscientious, and a hard worker, and before we began the march he had stocked each of us with a good personal supply of quinine and other basic medicines. He had us taking various medical supplies on our person to turn back to him on arrival at the destination so that we might have some medical supplies in our first camps.[8]

About noon he came back in a bad state of nervous agitation and stated that some of the Filipinos that had been picked up by the detail and carried to their graves were not dead. Some had attempted to crawl out of their graves and had been bayoneted or knocked in the head by the Japs, while others had been pushed back into the holes and covered up without the fatal blow.

"They are still doing it," he said, "and you can step out there and see it."

But none of us cared to look voluntarily on such atrocities. A soldier has to face too many horrors to voluntarily look upon them. An American prisoner of war, about half conscious, suffering from diarrhea and almost covered with his own discharge, almost black with flies, and naked from his waist down, lay close by. The Jap police detail came along and wanted to knock him in the head, throw him in the latrine close by, and cover him up. We could smell the stench and see part of the hands and feet of a couple of prisoners whom they had already buried there. We persuaded them that this was an American who was still living, and should not be so treated. Two Americans died that afternoon that were lying close to this man, but when we left next morning he was still living. We understand from others who remained and joined us later that the Japs finally, in the case of the diarrhea patient, succeeded in their murderous design.[9]

That afternoon three or four Japs came up in a truck looking for canteens. Someone passed the word quickly that if we would break the chains on our canteens they would not take them. They were too close on me to allow me the opportunity to break mine. So they gathered my canteen along with about 30 to 40 others, strung them on a rope, threw them on the truck and went on their way. This left about half of our II Corps group without means of providing themselves with drinking water. Colonel Dougherty and Colonel Pat Callahan shared their water with me on the next day's march at the end of which I found a Filipino soldier who was carrying two canteens and bought one for ₱3.00. This was the best investment I made while a prisoner of war.[10]

Next morning, we were fed a mess kit of steamed rice with salt, a canteen cup or canteen of water, and formed up about 9:30 a.m. to begin the day's march. Why they chose to hike us in the heat of the day we never understood. Colonel Garfinkle and Captain Avery were sick and weak. They fell in at the head of the column. By this time we had learned that they bayoneted or shot those who fell out but that if the weak or sick remained in camp and did not start the hike that they would give them a ride part or all the way to the next stop or to an advanced camp site. In some cases when starting from the camp alone or in groups of twos and threes, the weak and sick were allowed to hike at will and without sentries. Under these conditions we persuaded these two officers to fall out and not begin the march with us as none of us felt strong enough to drag them. We felt that there would be enough grief with those who began feeling strong and gave out during the day.[11]

The day's march was long, hot, and exhausting. Halts were too infrequent, about every three or four hours. I do not remember being given any opportunity to fill our canteens though we passed several artesian wells in the barrios along the roadside. I remember one or two people being beaten and abused for breaking ranks at some of these wells and filling their canteens. Natives who attempted to approach our column and give or sell us fruits or food were beaten off or shot by the Jap sentries.

I walked and prayed with each step that I not fall out with the heat. I was afraid I might fall out with heat exhaustion and be shot or bayoneted by the murder squads that brought up the end of the column. I had a few salt and saccharine tablets that I had purchased for use at Camp Wheeler, Georgia. I used them sparingly. We were so low physically that a small taste of chocolate or a lump of sugar from our C-rations would boost us up as much as a shot of whiskey would do in normal times. At a curve in the road there were a number of shots. I could see some groups of natives running through the trees but could not tell whether it was a break on the part of some of our Filipino prisoners or the Japs driving off some native vendors.

It was not an uncommon sight to see a prisoner lying along the roadside with a Jap sentry trying to get him up and in the march again. A few minutes later you would hear a couple of shots, look back and see the Jap sentry walking fast to regain his place alongside the column, with the prisoner lying still by the roadside or other Japs tossing his body into the roadside ditch. Some of the patients in our hospitals had joined the columns, clad in their pajamas, and several of their bodies could be seen in a bloated condition lying alongside the road. Earlier I had seen one legless hospital patient pushing himself along on a platform mounted on skate wheels. I have often pondered his fate.

Strange people! If a captive made a conscientious effort to save his life by hiking and keeping up with the column and because of physical infirmities could not do so he was clubbed to death, bayoneted, or shot. But if a person became disheartened and attempted to commit suicide they would save his life by not permitting him to do so. I saw Lieutenant Martin who lived in Manila prior to the war, who had been suffering from a bad case of arthritis, break on this day from the column and throw himself in small stream to drown. A Jap sentry ran down to the stream and pulled him out of the water. Our column marched on and my guess was that they would not let him accomplish his purpose. I was correct, for sure enough I met and talked and lived with him in Bilibid some 26 months later. Colonel Steele, who had an attack of pneumonia and was a patient in Sternberg General Hospital at the beginning of the war and who had not the opportunity to recover normal strength, had fallen out. An officer was with him. I was uneasy about them so I persuaded the sentry it was time to halt our column for a rest. He moved us on a hundred or so yards further and halted us.[12]

The guard was changed and we pulled into Orani about an hour before sundown. The new guard had quickened the pace, as was usually the case, and this had taken the strength out of us. It is usually very hot just before sundown in the tropics, and this day was no exception. We were halted in the streets of the barrio for about half an hour. Here a young captain fainted from heat exhaustion. Another colonel and I revived him and helped him into the compound if such a complimentary name can be given the squalid lot in which we were to spend the night. We were halted at the gate and a Jap looter tried to get my field bag away from me. I refused and as the argument got intense we were marched into the compound leaving the looter behind, I with my field bag, and the last of my personal possessions safe.

The lot was nothing more than a small cow and hog pasture in the back of a Filipino yard. The tide from the river pushed up and covered about a fourth of it when it was high. The tide was low when we went in and many during the night woke up to find themselves sleeping in an inch or more of water with all their possessions soaked in water with human and animal dung. I fortunately was bedded down on the high ground. The lot was as filthy as any Japanese heart could wish, and was covered with human dung and debris, showing evidence of many thousands of prisoners having been crowded into it. We were permitted to fill our canteens at an artesian well in the Filipino's back yard just outside the pasture. After a supper of one mess kit of steamed rice without salt we made down for the night. All we had to do was to spread our raincoats to lie on and use our field bag for a pillow. The Japs had taken all our other belongings.[13]

When I awoke a little after daylight, a G.I. who had been a helper at II Corps was swearing as he had been caught in the rise of the tide and was brushing off the fresh human and cattle wastage from his clothes.

He remarked, "I have reached the lowest depth of degradation."

"Don't swear about it," the sergeant major remarked. "It is your own fault. If you had never learned to read and write you would not have been caught in this mess."

You can always trust the G.I. for his sense of humor. It was my lift for the day.

After a breakfast of a mess kit of steamed rice and a canteen of water we were off for an early start. We were told that we would hike to Lubao that day. It was the only time they did not start us out in the heat of the day. The reason—a two-day hike in one day confronted us. At each camp site we picked up hundreds of Filipino army captives. Now the column appeared to be about a half mile long with the Americans bringing up the rear. The morning was hot and the atmosphere was oppressive. We marched from about 7:30 to 10:30 a.m. before we were given the first halt. This was on a long curve in the road just south of Layac Junction and the stream and bridge south of the road forks. There was an artesian well in the field about a hundred yards from the road. We went over and bathed our faces and hands, got a drink, and filled our canteens.

During the remainder of the halt we occupied ourselves in going through our field bags and throwing away every surplus ounce. A change of khaki clothes, underwear, and shelter halves were discarded. We were up against it and an extra pound might mean death. Our two days of C-rations were all used up. I pared down to one change of underwear and socks, papers, a face towel, and my toilet kit. I even went through my meager toilet kit and threw away one of the military hairbrushes my older daughter had given me on my 49th birthday.

Colonel Pat Callahan discarded his load one item at a time until he had only an empty field bag. He tried to give this away but could find no taker.

"It's a perfectly good bag," he said, "almost new," but no one wanted it.

Soon the column was again in motion with the men slowly dragging themselves along the road. We crossed the Culo River on a temporary bridge, our forces having blown the permanent bridge on the retreat to Bataan. Layac Junction, where the paved road forked for Olongapo, was deserted. Soon we passed under a sign across the road, announcing the border of Bataan and Pampanga provinces. I think everyone was glad to leave Bataan, the province of our suffering and humiliation, and all no doubt prayed and hoped for better luck in the provinces ahead. But this was only the beginning of sorrow and death.[14]

The men in the column began to fall out rapidly from heat exhaustion and many were dragging along, managing just to keep up. The guards were more sympathetic than usual. They slowed the pace and permitted a few Filipinos to stand along the side of the column and sell us things to eat as we passed. I bought a big ball of rice wrapped in a banana leaf. A small piece of dried fish was in the center. It was the first I had ever eaten, and it was good. I also got some fruits and something sweet. Another colonel received the opportunity and bought about ten or twelve pesos worth of lunches. He distributed them to the officers. They voluntarily offered to reimburse him when we halted and could get change, but only one or two ever did. The veneer of civilization is very thin, and people soon lose their sense of obligation when faced with hunger, hardship, and starvation. Under such circumstances the generous, brave, and unselfish are the men all too often left behind.[15]

It was noon and the heat was insufferable. The Hacienda de Rook was just ahead and was an emergency camp site for the Japs. They marched us in, putting the Americans in one side of the cattle lot and the Filipinos on the side next to the road gate. It was shady here and there were two spigots of running water from the hacienda water tank. We were told we would remain there until 2:00 p.m. so we made down to rest. Steel, Doane, Callahan, Compton, Stowell and I were together. At 2:30 p.m. we were served steamed rice and salt and told we would remain overnight and finish the march to Lubao next morning. Colonel Pat Callahan and I had made friends with a Jap sentry. He gave us a can of Vienna sausage or fish to add to our meal and it was a great help. Next morning he gave us a small can of pork and beans. We ate it between us and this was all the breakfast we had. The Japs had promised us breakfast but put us on the road to Lubao about 10:00 a.m. without it. It was a long, hard, hot march without food and took us until 4:30 p.m. to complete it.[16]

The column of Filipinos that preceded our little group seemed to be about three-fourths of a mile long. They were kept going steadily all day without a halt which would have been our worst day but for one or two features. First, we had persuaded the guard to put us at the end and let us march with a gap in the column that permitted us to get frequent short halts. Second, the guard for the first half of the day's march was under a sergeant who spoke good English, was a thorough gentleman, and showed us every consideration. We persuaded him that we were weak but willing and that the pace must be slow and the halts short but frequent. This was the second decent Jap I had met. He was a little sergeant, bright and intelligent, and spoke perfect book English. He was of the better class of people and had a high school education or better. We tried to reward him for his kindness with money and wrist watches. He declined saying he was a professional soldier, "a gentleman like yourselves," and hoped someday to be an officer like we were. The only fault we found with him was that there were too few of his kind. Most of those we came in contact with were of the lower peasant, ignorant, brutal type.[17]

During the day on more than one occasion, the guards, realizing we had not had breakfast, permitted us to trade with the native vendors. Allen Stowell and I bought a bunch of peanut candy and what a lift the peanuts and molasses gave us. A little further on we bought hard boiled duck eggs, rice balls, and small cookies. These things sustained us for the day. The Filipinos in the column ahead of us were constantly lagging behind and straggling through our column and giving the Jap sentries much concern.

Just before we came to our second halt a Jap sentry was working with a Filipino who was not exhausted but had to be coaxed along the road. The sentry got him back into his column once, but then he lagged back through ours to the rear of it. We halted and fell out by the roadside. Soon the sentry accompanied by another Jap sentry got the man to walk to about the center of where our column was resting. The Filipino sat down in the middle of the road. They pulled off his pants, got him up, and marched him between them to the rear of our group where I was sitting to a break in the tall cane by the roadside. They took him through this break in the cane to a place in behind it and about thirty feet off the road to my back. We heard the crack of their rifles, about three or four shots. The two Jap sentries came back, the Filipino did not. Later in the day I saw them shoot two Filipinos by the roadside.

From the Hacienda de Rook to San Fernando these dead bodies by the roadside became thicker and thicker. At one place I saw some 75 to 100 lying on one small spot. When we first began to see and smell them on the first day's march out of Bataan I thought them the bodies of people who had been killed by traffic, but now I began to realize more and more that it was nothing more than plain murder, premeditated and planned by the high command. I have asked a number of officers who marched out of Bataan how many bodies they estimated were along the roadside and the replies have ranged from 200 to as high as 800. Those who were the last to march had the largest estimates.

We arrived at Lubao about 4:30 p.m. in an exhausted condition. Here we met the first Filipino collaborators dressed like ex-Philippine Army soldiers who spoke some Japanese and some English. They were buttering their bread by helping the enemy. We climbed on one because he told one of our sick colonels that if he didn't buck up he would be shot. At the gate to the compound we were all told by another Filipino collaborator to turn in our knives, razors, and razor blades or else we would be shot. As I had lost my Gillette razor at Orion, I reasoned the blades would do me no good so I turned in the few packages I had left. A pity I had not kept them, as we were later issued razors at the rate of one per squad; a nice way to spread barbers itch and other skin diseases.[18]

Here Lieutenant Colonel Drummond, our II Corps surgeon, was forced to part with his precious medical chest that had been so carefully and tediously brought out of Bataan. It was thrown on a large pile of such seized chests, all of which must have contained enough medicine to have saved several thousand lives in the great dearth of medicine and food that lay ahead of us at Camps O'Donnell and Cabanatuan. But the conquerors were not content. They had to rob us of every vestige of food, medicine, and clothing, all in rank violation of international law.

At Lubao, our quartermaster had constructed a large sheet-iron warehouse in the last days before the war. It appeared to have been about finished and had not been stocked. It had been planned to make this and the Los Banos QM as distributing centers. We were marched into the enormous warehouse and bedded down on the concrete floor. A number of other American officers and soldiers joined us. We had a section to ourselves, and the Philippine Army captives occupied the remainder of the building, while apparently some four to five thousand additional Filipinos were camped around in the yard that was enclosed with a barbed wire fence. We were fed steamed rice and salt and given water after which we dragged our tired bodies back into the warehouse and went to sleep.[19]

About 9:00 p.m. there was a great commotion. The Japs were crowding all the people in the yard into the building. They overflowed the standing room in the aisles and filled the building like packed sardines. The stench from body odors was terrific. The doors were locked. We were afraid of a repetition of the "Black Hole of Calcutta." No one would mention it but everyone thought of it. It was insufferably hot and close in the building, but a merciful God was on our side. We were in the middle of the dry hot season when rain is very rare. Soon the wind arose followed by a long heavy downpour of rain. The building cooled off and we realized the top of the building was so high above our heads that there would be adequate ventilation.[20]

I fell asleep. At about 2:00 or 3:00 a.m., I was conscious of the opening of doors and the moving of feet; when I awoke at daylight the building had been cleared. We took our field bags with us through the mess line where we were served steamed rice, about two-thirds cooked, and water. We assembled and ate it in the road where we were to form up for the day's march. Colonel Steel, who was not feeling well, planned to stay back and try to get a ride later in the day but the Japs refused, saying the building must be cleared and all must be in San Fernando as soon as possible.

The Filipinos had been marching since before daylight and very soon we were off. It was the second time we started a march early in the morning. By this time we had picked up a large number of Filipinos. We could never at any place during the day actually see the head of the column and as usual we were at the end of the column. There were no halts during the day and no regular rate of march. The column sped up, slowed up, and lagged as a long, poorly regulated one always does. This makes it exceptionally tiresome for those at the rear end.

I began the day without water as I had used all I had with the poorly cooked rice breakfast. Soon we passed an artesian well on the off-side of the road. The sentry permitted me to fill my canteen and get a drink. He then gave me a handful of Japanese hard bread. It was the same as ours, made of white flour and a little larger in size than our square oyster crackers. Those in the column ahead had poor water discipline and large groups of them were being run away from the artesian wells all day by the Japanese. I saw a number of men beaten and two shot. It was a long, hot, difficult day's march without food except for a breakfast of rice and water. No authorized halts, and no time at which all could fill their canteens. The column often halted and we sat down on our field bags in the middle of the road only to be ordered up and made to march almost in double time to catch up. We passed through numerous villages and the women threw us all sorts of fruits, sugar cookies and things to eat. I got about three or four cakes (brown sugar) and a small piece of watermelon, which I ate, rind and all.[21]

The villages and little towns were again well-populated with women and children. I had seen many of them come as refugees into our lines while we were fighting in Bataan, the old men and women and children. But of all the women I saw no presentable one between the ages of 16 and 30. I asked about them and was told that they had been taken away from their families by the Japs for use in houses of prostitution. In our refugee camps in Bataan there had been almost no young Filipino women. The Japs had permitted the other people and children to pass through their lines to reach us because their number would rapidly decrease our food supply.[22]

An hour or so before dark we arrived at San Fernando, Pampanga tired, foot sore, and half-starved. A big market and wooden school house were used for the prisoners. The Filipinos were put in the market and the Americans in the school house and yard. I slept one night on the porch of the school and one in the school yard. We were fed two meals of rice a day.

San Fernando, the capital of Pampanga province, was the largest town in our route of march. It was an important trail and road hub. The war had more or less passed it over because it was out of the bombing areas of Bataan and Corregidor and had become a beehive of Japanese activities. Some of the Japs' wives, clad in handsome clothes, rode in apparently seized American cars to view our bedraggled and starving column as we marched from Lubao towards the city. The Filipinos were there, plenty fed up with the Japs, except for a half dozen or more former Filipino soldiers who had turned coats and were strutting themselves before the Japs.

It was here that a Jap sentry asked me for my pocket book. He spoke a little English. I pulled it out, opened the card and photo section, and began to show him pictures of my wife, two daughters, and home in Durham, North Carolina. It seemed to entertain him well and I escaped giving him my few remaining pesos. To us the worst part of the Death March was behind.

At this place three or four Americans including a reserve lieutenant colonel who came on the *Coolidge* with me died along with a number of Filipinos. The burial details went outside in the city to dig graves. They were permitted to stop and shop at the local markets and came in with canned goods and fruits, but they would not share them with fellow prisoners. The Filipino doctors who were also war prisoners and were running the first aid station in the school house had outside connections and they brought in all sorts of food but did not share it even with the others that were working with them. This type of selfishness seemed unpardonable to us, but it was very common in prison life among the starving and we soon became hardened to it. A Filipino boy who came to the fence and sold us food was caught by the Jap guards, brought into the yard, tied up in front of us and beaten for several hours.

After two nights and one day we were marched out at daylight to the railroad station. As we passed through the gate going out those American officers and soldiers who were lagging behind in the column were struck across the back with whips or paddles and cursed by a few Filipino collaborators, who had very quickly sold their birthright for a mess of pottage. This made us temporarily uneasy about the loyalty of the Filipino people, but the Death March that we were completing and the terrible days ahead at Camp O'Donnell were to mark the turning point of all decent people against the Japs. It is not in them to treat people kindly, nor seem to be able to be decent and kind to each other.

They had made great headway with their Asiatic Co-Prosperity Sphere and their propaganda had unquestionably impressed some Filipinos. Had their soldiers and commanders acted it out they might have alienated the loyalty of many Filipinos from the United States. There was no reason why the Filipinos should have been put through the Death March and the stragglers shot like rats. There was no excuse for their being confined for months at Camp O'Donnell without proper food and medicine. Our 40 years of kindness bore fruit and our friendships were soon cemented forever. Had the Japs registered all Filipino soldiers near the point of their surrender, turned them free, encouraged them to work and restrained their soldiers from brutalities aimed at the Filipinos, the return of our forces to the islands would have been far more difficult.[23]

At the San Fernando station we were crowded into small box cars and moved north with about 100 men in each small box car. When the train stopped in a few small towns the native vendors sold us such foods as they had. It was mostly steamed rice, boiled camotes (sweet potato), dried fish, rice cakes, fruits, and fried bananas. The Jap sentries beat the natives if they caught them making a sale. About 11:00 a.m., we arrived at Capas, a very small town a few miles north of Fort Stotsenberg and Angeles, where we were unloaded, formed up and marched away. The natives here were not permitted to sell us anything if the Jap sentries could prevent it. Large signs in English and Tagalog were posted stating that visitors would not be permitted at the prison camp until arrangements could be made with the provisional governors. This was a false lead for we were never permitted to see visitors during our prison life.[24]

The hike to Camp O'Donnell was made in short order, being only five miles from the station. Here we were halted, formed, and caused to stand a long time in the hot sun to be searched again for anything that should not be brought into the camp. When the search was over we were addressed by the camp commander, a slant eyed, stubby, fat Jap captain whom we called "Baggy Pants."[25]

"You are my enemies, I should like to kill every one of you, but you are the property of my emperor and my Bushido forbids it. I should like to carry you to my country and let you see the great damage your embargoes have done to us. We are at war and the hatred you have caused will not be forgotten for a hundred years."

Then he raved on for about five minutes trying to make us great criminals, and I believe he made a very good case against us, in his own estimation.

He was one of the most misshapen and overdressed soldiers I have ever looked upon. I could hardly classify him as a member of the human family save for his feet that were hidden in handsome dress boots about two sizes too large and reaching almost to where his knee caps belonged. His pants bagged at the knees and covered the top of his boots, and there was enough extra room in the seat of his breeches to hold a nail keg. His body was large and humped like that of a gorilla and his head without any direction went up to a sharp peak at the back like a monkey's. His greatest resemblance to a human was that he could speak and he blabbered away at us with a facial expression that resembled a raving idiot.[26]

He was only commencing on the long trek of neglect, lack of medicine and food that was to take many lives for which the Japanese later rewarded him with a governorship of one of the southern provinces in Luzon. This was only the beginning of the harangues we were to be subjected to as prisoners. Some of the camp commanders went so far as to tell Americans that the Emperor owns everything but your breath and that can be taken away from you any time, instantly.[27]

After he finished and disappeared, General Funk, General King's chief of staff, came down and made a short talk. He told how we would be given three meals of rice, salt, and soup a day and soon we would be fat with rice bellies. Little did he know that while some would gain some flesh none would ever fully recover their normal strength and endurance on the food we were to get. After this we were assigned to barracks and the Death March to us was a matter of history, but the things it had taken out of us would be long in rebuilding and in some cases never completely replaced.[28]

We had not lost a man in our II Corps group of seventy officers and men, but we had many lucky breaks from the beginning to the end. Our group had been small and we started with two and a half days of C-rations on our persons. Our daily hikes had been short, rests in some cases more frequent than for others not so fortunate, and we came at the end of a long column of about 80,000 prisoners and were no strain or irritation to the Japanese.[29]

There were many opposites in the Death March. Some organizations were permitted to load up their trucks and ride from Bataan to O'Donnell. Others were herded by the thousands down the road, bareheaded, without water or food and forced at the point of bayonets to hike all day without a halt or rest period, and to continue like this for 80 or more miles from Bataan to San Fernando.

We had hiked a day and a half, had a two day rest at Balanga, and then hiked four continuous days to San Fernando, where we were given two nights and one day's rest and moved by rail the remainder of the way, except for five miles from Capas, the rail station, near O'Donnell. We had begun on the 16th of April and arrived at O'Donnell on the 25th—ten days en route. During this time we had been given one meal of raw rice and thirteen meals of cooked rice, an average of 1.4 mess kits of plain rice per day. We had traveled 85 miles and spent one morning crowded in box cars from San Fernando to Capas. Many others had not been so fortunate. Colonel Garfinkle, Captain Avery, and others who were sick and had been left behind in the camp sites came into O'Donnell within a few days.[30]

Section II

Death's Prison Camps

> I am well, medicine and toilet not sufficient, pocket book empty. Am thin and weak from rice diet. I need money badly. Can you find a way to send it? 100 pesos per month for a couple of months. If you can find a safe route send all at once. If not send small bills after.
>
> **—David L. Hardee to Carl E. Olson, August 26, 1942**

Having survived the march out of Bataan, Hardee and his fellow POWs now entered a new period of horror. Camp O'Donnell was 617 acres enclosed by a tall barbed wire fence. Inside the wire approximately 9,000 American and 50,000 Filipino prisoners lived in and among the incomplete bamboo and nipa roofed barracks of a former Philippine army division. A small stream ran through the camp, but the only source of running water for many prisoners was a barely functional faucet, and prisoners waited in line for hours just to fill their canteens.

The camp lacked even basic sanitary facilities, and many of the prisoners were already suffering from dysentery and other illnesses. Within days human waste nearly covered the grounds. The Japanese eventually provided some shovels, but the men were too weak to do more than dig a slit trench. Big blue bottle flies descended upon the prison camp like a biblical plague, swarming over the living and the dead, carrying disease from man to man, and filling the air with a menacing drone.

Roughly one of every six Americans in Camp O'Donnell died—almost 1,600 succumbed between April 1942 and January 1943. Filipino deaths were

Part of the remains of Camp O'Donnell; Cabanatuan featured similar buildings. Vermin of all sorts infested the barracks, and the bamboo and nipa roofing provided little protection from the elements. **Source: NARA.**

estimated at closer to one out of two—over 21,000 men died from April to July 1942 alone.

Surviving each day severely tested every man. The prisoners converted a hut adjacent to the camp hospital into the Z, or "Zero" Ward, where prisoners too weak to stand were taken to die. Willpower often became the deciding factor between life and death. Men who had withstood the march to camp often chose to stop fighting, and they died within hours. Older men such as Hardee, veterans of the First World War or of conflicts in Asia and Central America, often withstood the harsh conditions at O'Donnell better than younger men, perhaps because the struggles of past experiences tempered their behavior.

Discipline and camaraderie sometimes broke in the face of the daily struggle to survive. Officers and some noncommissioned officers had notable advantages over the junior enlisted personnel, such as contacts in the black market and hidden reserves of cash smuggled into camp or bank accounts in Manila. Rank always had its privileges, but in Camp O'Donnell it could be

Filipino prisoners at Camp O'Donnell carrying out the dead for burial. The death rate at O'Donnell forced the Japanese to move the POWs to prison camps in Cabanatuan. **Source: NARA.**

the difference between life and death. Hardee drew upon his bank account to purchase food and medicine for himself and to provide aid for close friends, but he does not mention providing aid to the former members of his unit. Furthermore, he criticizes other officers for abusing their rank or authority and condemns the black market on which he relied for survival. Life at O'Donnell was a desperate competition—survival of the fittest—and the will to live almost invariably quashed the impulse for altruistic gestures.

In May the situation changed for the Bataan survivors. Senior Japanese leaders inspected O'Donnell that month and, disturbed by the death rate, decided to close the camp and relocate the prisoners to "better" facilities in Cabanatuan. The American survivors of O'Donnell moved in early June to Cabanatuan Prisons 1, 2, and 3, which were also former Philippine army facilities, albeit closer to completion than had been O'Donnell with slight improvements in accommodations. The American survivors of Corregidor, which had fallen on May 6, were shocked at the condition of the former Bataan fighters when they encountered them in June. Despite the infusion of healthy men with strong

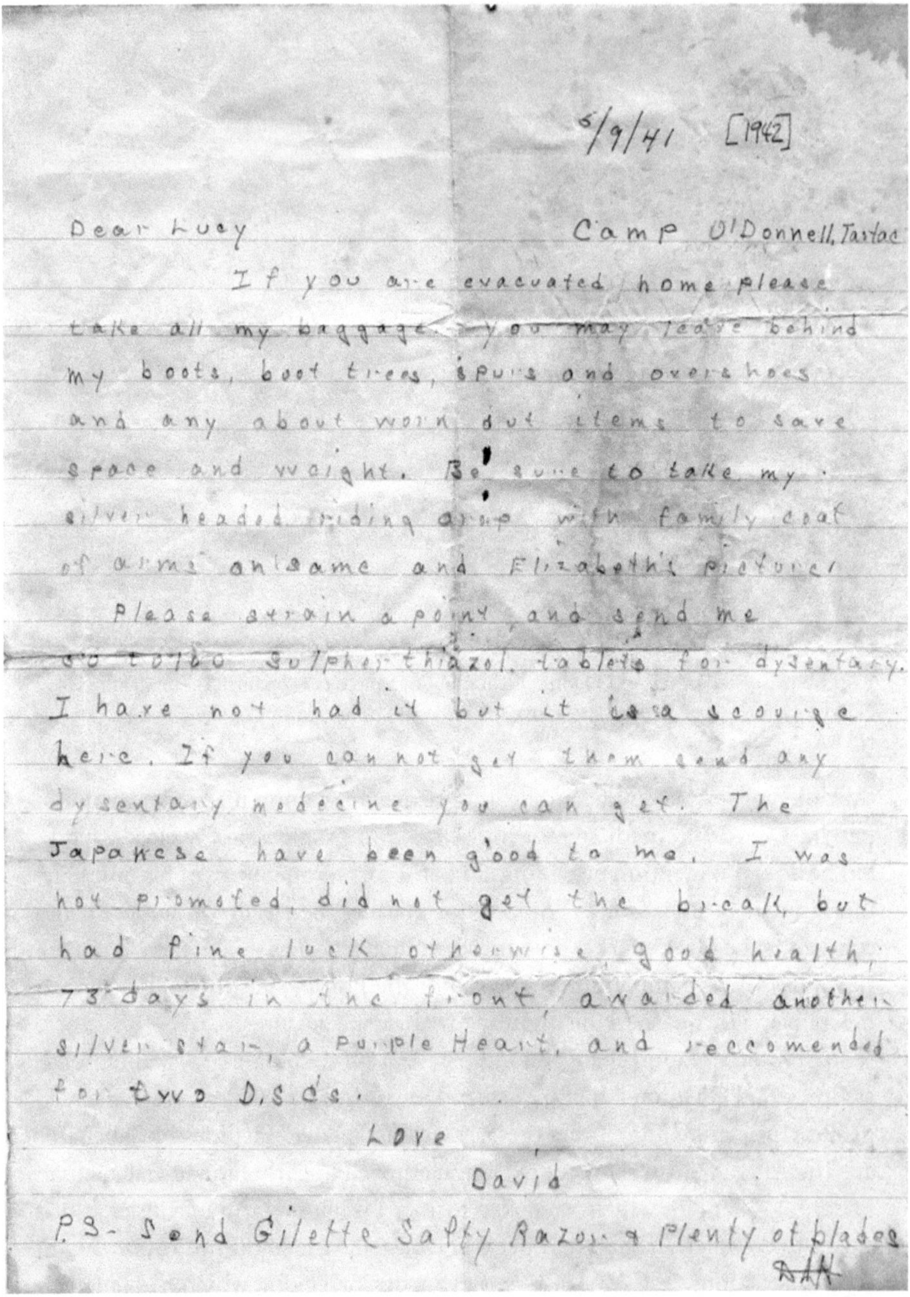

5/9/41 [1942]

Dear Lucy Camp O'Donnell, Tarlac

If you are evacuated home please take all my baggage. You may leave behind my boots, boot trees, spurs and overshoes and any about worn out items to save space and weight. Be sure to take my silver headed riding crop with family coat of arms on same and Elizabeth's pictures.

Please strain a point and send me 50 to 100 Sulpher thiazol tablets for dysentary. I have not had it but it is a scourge here. If you can not get them send any dysentary medecine you can get. The Japanese have been good to me. I was not promoted, did not get the break, but had fine luck otherwise, good health, 73 days in the front, awarded another silver star, a Purple Heart, and reccomended for two D.S.Cs.

Love

David

P.S.- Send Gilette Safty Razor & Plenty of blades

DAH

A note Hardee sent from Camp O'Donnell to his sister imprisoned in the Santo Tomas Internment Camp in Manila. **Source: State Archives of North Carolina.**

morale, a slight improvement in prison food, and some provisions of medical supplies by the Japanese, the death rate soon matched that of O'Donnell. By November 1942, approximately 2,400 Americans had died at the camp. What battle had failed to achieve, starvation, disease, and brutality accomplished.

The American prisoners were stunned by the cruelty of guards and the inhumane responses of prison camp administrators, not only to prisoners, but also to their own soldiers. Slappings and beatings at the slightest infraction of prison rules became standard. To deter escape attempts, captors organized the prisoners into ten-man squads—"blood brothers"—and made clear that the escape of a single prisoner would bring about the execution of the remaining nine in his squad. Few tested the system, but those who did paid dearly. Hardee bore witness to the torture and summary execution of three men, details of which seem almost surreal.

International protests to the Japanese regarding adherence to the 1929 *Convention Relative to the Treatment of Prisoners of War* signed in Geneva, Switzerland, proved pointless. In response to inquiries in early 1942, the Japanese government announced on January 29 that they would observe the convention *mutatis mutandis* (with necessary modifications) relative to the treatment of prisoners; in essence, the Japanese ignored the convention, using the prisoners for their own devices. Even amid depravity, the prisoners began to construct, as best they could, a sort of normal life at Cabanatuan. Mental diversions from captivity emerged in baseball games, theatrical performances, reading, crafts, gardening, and contests, as with one in which prisoners competed to see who could catch the most flies, in exchange for prizes.

In May 1942, Hideki Tojo, then Japan's prime minister and its minister of war, decreed that Allied prisoners would work in order to eat. Authorities in the Philippines had been using American work parties across the archipelago since April. Some prisoners volunteered for work details at the promise of time away from the camp and opportunities to interact with the Filipino population to acquire vital sustenance, resources, or simply valuable news on the war.

In the late summer of 1942, the Japanese completed their registration of prisoners and decided to increase the use of POWs in industrial work, issuing orders to begin dispersing prisoners throughout the Far East. In October, Hardee joined a group of 1,000 prisoners destined for the Davao Penal Colony (Dapecol) on the island of Mindanao. Nearly 2,500 acres of cultivated agricultural land surrounded by forbidding swamps and impenetrable jungle, the penal colony would provide food not only for the prisoners but for the Japanese army on the island. The prospect of plentiful water and food gave Dapecol an Elysian appeal compared to O'Donnell or Cabanatuan. After an unpleasant but fairly uneventful voyage aboard one of Japan's hellships, the relatively small band of Bataan and Corregidor survivors prepared for another long, hard period of incarceration.

CHAPTER 6

Camp O'Donnell

Camp O'Donnell was the place used by the Japanese for the assembling, registration, and classification of prisoners of war. I remained there forty days until about June 5, 1942 when I, with many more of my group, was moved to Cabanatuan. The camp was a Philippine Army camp, and about 75 percent completed. We had moved a few troops into it after the war began, and the water systems and roofs over the kitchens and the hospital were the most unfinished items.

The combination mess halls and kitchens were covered with nipa over the mess hall section, but over the kitchen section where sparks would soon ignite the nipa, no covering had been placed. The hospital was nothing more than a shell. The water tank was incomplete and to fill a canteen one had to wait in line in a tropical sun sometimes for as long as two or more hours. "Sweat the water line" was the common expression for it. Clothes were for the first few weeks laundered in an old muddy sump hole. The American prisoners were quartered in the hospital section while the Filipinos were given the remainder of the camp, with the exception that another large group of Americans were in a section we referred to as the air corps section, but contained several thousand troops of all types.[1]

For the first couple of weeks I was quartered in a barracks and slept on the floor, initially on a raincoat given to me by Major Thomas B. Smothers, a regular infantry officer from Winston-Salem, North Carolina. He slept by me for a day or so, and was then sent by the Japs back to Bataan to help police the battlefields. About the third or fourth day I was issued a blanket by Warrant Officer Jack Curry. I had known him for years and while working at USAFFE had drawn the order that promoted him from staff sergeant to a warrant officer.[2]

We had steamed rice three times a day and some salt. Usually it was accompanied with oleomargarine at breakfast and a vegetable and boiled camote soup for the other two meals. We had a little brown sugar occasionally but no meat and very little grease. Lieutenant Colonel Drummond had been forced to turn in our medical kit at Lubao, as had all the other surgeons either there or elsewhere. The hospital had little or no medicine. There were not enough tools to dig enough latrines. Those that were dug were open ones, with no lumber for covering them. Flies were rampant. When you drew your food you ate with one hand and beat them off with the other. Everyone was weak and hungry. The starvation days in Bataan and the Death March had weakened all and would soon take its toll. Lieutenant Colonel Louis E. Roemer, an old friend who lived next door to us at Fort Howard, was there when we arrived. He helped me by giving me a sheet, some clothes, and other odds and ends. He said another day or two of marching would have done me much permanent injury.[3]

The men were weak, hungry, homesick, heartsick, and despondent. We were so numbed by the Death March that we could only eat and sleep. Despair, diarrhea, and dysentery seized them and the death rate began to mount. At first there were only a few dead each morning, but in about two or three weeks after my arrival it was very common to see from 50 to 75 dead bodies each morning lying under the hospital or around in the yard. Burial details carried them to the growing cemetery all day long. Chaplain Sam Donald, my regimental chaplain in Bataan and a classmate of my brother Robert at Duke University, would read the burial ceremonies, not for one but for scores at a time. They were put in long continuous trenches, a body every three feet, with an identifying wooden cross at the head. One detail was kept continuously busy digging these trenches and another closing them. I watched the Filipinos carry their dead out to the cemetery. I could see the long endless procession from my shack. In one hour I counted 125 bodies being carried out and this was not one-third of the toll of the Filipinos dead for one day.[4]

A most noticeable thing about the grim reaper—he laid his hand most heavily on the younger men while the older men as a rule survived. Our War Department teachings and past experiences in campaigns had been to the contrary, so our policies had been to eliminate the older men from the battle line. Here their theory was disproved so far as hardships from marching, exposure, and starvation were concerned. Young flesh had less resistance and burned out quickly under pressure of heat and starvation. Young men were more easily discouraged, because for the first time many were meeting adversity, while older men had gone through many hard knocks. Young bodies were tender and had little surplus; older bodies were tough and had old gristle that furnished fat for the body for weeks. The older men realized the seriousness of the situation and as soon as captivity began they saved every ounce of energy and applied it only at the places needed. Some almost refused to talk as that consumes nervous energy.

Personally, adversity and disappointment had followed me closely, and if they ceased to follow after me I would abandon hope and die of loneliness. Many of these younger men had not learned the deep lesson of life that happiness is a thing that springs from within. External surroundings may alter and put a damper on it, but hope should spring eternal in the human breast, and the stubborn will to not let the Japs beat us and to live on no matter how hard they made conditions pulled many a person through places where it would have been much easier to fall on eternal rest.[5]

Our American contact officer begged for food and medicines. Captain "Baggy Pants" and his Jap staff did not seem to be in the least concerned. We were being treated as captives; maybe we would someday rise high enough in the world to be prisoners of war. So long as we were in the status of captives they waived responsibility for our lives. They had refused to accept our lists of surrendered men as drafted for our II Corps group in Bataan. They did not want to know our names or how many of us there were until they had enjoyed the privilege of starving and killing as many of us as possible while removing us from the combat zone and registering and classifying us. From our registration cards, the list was made for official report to our War Department through neutral countries, after which they would change our status from captives to prisoners of war and begin our pay. The more prisoners they murdered and starved meant the more they would not have to register, report, and provide for and could just claim as killed in action or died in Bataan.

Later in their efforts to win over the Filipinos they tried to blame the deaths at O'Donnell and Cabanatuan on our starved and weakened conditions in Bataan but the entire world knew it was a lie. We were weakened from hunger but not disease and hard fighting in Bataan, and under the rules of all civilized peoples this imposed on our captors certain obligations of care and medicines. Japan had never made war with a first-class power before and did not care to recognize this obligation. In fact, I have always believed they intended to treat us as they had often been accused of treating the Chinese—drive us into a compound and let us starve. This I believe they would have done had it not been for the pressure of influence through neutral countries. All their propaganda they had dropped from airplanes in Bataan trying to coax us into surrender with promises of good food, good treatment, and care as provided in the Geneva agreement were lies and we recognized them as such as soon as they began to drop this propaganda to weaken our fighting morale.[6]

I surrendered on April 9, reached O'Donnell on April 26, and was picked up as a prisoner of war as of August 1 when my pay began. The official notice of my capture and internment reached home in December. I received my first pay in April 1943 and was given the privilege of the first card home in December 1942 or January 1943. Our first Red Cross relief reached us in March 1943 and our first mail from home began to reach camp about July 1943.

For the first week or so at O'Donnell we were very much concerned over the fate of Colonel Ralph Hirsch, Field Artillery, and Colonel John W. Irwin, Infantry, and very much grieved to know that three others had been clubbed, bayoneted, or shot on the Death March. The one who had been unmercifully clubbed came in suffering from a concussion and died a few days after his arrival. Colonel Doane attempted to save a few personal things for his wife and I hope finally succeeded in getting them through his long trek of prison life. Those who had been bayoneted and shot of course died en route and failed to make it to O'Donnell.

The two whose fate was undetermined gave us the most concern. Colonel Hirsch, an artilleryman on General MacArthur's staff, had arrived at Camp O'Donnell with his group, all of whom were at the point of collapse from physical exhaustion. After the routine Jap sun treatment of about an hour waiting in formation for the humiliating harangue by Captain "Baggy Pants," this group like all others was treated to a "shake-down" inspection by the Japs. They found on him a few Japanese yen that he was possibly carrying as souvenirs. After much jabbering among the Nips, they put him in their guardhouse, to which none of us captives had access or communication. When we did get communication through the Japanese camp headquarters, this officer had disappeared in thin air. We never knew whether he had been executed or died of exhaustion while in the guardhouse. Most of us believed the latter.[7]

Colonel Allen L. Stowell, his brother in law by marriage, and I looked long and earnestly for Colonel Irwin, who had been a friend of mine for many years. He started the Death March about April 10 in his command car that was soon taken away from him by the Japs and he was compelled to walk. About Layac Junction one person said he was lagging behind the column and the heat and nervous strain temporarily deranged him and he begged people to kill him. We could trace him no further than Layac Junction, a point about half-way along the route of the Death March. In the later part of 1944, while at Bilibid, I met one of the signal communications men of my old Provisional Air Corps Regiment. He told me that he saw a Japanese sentry strike him down with a club or rifle just before they got into Lubao. He knew Colonel Irwin well at sight, and I am sure the man was telling the truth. Lieutenant Colonel Ralph T. Garver, Adjutant General Department, also lost his life in like manner on the march.[8]

There were many other heart-breaking reports of other officers and men whose lives had been taken by the Jap murder squads that policed the column for those who from sheer exhaustion could go no further. The exact toll of this retrogression to barbarism will never be known and will always be a matter of speculation. It greatly overshadowed the number of deaths in the last days of fighting in Bataan, and was in turn over-shadowed by the great number of inexcusable deaths in the concentration camps prior to our registration and classification as prisoners of war. There is little to segregate and classify these uncalled-for losses of human life. The Death March itself was inexcusable. International law provides for a forced march out of the immediate combat zone. After the surrender of Bataan, this combat zone ended at the extreme range of the guns at Corregidor, for the Japs had completed mastery of the air.

We have often wondered why the Japanese high command did not plan a concentration of the captives about Lamao, one day's march from battle positions to Bataan. They could have easily done so, organized to take care of us, and moved us by easy marching stages, with food and watering stations on the way. They could have carried us in this manner wherever they pleased with little loss of life—but not the Japs. The longer we lived with them the more brutal and unpredictable they seemed to become.[9]

When we had been at O'Donnell about three weeks, the full colonels and generals with their orderlies were removed to a separate camp at Tarlac, in the province of Tarlac, in preparation for a station in Formosa. The last we heard of them they were loaded on a boat at Manila sometime about the middle of August 1942. I hated to see them go. They were my army crowd with whom I had been brought up, and except for a few lieutenant colonels who like me had not been promoted, I had few old associates left. Many of my friends expressed deep regret that they could not carry me along but the Japs were to be reckoned with. It was with deep emotion that I told many old friends goodbye. We felt that they were being singled out for better treatment—the Japs themselves had boasted of the fact and declared that it was a great honor to go to Japan where life was better than in the Philippines. I felt like one left behind. We knew their treatment would be rough enough but wondered what was to become of all junior officers and G.I. Joes who were left behind.[10]

The detachment leaving O'Donnell plus those congregating already at Tarlac numbered over 150. We made estimates of their chances and felt that from 90 to 95 percent would survive and be restored to home and country when America won the war. We never doubted on that point. Our estimates were not far off, for better than ninety percent lived through it. Of those left behind the figures for the survivors are ghastly and almost in the reverse. In fact, there are so few of us alive that remained in the Philippines any length of time that now when we meet each other and talk about the loss of our comrades we can console ourselves only with the thought that we are walking on velvet and living on borrowed time.

It is an ill wind that blows no good. The colonels and generals had vacated lots of good houses. Lieutenant Colonel Compton and I moved into the house vacated by General King and his staff. We were soon joined by Lieutenant Colonels John J. Atkinson and Richard G. Hunter of the field artillery. Hunter was sick from malaria and dysentery but with careful nursing we pulled him through. Dick Hunter had been on duty with organized reserves in Raleigh and married a girl from Warrenton, North Carolina, and I was to see much more of him and Compton in our prison life.[11]

I went over and got my old orderly, Corporal Gerken, of the Provisional Air Corps Regiment. He came over and brought two of his friends. They became our helpers and were the prima donna merchants of Camp O'Donnell. They went out on detail working on Japanese trucks at various jobs. When the trucks stopped in the villages, they bought canned goods and various fruits and brought them into camp and sold them at from 100 to 200 percent profit. They worked for us and continued this business on a small scale, keeping them and us supplied first and selling the surplus. We were fat and protein hungry, and were losing weight and strength rapidly on the rice diet. It was a real life saver to get some corned beef, canned fish, pork and beans, fruits and sweets.[12]

We were in the course of a forced transfer from a wheat and meat to a rice diet. This transfer takes months and a person's physical being undergoes a change. All suffered with diarrhea and many of the heavy meat eaters could never successfully make the transformation. So the little nick-nack of what we used to eat helped us greatly in the transformation. As a sample of our black markets, Lieutenant Colonel Hunter could get nothing to remain in his stomach and he paid eighty cents (gold) each for a few fresh eggs that had been smuggled in. They marked the turning point and undoubtedly saved his life—at least prolonging it for a couple more years of humiliation, slavery and suffering until it was taken in the torpedoing of one of the Jap hellships toward the end of the war.

I landed at O'Donnell with ₱16.00 in my pocket, and initially no way to get any money. Doane loaned me ₱50.00 and Gerken cashed checks for me for ₱125.00. This money and the food Gerken and Sam Schulman brought in not only saved me from dire starvation and death, but enabled me to build up some of the flesh and strength I had lost in Bataan and on the Death March.[13]

We watched the Japanese air activity, saw the big transports come over, and guessed to the day the fall of Corregidor. This was soon confirmed by their newspapers. They were good at informing us of any news that would keep us depressed. I had estimated when we marched out of Bataan and laid Corregidor bare to hostile artillery fire that its garrison would hold out for thirty days. It resisted for 27 days of merciless pounding, days filled with despair and anguish for us as well as its heroic defenders.[14]

I had diarrhea twice but on each time I was lucky in finding a doctor who had a few sulfathiazole tablets and cured it right up. The Japs began to tell us that we were to be moved to a camp on the other side of Mount Arayat as too many were dying at O'Donnell. The sick were to be left behind and the well moved. We were moved in groups and Atkinson, Hunter, and Compton were in the first group that left by truck on the first day. I was sick and deferred my move to the second day. We were marched to Capas, put on the train again, closely packed in box cars. We headed for Manila and turned to Bigaa back to a track to the north. I was much in hopes that we might go to Bilibid where I could get in touch with my sister and family, who I judged were at Santo Tomas. My morale reached bottom when the train switched back in the opposite direction.[15]

After a while I cheered up with the thought that it could not be worse than what I had lived through, the Death March, and the 40 days at O'Donnell. It could not be worse, this I was sure. We spent the night in another squalid, filthy lot in the town of Cabanatuan, and the next morning after a rice breakfast we hiked to the camp some eight miles away. The hike was conducted with regular halt periods and was not difficult.[16]

CHAPTER 7

Cabanatuan

The camp at Cabanatuan was another unfinished Philippine Army camp of the same type as O'Donnell. I was the senior officer in the group that arrived that day and was placed in command of a battalion of one thousand men who came with me. Lieutenant Colonel Jasper Brady, who commanded the 31st Infantry (U.S.) in the later days of Bataan and with whom I had served at Plattsburg, New York in 1923, was group commander. Soon he was outranked by Lieutenant Colonel Atkinson, the only time I knew this to occur in my prison life. The battalion organization was soon abandoned by the Japs and I became just a private prisoner of war.[1]

Here we were placed with the officers and men of the army and navy who had been captured at Corregidor and we soon learned the story of the fighting there. It was a good time to reminisce about the battles of Bataan and Corregidor and exchange views and opinions. Many of us coveting our freedom dreamed of escape, but most of us who came from O'Donnell, and were survivors of Bataan and the Death March, did not possess the strength to run even if we had been able to find the opportunity. The prisoners of Corregidor were in very good shape as compared with our men as they had not gone through anything comparable to the Death March. After the surrender they were crowded together at a place on the beach near the 92nd Garage. About 10,000 were held in this concentration from May 8 to 23. The first day they had no water, but on the second day they ran in a small pipeline. Food was brought in twice a day. The flies were very numerous and the men being held were too closely concentrated to properly observe sanitary regulations.[2]

On May 23, most of them were loaded on a boat and unloaded on Dewey Boulevard somewhere below the Polo Club, and were marched about two or three miles through Manila to Bilibid. From Bilibid they were carried to Cabanatuan by rail. They had been in camp about ten days when we arrived and were in good condition compared to us. Here I saw Lieutenant Meade H. Willis, Jr. of the Navy, and Lieutenant Julian V. Lyon of the Marine Corps, both of whom I had known since their birth. They were both in good health and good spirits. Meade was spending a good deal of time reading and I remember he spent some time reading *Quo Vadis*.[3]

I envied his ability to sit quietly for hours and read, as well as the privilege of a good book, smuggled by hook or crook into the compound. My nervous system had not yet settled down enough to enjoy this phase of entertainment. Later I was to enjoy it and passed many hours in attempting to be the full man the writers proclaim. Lyon later went with me to Davao, while Meade was sent on to Japan before we were returned from Davao. Both were finally saved out of the wreck of things.[4]

Atkinson, Compton, Hunter, and I never lived together again. Atkinson and I were in Group 1, but never lived together. Compton was in Group 2 and lived about a half mile away but in the same compound. We saw each other often but did not get to live together again until some months later at Davao. Hunter was sent to the hospital; he had been at death's door for weeks at O'Donnell. Soon he began to improve at Cabanatuan and came out of the hospital. He and I got a small room together at the front end of what had been originally built for a regimental infirmary. The room was not large enough to take care of three people and we were permitted to occupy it undisturbed.[5]

The room overlooked the main walk through camp, the main road, the mess hall, and the ration shed. We were well and comfortably located. I built a bunk 14 inches off the floor and made a mattress of split bamboo. I was never prouder of a piece of furniture in my life, and this served both as a mattress and springs while Hunter had a folding cot. Both of us had mosquito bars and pillows, shelter halves and a blanket and we were very comfortable. Hunter was still sick but by the end of the year he had begun to recover his health.

Lieutenant Colonel Compton was given a job by the Japs taking care of three or four Coleman-type gasoline lanterns at the Jap guard headquarters. There was a Jap sergeant major there in charge with a handle-bar moustache. We called him "Handlebars." He was appreciative of Compton's services and purchased canned goods and food for him every few days at Cabanatuan. He became a little merchant in selling this food to others and kept Hunter and I partly supplied. Gerken and Schulman, our orderlies from Camp O'Donnell, were also in the mercantile business and they were very helpful. We bought from both with cash and on credit and I will be grateful to them for the remainder of my life.[6]

Cabanatuan at first seemed to be commanded by Jap noncommissioned officers who worked under a Jap lieutenant whose headquarters was at Camp No. 3, another smaller camp a bit closer to the Sierra Madre Mountains than our own. Conditions were wretched, but we were to have a new camp commander, a Lieutenant Colonel Mori, a reserve officer of the Japanese Army. A smile came to the grim faces of some of the old-timers of Manila. Yes, they knew him; he was their good friend who for many years had operated a bicycle shop in Manila. He had served their children many times and was very friendly and accommodating. When he arrived things would be different. They could talk to him in English, and he could solve many of our problems. They looked forward to the day of his arrival. That day soon came and he made an inspection of our messes and barracks, but his face was stony, his voice authoritative. He recognized none of his old Manila customers, and as was the usual custom all business and conversation with him must be clothed through the dignity of a Japanese interpreter.[7]

Yes, it was so. I, Lieutenant Colonel Mori of the Imperial Japanese Army, have so decreed it.

"The blankety-blank old spy in disguise among us all these years," some of the old Manilians murmured.

But there was one thing about the lieutenant colonel we soon recognized. There was no difficulty in knowing what he wanted, though it was too often inimical to the best interest of the prisoners, so conditions grew steadily worse. Whenever they seemed unbearable, he persistently started a rumor that we would soon be exchanged. Until we became wise to it we lived for weeks on such a report. On one occasion, our group leader was called to Jap headquarters after dark and told that the Tokyo government had just made the United States government such a liberal offer of exchange that they were sure of its immediate acceptance. We could hardly sleep for joy. Men broke out their last or only can of meat and ate it in celebration, only to realize later that it was another Jap lie told to encourage men to not attempt escape and live with guerrillas.[8]

Our American prisoners gradually got a store in operation. We called it the "commissary" and operated it by pooling our money and orders, and about twice a week the commissary officer, one of our fellow prisoners, would be carried to Cabanatuan by the Japs and purchase such items on his consolidated list of orders as could be found. Corned beef, canned fish, Vienna sausage, canned milk, sugar, salt, guava jelly, crackers, and tomato ketchup were the favorites in eats and all kinds of tobacco were always in demand. As the commissary grew in the volume of orders there was never any stock kept on hand and the black market with its exorbitant prices disappeared. A few prisoners flourished on the black market. They could sell anything they could get in, and never sold for less than 100 percent profit. Usual prices were from 200 to 400 percent. I have seen corned beef sell for $15.00 per can.

Some of these smaller merchants withstood the Jap beatings and made several thousand dollars. The accumulation of their money was a great liability, for they never knew when the Japs would discover it and rob them. They soon resorted to scattering their capital out among their friends, G.I.s and officers in the form of credits, I owe yous, and post-dated checks good upon arrival in the United States. The commissary prices, such as corned beef ₱1.00 (50¢), small canned fish 40 centavos (20¢), large canned fish 70 centavos, sugar 10 centavos per pound, live chickens 80 to 90 centavos, soon put the skids under the black market and our little merchants.[9]

It was none too soon for the personal good of the little merchants for green-eyed jealousy, when starving men see others with more food then they have, soon raised its ugly head. They were denounced by many of their fellow prisoners who patronized them and like dogs turned to bite the hands that were feeding them. I always took their side for they were increasing the income of food to a starving camp and took many a blow from the Japs for it while their critics were doing nothing to increase the food income. A number of them, senior officers at that, resorted to bribing the cooks and kitchen police with cigarettes to bring them salt, sugar, and burned rice, flour or any kind of food from the kitchen. This was not less than stealing from their fellow prisoners.

I knew one of these ingrates to go to a fellow officer who was a little merchant with a ten dollar bill. Dollars were at that time forbidden by the Japs. He offered to change the ten dollars for ten pesos. His offer was accepted. Then he talked of preparing charges against the little merchant as if any court martial would listen to such childishness. Money, however, became scarcer and scarcer. I began to get notes from my sister and brother-in-law in Manila and finally got ₱50 from them with more to come, but the grapevine communication was cut. The Filipino well diggers finished the wells and were dismissed. Before I could reestablish it I was moved to Davao.[10]

Two extremely bad features of the store or commissary were badly in evidence. One was staff purchases condoned by the Japanese and the other was R.H.I.P. (rank has its privileges). About two trips per week were made by the commissary officer to town. The first was for staff purchases. The commanding officers, if they can be termed such, and various members of their staff to include camp maintenance and mess officers, constituted a small percent of the prisoner total. For them to have the privilege of spending all they wanted, get many items not open to the general run of prisoners, and build up sizeable stocks of food with others dying of starvation caused them to be called names that are unprintable.

R.H.I.P. was said to be an old army custom or rather an old Spanish custom I had never heard in my 25 years of service. It was introduced by one or two senior officers (artillery) for whom I entertained little respect. On the contrary, in the infantry, we had been taught to take care of our men first. R.H.I.O. (rank has its obligations) was our motto. Every time the commissary got an item in small quantities and not enough to fill everyone's order, R.H.I.P. took a hand and often the juniors got nothing. The baseness of human nature when men are hungry and face the prospect of immediate starvation, reverting to the basic law of survival of the fittest, begs description.[11]

Colonel Hunter and I had a little money between us. We could keep enough on hand for extras to add to the rice diet to run us a week or ten days ahead. At one time we even had sugar, cocoa, canned milk, meats, guava jelly, and a can of Washington crackers and we stretched them out further than you can imagine they would go. We began to rebuild, but many others were not so fortunate. Camote vine tops were added to our soup components and some of the better vegetables, such as string beans and egg plants, disappeared. The hangover from O'Donnell where we parted with the Filipinos began to appear. The thin rice diet, innumerable flies, and the filthy condition of the latrines with not enough tools to construct others began to tell. The death rate increased and finally surpassed O'Donnell.[12]

Some 2,000 Americans were buried at O'Donnell, and a corresponding number of graves were being filled at Cabanatuan. All sorts of fancy names were given to the diseases, and starvation and a lack of medicines were at the bottom of it all, connected with the sadism of the heathen who for a long time took the view that it was easier to count a grave once than to count a line of captives twice daily at morning and evening roll call—*tenko* as they called it.[13]

No one knows whether it was the influence of the Battle of Midway that happened about this time, or whether it was the pressure being brought upon them through neutral countries, or the consciousness that win, lose, or draw they would still have to live in a world of human beings, but when the death rate at Cabanatuan reached its height they seemed to relent the fact that they had turned down the offer of medicines and food from relief agencies in Manila and talked about scattering us out.[14]

"No more big camps," they said.

Yet, with their relenting they still did not permit the relief supplies to come in, or the Filipinos to sell openly to us or through the fence, which could easily have been done. Such a course would cause the great Imperial Japanese Army—the conquerors of the Asiatic Co-Prosperity Sphere—to lose face and they could not afford to do that. We saw then once and for all that they preferred to lose the rear part of their anatomy rather than lose face, and they finally lost both. We had hopes that the smaller camps would mean less crowded conditions but not so. They never seemed to be happy unless they were crowding prisoners of war on top of each other like sardines in a can.

In the diet there was almost a complete lack of meat, fats, and cooking oils. After we had been in Camp Cabanatuan about a month to six weeks word went around that we would have meat for lunch. When it appeared it was nothing more than a little visible grease and a flavor in the soup. A lieutenant colonel from Corregidor came down the aisle of the mess hall with his face beaming. He had received a piece of actual meat that he sincerely and joyously exhibited to his fellow prisoners. It was a piece of carabao meat about the size of a silver quarter. About 50 pounds of meat, weighed bone and all had been issued per 1,000 prisoners. All of our cooking was done in large iron cauldrons. This meant boiling alone; no provisions were made for baking. They did not long expect to issue us things that could be baked.

For the first few weeks at Cabanatuan we had small issues of seized flour. Our workman devised bake ovens out of racks, mud, and oil drums and did some very good baking. This displeased the Japs very much. Later the baking was largely restricted to rolls that were distributed to working details and to the staff. The storehouse for flour that had been seized in the islands was across the fence and road where Hunter and I could see it very clearly. We watched the issue very interestedly. When it came to the end we watched for a face-saving gesture. It came in the way of a severe criticism of American conduct and demeanor. Until the American prisoners learned to conduct themselves better there would be no more flour issued to them. The simple fact was they had no more flour to issue.

It was here we were to witness a typical propaganda stunt. The mess sergeant of one mess prepared at Jap direction a nice meal of chicken, eggs, fruits, and vegetables and set a handsome table with prisoners sitting at it. A photo was snapped, the Japs grabbed the eats and no doubt they advertised American prisoners fed on chickens, eggs, vegetables, and fruits. A matter of fact we had chicken and eggs at the Cabanatuan mess once during my stay there. The issue consisted of 3 chickens and 18 eggs per 500 prisoners.

One afternoon I walked down to Group 2 to talk to Jack Curry, a warrant officer friend of many years standing. He was well except for minor complaints and was much downhearted. I tried to cheer him up, but did little if any good. That night I dreamed of being in front of a big department store in Winston-Salem, North Carolina, greeting old friends. As I turned to walk from the corner towards 4th Street, I met his girlfriend whom I always knew as Jane, and told her he would not be back. When I saw the tears begin to flow down her cheeks, I broke off the conversation by promising to come to her office in fifteen minutes to tell her the details. Next morning this dream haunted me until about 10:00 a.m. when I returned to his barracks and asked for him. He died during the night and the burial detail was then returning from the cemetery.[15]

About this time a small group of our Americans showed contempt for the sacredness of the barbed wire fence that surrounded us. They continued to go through it and bring in food purchased from Filipinos. They were placed in arrest in barracks by the Japs. Some of them broke their arrest and were caught in the act of coming back through the fence with canned goods and native fruit they had purchased. The Japs shot six of them, some of our men being compelled to witness it. They complained of the gruesomeness of it for the men were not blindfolded, the Japs were poor marksmen, and the men were permitted to suffer while lying on the ground awaiting the relief of death.[16]

Cabanatuan was also, like O'Donnell, a place for the registration, classification, and interrogation of captives. This work was begun but not finished at O'Donnell. We were captives until registered and accounted for to our War Department through neutral countries. They did not hold themselves responsible for our lives until this was fully accomplished and we were transferred to the status of prisoners of war and a pay roll was begun for us. Hence, the Death March from Bataan and the long delays at O'Donnell and Cabanatuan in accomplishing this simple piece of army paper work. It was finally accomplished about August or September, we having been captured in early April. This delay caused many deaths to be erroneously charged to the Death March.[17]

The interrogations were long and tedious, sometimes harassing, for some of the officers, particularly the air corps pilots, radio, and signal officers and men. On my registration I put as little as possible. Name, rank, and specialties in civilian and military life were the minimum requirements. Some of the G.I.s and junior officers worked for hours and turned in pages on their specialties and various qualifications. I reasoned with many of them about it that the less these people knew about one's qualifications the better off the individual would be. Some saw it my way; others did not and later paid dearly for their many highly specialized qualifications—radio and code men particularly. I did not say anything on my registration card about having worked at General MacArthur's headquarters. If I had they no doubt would have harassed me continually for things I did and did not know. I figured the less they knew the better for me. Under duties was listed my last assignment: "Executive Officer, Provisional Air Corps Regiment." Under civilian or business attainments: "none—professional soldier."[18]

They did not know what the name of my regiment meant and much to my delight they never troubled to find out. They were always looking for an American division on Bataan, and were much surprised that we had none. The 31st Infantry (U.S.) and our partially organized air corps regiment that fought as infantry were all the front line American regiments in Bataan. Whether they knew this or not, Colonel Doane and I did not worry. I was never called up for questioning and do not believe he was.

Here I learned to like burned rice. It is the burned crust that sticks to the cauldron, and was much in demand among the prisoners after they had been on a rice diet for some months. It was a flavor like the crust of ash cake or burned corn bread. Private gardens inside the compound were authorized and prisoners who could get seed began to cultivate little plots. In many cases they did great good. The Japs were great in devising schemes to deprive prisoners of the fruits of their labors: transfers, moving fences, changing boundaries, putting places off limits, anything to be obstinate—"a servant when he is king."[19]

CHAPTER 8

More Prison Life at Cabanatuan

The first big Japanese holiday that came after we were assembled at Cabanatuan was celebrated by them with a big athletic event to which all our senior officers were invited. They marched us under guard across the road to the guard company area where platforms and rings were constructed for their events. The men put on a number of jiu jitsu wrestling matches, jumping and like stunts. It appeared primitive to see their men make attacks at each other to try and force the opponent out of the ring. At the conclusion they had two American prisoners, former wrestlers, demonstrate our modern wrestling methods and the men got a big hand not only from the Americans but from the Japs.[1]

As strange as it seemed to us, the Jap prizes to their soldiers as event winners consisted almost entirely of food. Two cans of corned beef or three cans of fish and two bottles of beer were large prizes. We could not help but contrast this with our American ways of giving such prizes as bronze plaques, watches, pen and pencil sets, and wondered how badly our athletic G.I.s would feel cheated to stage a competition for such prizes as the Japs gave. As the events closed dinner was announced, the table being spread under a tent close by the athletic arena. The tent and tables would accommodate all the Jap officers and noncommissioned officers and about thirty Americans. The tables were well-spread with a sumptuous meal as contrasted with our customary soup and rice. The American prison staff was invited to fill what seats remained vacant after the Japs had been seated, and they were treated to a good meal with beer or tea for beverages. But the Japs made no attempt to feed the other couple of hundred Americans and were lacking in the decency to march them back to the compound for their dinner of rice and soup. They made them wait and with drooling mouths watch the others partake of a feast.

At this time they secured a group of about 200 Formosan recruits for training to become our prison guards. We watched this process day by day and made mental notes comparing their training with our own training methods. They hardened their men by running them excessive distances before breakfast and with long night marches, usually in bad weather. They were short on bayonet practice, using only the long point. They were long on slappings and beatings and their petty officers beat the recruits without mercy on what appeared to be the slightest provocation.[2]

Our men soon pooled the papers, magazines, and books that by various hook or crook had gotten into camp. It made a sizable library and the only the requirement to be a member was to have a book. I got one and joined. After three years of service they were good museum pieces with their many mends and patches.

In the early days at Cabanatuan, when no one was working except those who worked in the kitchens, brought in firewood, and policed the camp, there was no objection to our providing ourselves with amusement programs.[3] Amusement officers were appointed for each group and shows were exchanged between groups. Lieutenant Colonel "Zero" Wilson worked up some very good shows for our group. His musical numbers with a large chorus of male voices were particularly good. Some programs followed the old patent medicine type and others radio broadcasting types. When the work programs went into effect there was not much time for rehearsals and the shows were discontinued.

It is always the privilege of a prisoner of war to escape provided he can do so. If he makes good his escape he is in luck. If he fails and is caught alive, then his captors have the duty to confine him in such a way as to prevent his escaping again. We treat our criminals this way, but it is not the Japanese code.[4]

Such sadism! All they seemed to know was the misapplication of force and inhuman brutality. The practice of all civilized people would have been to use only such restraint as was necessary by putting them in a stronger enclosure. The simple duty devolving upon them as our jailers could require little more. They did believe in mass punishment to prevent escape and the penalty of death for those who attempted it. Little attention was at first paid to escape at O'Donnell, possibly because we were still captives and the Japanese themselves did not know the exact number. As time went on and we became prisoners of war, they began to lay a great deal of stress on not trying to escape. Everything was *not* with us. It was mass punishment for all when a small group badly infracted the rules and there was never a reward for good conduct.[5]

There was however an epidemic of escapes in the early days at Cabanatuan. Some were weak hospital patients who resented dying, sick of starvation, in prison and believed if they could get out they could survive. Several were found dead in the weeds and grass close by the hospital. Others were stronger and made good their attempts, often to turn themselves back in because they could not survive on the outside. They were oftentimes beaten, sometimes not; no definite rule seemed to be followed at this time. Many returned escapees had placards hung on their chest and back reading "I was a fool and tried to escape." They were each followed by another prisoner guarding them with a large club threatening to strike him on the head or back but never doing so. They appeared weird and as pertaining to the superstitions of witchcraft as we saw these men moving about the camp half clad in dirty rags with a fellow prisoner shadowing them with a club, and always acting as if he were going to strike a death blow but grinning because he and all of us knew that he would not do so.[6]

The Japs prominently posted in all barracks and shacks at Camp O'Donnell when we were first captured a large printed poster. This read in substance as follows:

All captives will be killed who —

1. Attempt to escape.
2. Impose upon or molest the civilians.
3. Set fire to or burn.

Signed — the Imperial Japanese Army.

We took this sign as a matter of course and so did the Japs until escapes became too common place, after which they lived up to the first provision to the letter. As to the second, we rarely came into contact with the Filipinos, but when we did all our dealings and conversations were along mutually sympathetic lines much to the disgust of the Japs. As to the third provision, it was useless for all of us felt that should the squalid shacks we were forced to live in burn we would be forced to sleep and live in the elements. Our captors were certainly no providers.[7]

Then the bad news came. They had made blood brothers of every ten men in some of the camps. If some of the ten escaped, the remainder of the compact would be shot. In Batangas where there was a small camp, there had been an attempted delivery by guerrillas. One man had escaped, so they had shot ten others. The Batangas camp was abandoned and the men transferred to Cabanatuan. They had not established the blood brother system there when the incident occurred. I talked to the officer whom the Japs forced to choose the ten men to be shot. He was all nervous and distraught about it. All the men were compelled to witness the executions. They were upset because the Japs, imitating the custom of civilized countries, had these men face a firing squad. They failed to blindfold them and their marksmanship was so poor that some of the men had to be shot several times.[8]

Our blood brother system was inaugurated with ten men to the squad, with everyone watching each other in fear of their lives. My squad consisted of field officers and I was not uneasy about any of them. The squad in which one of my friends, Major Charles F. Harrison, Jr., was placed was uneasy about him and the other nine took turns at watching him. Events later proved them correct. No one knows a man better than his squad mates.[9]

The Jap commander spent the best part of the day having the returned escapees demonstrate to the prisoners that it was not worthwhile to escape. Colonel Horan, previous C.O. of Camp John Hay (Baguio) who had lived for some months as a guerrilla before being captured, was compelled to head the show with a long prepared, censored speech, showing that the guerrillas could not make it, that they were starving, living off roots and berries, and the much hated rice was to them a luxury. Therefore, escape and life in the hills was futile. He was followed by several junior officers who at one time or another had escaped and turned themselves in.[10]

Colonel "Zero" Wilson had a good show that night and the Jap commander made attendance compulsory and put on the escape song and dance to everyone before the evening show began. He tried to be a good fellow and wind it up with news flashes. One of them was to the effect that large portions of the American navy had been destroyed by the Imperial Japanese fleet in the Southwest Atlantic Ocean. This would have been between Africa and South America and we wondered what fool thing they would pull on us next. The Battle of Midway had been fought some time before; Guadalcanal was just behind, and we wondered how much of this blood brother scheme would turn into real murder. It was soon to be tested.[11]

We had a perimeter guard of prisoners of war placed just inside the fence. It was the Japanese idea that we should restrain each other in the matter of escape. The fence at this time was nothing more than a three strand barbed wire fence of the common cow pasture variety. Lieutenant Colonel Lloyd C. Biggs and Lieutenant Colonel Howard Edward C. Breitung had about ₱1,500 to ₱2,000 accumulated from various sources and so they and Lieutenant Roy D. Gilbert of the navy decided to attempt an escape. None of the survivors of O'Donnell had enough physical strength to attempt such a course. They gathered together their possessions and all the canned goods and medicines they could muster and just at dark the night following the big demonstration they attempted to get by the American sentry on perimeter guard.[12]

A loud argument ensued. The Jap sentry came down from his tower, sensed the trouble and gave the alarm. These three men were caught red handed in an escape attempt. They admitted it, but Lieutenant Colonel Biggs is said to have argued with the Japs that they could do nothing with him because he was a lieutenant colonel and because international law forbids punishment without a trial. It seems that the Japs decided they would show us what they could do by way of making an example of them.[13]

Meanwhile matters were very tense with us. We wondered if they would shoot all thirty men in the three squads because of the attempt of these three to escape. They decided to punish only the offenders with death and the blood brother system was proven ineffective so far as shooting the entire squad was concerned. They took the three offenders to the Jap guardhouse and "worked them over" from about 7:00 to 10:00 p.m. Such cruel beatings none of us has ever witnessed or heard. I did not go to see it but could hear it from my room. Jiu jitsu, beatings with planks and sticks, slaps and kicks on their shins, in their privates, over their kidneys, throwing them over their shoulders, nothing was barred. Their sufferings must have been intense. None of us slept that night.[14]

Next morning about breakfast time the three were marched along the road that ran parallel and just outside the long side fence of the camp to the main road. At the junction with the main road there was a Japanese guardhouse on the opposite side of the road, facing the camp. A sentry to watch the camp and control traffic, when there was any to control, was stationed at this road fork by the guardhouse. Here the three prisoners were tied up to trees or posts. They were scolded, slapped, and beaten with whips and boards by the Japs. The sentry on the post made every Filipino that passed during the day beat them, and if the native did not strike hard enough to suit the Jap then the Jap would in turn beat the Filipino. The guard was changed every hour, and members of the old and new guards took turns at scolding and beating them again. At a post close by hung the head of a Filipino. He had been a guerrilla and we were shocked a few days before when a Jap combat squad came into camp with this Filipino head hanging from a pole and displayed it with much gloating over the destruction of an enemy.

About nightfall, after taking these intermittent beatings all day, I saw them marched back to the guardhouse inside the compound. They had been so weakened they could hardly walk. Observers who were close by stated that Lieutenant Colonel Breitung's ear had been cut off and was hanging down on his shoulder, and Lieutenant Colonel Biggs' left eye had been torn out and was hanging from its lower socket; results of the lash from their black snake whip.

The next morning a squad of Japs marched the three of them back to the road junction where they had been tied up the day before and repeated the former day's performance until about ten o'clock. None of us had slept in the camp for almost two nights. None of us carried on conversations above a whisper. A spirit of pity and grief accompanied by solemnity and death permeated us.[15]

About mid-morning, a truck left the Jap guardhouse filled with a squad of soldiers, guns, and ammunition. The lieutenant rode on the front holding his big samurai sword. By their holy Hirohito how they loved their samurai swords and Mother of God how we despised them. The truck stopped at the spot of the three sufferers. They were untied and thrown in while unconscious. It drove on to a little spot of woods just outside the southwest corner of the compound. We heard two volleys, listened attentively, but did not hear a third. When the truck came back someone asked in broken Japanese about the third prisoner, in the hope that amnesty has been granted.

"No, no, Lieutenant Colonel Biggs was the leader; he had talked back to a representative of their God and Emperor. He did not rate shooting. His head had been cut off with the sword."[16]

It would have been just as humane and much quicker to have put them on a Roman cross and crucify them. The escape involved two barracks. One with army officers, about 25 people packed in excessively close, and the other a naval barracks of about 150 men and officers. The Japs sentenced these barracks to 30 days confinement. It was a joke at first, but the Japs never relented on the sentence and before the end of the 30 days all were pale, pooped, and considerably weakened by their confinement. This was, however, an improvement over their announced plan of shooting their 27 blood brothers.

CHAPTER 9

En Route to Dapecol

Food became scarcer although there was always a heaping mess kit of rice three times a day. Sometimes there was a spoonful of brown sugar for breakfast. The soup for the other two meals became thinner and thinner, with less and less grease, and occasionally a little meat. Camote vine tops replaced much of the better vegetables used in the soup, and flour issues were discontinued. Medicine was scarce and the Japs had brought in little if any. We were still stretching the meager lot brought in by hook or crook from Bataan and Corregidor. Sanitary conditions were not improved to any great extent though covers and seats had been built for the latrines. Flies were almost as bad as at O'Donnell. Had it not been for the rainy season they would have been worse. The rainy season seems to prevent rapid propagation in flies and mosquitoes.[1]

The hospital was in a compound across the road. It was filled and overflowing with beriberi, dysentery, and malaria constituting the most common complaints. Many died of malaria for want of a few hundred grains of quinine. Deaths from cerebral malaria—the most painful form—were frequent. I shall never forget my attempts to get it for Hunter, but I succeeded and it no doubt saved his life. The Japs accepted a small shipment of medicines from some relief agency in Manila. I watched them unload it but with apparent indifference. They let it remain there for nearly two weeks before it was issued to the hospital and then it was given to them in driblets.[2]

Then the Japs made plans to scatter us into smaller concentrations. A detail of 1,500 air corps technicians was made up to go to Japan. Another detail of 1,000 officers and men was made up to go to Davao. Hunter and I were drawn in the latter detail, so were Lieutenant Colonels Compton, Dencker, Amoroso,

Conzelman, Duke, Miller, Kerr, Cain, Witten, Luikart, Commander McCracken of the navy, and many other officers whom I knew well and respected.[3]

The camp was so well combed for the best of the airplane mechanics that they believed they were going to Japan to work in airplane plants or to do repair work or some kind of labor around the airfields. The Japs promised better climate and better food. I later learned that this detail upon arrival in Japan was divided and part were sent to work in the mines of Manchukuo or Korea and half of them died of starvation, malaria, and respiratory diseases in the first winter. The Japanese response, published in the *Japan Advertiser*, possibly in rebuttal to protests by our own State Department, was that "they have no complaint, they have nice graves."[4]

The detail of 1,000—half officers and half men—was made up with Hunter in command and myself as executive officer. We selected our staff well, so far as those selected at Cabanatuan were concerned. American headquarters made up the list of those to go, half sick and half well. We were told it would be a recuperation camp, with better climate, better food, and to carry half of the personnel that were on the light sick lists as they would get well. This was nothing more than the usual Japanese bait that was thrown out to make men clamor to go on the details they offered.

The afternoon before we were to leave everyone was all marched out of the camp to an open field for inspection by the Japanese officers who were to accompany us. They rejected several of the sickest and weakest and we called on American headquarters for replacements and received them. The task of being a commander or staff officer for the Japs and your fellow prisoners is by no means a pleasant one. If you make good with the Japs you displease your fellow Americans with whom you have to live the rest of your life. If you please your fellow prisoners, you displease the Japs. There is no compromise between light and darkness, good and evil. I recommended to Hunter at the beginning that we take the job, organize our staff, protect the prisoners as best we could on the trip down, establish as many favorable policies as possible in the first few weeks of the new camp, and then retire to the position of private prisoners of war.[5]

There was little means of doing anything with troublesome and undisciplined prisoners. It would not do to turn them over to the Japs. They were too unpredictable for either they would turn them back with a mild admonition or subject them to some cruel and unusual punishment. All prisoners in their guardhouse, no matter what the offenses, were awakened and caused to stand on their feet every hour of the day and night. It was said that their cure for stealing was breaking both arms of the culprit and throwing him in the guardhouse for 48 hours before medical aid was permitted. They had many offenses punishable with death, and their officers and noncommissioned officers slapped or beat their privates upon slightest provocation.

The next morning we marched out. Our baggage, except for our field bags, was carried on trucks. It was goodbye to Cabanatuan as a prisoner of war for me. It was not for some who were later returned there. I had been there four months and three weeks, having spent 40 days at O'Donnell. I arrived there about June 6, 1942, and departed October 26, 1942.

We spent a day en route to Manila, a night in Bilibid, two days on a boat in Manila waiting to sail, then arrived in Cebu about November 1, left Cebu about November 5, and arrived at Davao Penal Colony on November 8, 1942. At the Cabanatuan station, we loaded our baggage and ourselves in box cars as previously. We were told that the Jap major would visit Santo Tomas the next day and carry any personal messages to our people there. I sent a message to Lucy, my sister, and her husband Carl Olsen. They received it.[6]

The rail trip to Manila was marked by Filipinos making demonstrations over us every time the train stopped at a village. They gave us the "V for victory" sign. They threw us fruits and eats and wept for joy at the sight of us. They had had enough of the Japanese tyranny and brutality. Our forty years of kindly rule over them had reacted in our favor; we could see that they loved us. Their families and neighbors had fought with us in Bataan and they had been liberated at O'Donnell. That is to say as many as had lived through the catastrophe. If the Japs really wanted to win the Filipinos over and incorporate them into their Far East Co-Prosperity Sphere, as they pretended, why did they not liberate the Philippine army soldiers in Bataan and treat them and their people kindly? But kindness is regarded by the heathen as a mark of weakness and it is not in the makeup of the Japs. At Bilibid we slept on a concrete floor in the old hospital building and in marching out saw several old friends to chat with them for a moment. These included Colonels Hutson and Mitchell.[7]

We were loaded on an old iron boat at Pier 7, the Million Dollar Pier. It was *Erie Maru*, built during World War I, and recognized by some of the prisoners as having been bought by the Japs from our ship's graveyard at New Orleans. We were loaded and packed into a hatch such as we would use for freight, but the hatch had been converted into a troop carrier by constructing double platforms for sleeping. We had a space about 30 inches by seven feet assigned to each of us. We could all lie down flat on our backs and that was all. We had sleeping mats of thin grass matting and bed bugs were numerous.[8]

During the entire voyage we had free use of our deck. On this deck were located the troop kitchens and two latrines. They were so few in number that men lined up from six to almost 50 deep for each closet. There were no bathing facilities for prisoners. We lay on the hot side of Pier 7 for two days while the ship finished loading and took on Filipino and Jap civilian passengers. The stay in Iloilo was only for a few hours during daylight. We pulled out at dark and arrived at Cebu early next morning. After a day and night at Cebu, all unloading and loading had been accomplished, and we were ready to proceed but the Japanese announced that a great battle in the Solomon Islands was in progress.[9] We had to wait for a green light from their navy. It was about three days before it came, and very hot in port while waiting, yet not as hot as in Manila. One of our men died and they carried him ashore and buried him.[10]

When the go sign came from the navy, we sailed through Surigao Straits to Davao in a day and a half. The crew showed their uneasiness of American submarines while sailing through Surigao Straits. We lay at anchor in Davao for a day and a night. No prisoner went ashore or got a glimpse of the city. The following morning we sailed up the bay and up a series of narrows to a big Japanese saw mill site called Lasang, and unloaded in lighters to begin our 30 kilometer hike to the Davao Penal Colony hereafter called Dapecol.[11]

We thought our voyage had been bad enough. We buried two at sea, sick cases that should not have left Cabanatuan, but it was the best voyage any of us were ever destined to take as prisoners of war under the flag of the red rising sun.[12] We had made the journey in ten days and without danger. The food was the best we had for any ten day period we experienced. There was plenty of well-steamed rice, corned beef seized at Cavite—a barrel of brisket a day—good, thick, rich vegetable soup and frequently a good boiled vegetable that resembled our American turnip. I liked to watch the Japanese cook steam the rice in large steam-served cauldrons. It came out as fluffy and nice as a hot baked biscuit.

Because it was dirty and hot, many of us slept on deck. Hunter and I slept on an old coal bin. We made the trip somewhat strengthened by the better food and with our lives. Kitchen details on the trip consisted of junior officers who got extra food from the Japanese kitchen for their labor and they were very liberal in dividing their extras with the less fortunate. Charlie Dunnagan from Yadkinville, North Carolina and Lieutenant Julian Lyon from Creedmoor, North Carolina were on the kitchen detail and looked after Colonel Hunter and me. This of course was a great help.[13]

When we arrived ashore at Lasang and were fed a meal of rice for lunch, we formed up to begin our hike. All baggage except what the individual chose to carry was loaded on trucks along with our weak and sick personnel. These trucks continued to run a shuttle service and pick up those unable to hike all the way. We were upbraided later by the Japanese Major Maeda in command of the new camp because we were weak and ineffective as over half of us had to be ridden into camp. It would have done our hearts good to have been able to slap him in the mouth and tell him that we were told to bring half of our number from the sick, and that if his men had no more to eat than we for the last six months they too would be in our condition or worse. But we were slaves and could say nothing without taking our lives in our hands, while he continued to rave on.[14]

"I asked for laborers, not walking corpses."

Despite his ravings he put us on reconditioning food for a short time, but even this was little above starvation levels. I made the hike all the way to the camp. We started at 1:00 p.m. and arrived at 2:00 a.m. It was well regulated, with halts and meals of rice and soup at intervals. I believe this heavy hike was the beginning of my hernia though it did not show up for some time. Upon arrival I felt a nervous chill from exhaustion coming on. The medic gave me a couple of aspirin tablets and I lay on the floor and slept for the best part of two days and nights getting up only for meals. Two Japanese officers, Lieutenant Hozumi, the "Crown Prince," and Lieutenant Yuki accompanied us from Cabanatuan to Davao.

The "Crown Prince" remained with us nearly a year as our company commander and Lieutenant Yuki remained in one capacity or another until the end of the camp. The "Crown Prince," so called because of a rumor of his close relation to Emperor Hirohito, was tall, well-proportioned, and as handsome a Japanese as I have ever seen. He was always properly, neatly, and almost meticulously dressed. His wardrobe was ample, of best materials and best tailored cuts. He wore shores at all times when out of doors, and never permitted himself to deteriorate into the slovenly tropical habit of going around his work and about camp dressed in scraping wooden shoes, khaki shorts, a white undershirt, and pith helmet or cap that so soon became the accustomed uniform of our officer jailers.

He was quick of speech and quicker of disposition—a sort of superior being who held himself aloof from the common herd. The punctiliousness of his appearance, his tall well-built figure, and his military swagger reminded me of the German officer, and his arrogance is equaled only by them. He was the only one we had from the line officers while prisoners of war that was of the type and seemed to possess the qualifications to be a good combat officer. But as the story goes he had been in combat somewhere in the New Guinea area and could never keep his command post close enough to the front to satisfy his superiors. He never slapped or beat a prisoner but often chastised his own officers or men. No, he would not disdain to dirty his hands on a prisoner, but rather permitted his officers and men to slap them around at will.[15]

Lieutenant Yuki was a different type, short, squatty and square, but not excessively so. He was an intelligent, neat and bright reserve officer with not too much military background, a good administrator, quick of perception, and with a kindly attitude towards all. He worked long and hard for our best interest and always had the confidence of the prisoners. I never knew him to strike an American, or resort to violence, or flare up in a temper. Rumors among the prisoners were that he was a Christian, but in order to obtain a commission in his army he was compelled to renounce Christianity, swear allegiance to the emperor, and demonstrate it by cutting off the heads of a number of Chinese prisoners. He was the supervisor of all work details for some months at the Davao farm project and even when put in disgrace by his fellow officers and placed in charge of the rice plantation, the dirtiest work of the farm, he still proved our friend for he never failed to have a carabao or Brahman steer ready when our too infrequent meat days came.[16]

There were a thousand prisoners of war at Dapecol when we arrived. They had been there about a week, having been moved in from Malaybalay by a short boat trip. Malaybalay was one of the large camps in Mindanao. Some of the prisoners had been assembled there after the surrender, but most of them had surrendered there. They had offered no resistance to the Japs, having surrendered to a small detachment on orders from General Sharp, and upon forced orders from General Wainwright while he was held under terrible threats as a hostage. The Japs had not invaded that part of Mindanao in force so they accepted the surrender and left them almost to date to live their own lives as they pleased. There was in camp and in the vicinity plenty of good food. They had their clothes, bedding and good housing, and had lived several months without any understanding of what it meant to be a Japanese prisoner of war. The Japs had even permitted them to bring their wardrobe trunks, bedding rolls, foot lockers and all heavy baggage to Dapecol. It was nice to find among them some old acquaintances—Marcus Boulware, Howard Perry, and Howard Edmands.[17]

It was difficult for this group at first to realize what we had endured at Bataan and Corregidor and what it fully meant to be a prisoner of war of the Japs. At first our stories of the heroic defense of these places sounded to them like fiction, and the Death March like a skein of imagination. The war to them so far had seemed far away, but our wrecked and emaciated bodies bore evidence of our stories. The cruelties of the Japs, when we were all too soon fed and worked as oriental slaves, soon brought them around to our viewpoint. Misery loves company and they, like ourselves, were to see it in abundance.

At first, however, despite Major Maeda's statement that this was a work camp, we were the immediate cause of their work and misery.

"If you guys hadn't come from the north, we would still be sitting pretty at Malaybalay," was a current remark until they appreciated fully the situation.

Dapecol had been started a number of years ago by the Philippine government as a big plantation project where convicts who were not criminals might be taught farming and trades. A large opening in the jungle had been initially cleared and each year the jungle was pushed farther and farther back. The ground was only a few feet above sea level and surface water was not over three feet from the top of the ground. A small river ran down through the settlement of small weather-beaten houses. Groves of coconuts, coffee, guavas, avocados, citrus, and bananas were in cultivation. Papaya grew wild, as did peppers, spices, and cassava. There were tremendous fields for rice, corn, camotes, and all types of vegetables. The farm was well stocked with warehouses and tools ranging from saw, rice, and sugar mills to tractors and on down the line of tools to the smallest garden hoes and plows. It was the ideal spot for a prisoner of war farm, and the climate with rainfall well distributed throughout the year was mild and suited for rice and trucking. Herds of Brahman cattle and carabao grazed the fields. It was a paradise if it could be worked and administered properly.[18]

Section III
Survival on Mindanao

I am interned at Philippines Military Prison No. 2. My health is excellent. I am not under treatment. I am well. Please see that letters sent thru Red Cross. Keep children on honor roll. Be cheerful. Lucy and family OK. My undrawn pay accumulating. Build rental house if suitable. Please give my best regards to all take good care of Mother.

—Japanese prison postcard from David L. Hardee to Elizabeth Hardee, received September 7, 1943

Although Hardee adopted an optimistic tone when writing to his wife, the nineteen months he spent at Dapecol would prove anything but comfortable. With no way of knowing how long they would be held, Hardee and the other prisoners spent 1943 and 1944 adapting and attempting to establish a daily routine of existence. During these months at Dapecol, Hardee paid witness to some of the only successful escapes from Japanese captivity, reflected on his Japanese captors, and experienced the deterioration of his own physical health.

The Philippine Bureau of Corrections had formally established the Davao Penal Colony in 1932 with an initial area of approximately 74,000 acres. The colony, surrounded by seemingly impenetrable jungle and swamps, served as a maximum-security prison, conjuring up comparisons to Alcatraz in California or Devil's Island in French Guyana.

When Hardee and his fellow prisoners on the work detail arrived they found conditions somewhat better than those at O'Donnell or Cabanatuan. The Americans were housed in eight barracks, constructed of wood and topped by metal roofs, which held 200 to 250 men each. The buildings were divided into two sides, then further divided into bays that could accommodate eight to twelve men apiece. A mess hall and latrines occupied separate buildings. Surrounding the barracks was a barbed wire fence. Guard towers stood at all four corners and were manned twenty-four hours a day. The barracks themselves had only a few small lights inside, but outside, lights illuminated the entire compound at night. Vermin remained a common scourge, and Dapecol's bed bugs proved impervious to the prisoners' efforts to eradicate them.

Like many of the men who had volunteered to work at Dapecol, Hardee had hoped for an improved diet. Under Japanese control, American prisoners worked in the rice paddies, orchards, and fields surrounding the prison compound, supposedly growing their own food. But he soon found that productivity gained him little. Prison administrators frequently denied the prisoners the fruits of their labor. They used what was produced to feed Japanese forces on Mindanao or sold the produce on the black market for personal gain. Japanese officials wrecked orchards and fields by grazing carabao in them, allowed harvests to rot in the fields, and permitted the jungle to reclaim previously

View of the abandoned barracks at the Davao Penal Colony as found in May 1945 by members of the USAFFE Recovered Personnel Field Team and guerrillas of the 1st Battalion, 130th Infantry. Hardee and his compatriots lived in the vermin-infested buildings from October 1942 until June 1944. **Source: NARA.**

cultivated areas. Whenever possible, prisoners stole food while at work and then smuggled fruits and foodstuffs into the camp.

The new camp's death rate was considerably lower than that at either previous site of Hardee's incarceration, but life there was not without hardship, and the physical strain finally caught up with him. In March 1943, while picking coffee, he suffered a severe abdominal hernia that left him debilitated and increasingly weak. Because the Japanese refused to provide surgery, and American medical personnel were unable to offer much relief, Hardee spent much of his time with the ill and handicapped within the confines of the camp, weaving hats and baskets from jungle vines or cogan grass. Frequently bedridden, Hardee relied on care from the hospital personnel and the kindness of fellow prisoners.

In stark contrast to workers at Luzon's prisons, Dapecol's Lieutenants Kempei Yuki and Osamu Yoshimura treated Hardee and other prisoners with greater consideration and humanity, garnering the respect of many of those held at Dapecol; however, camp commander Major Kazuo Maeda, some of his lieutenants, and civilian interpreters actively sought to demonstrate Japanese superiority to the prisoners through constant harassment and brutality. The displaying of propaganda newspapers and efforts by some of the Japanese to hinder or completely deny even trivial sources of improved morale did not break the spirit of the prisoners. Occasional mail, a camp library, religious services, and other diversions helped prisoners overcome boredom and maintain morale.

One source of diversion for some prisoners was the planning of escapes. These proved marginally successful at Dapecol, although most of the remaining prisoners remained unaware of their comrades' good fortune. Contrary to Japanese belief, the surrounding jungle was not impenetrable; several groups of prisoners managed to find their way into and through it, link up with Filipino guerrillas, and make contact with American guerrilla leaders. Three men who succeeded, Major Stephen Mellnik, Commander Melvyn McCoy, and Captain William Dyess, eventually voyaged by submarine to Australia and revealed to General MacArthur the horrors of the Death March and the prison camps. Dyess's account reached U.S. news outlets in January and February 1944, horrifying Americans and filling them with unshakeable resolve to make the Japanese pay for Bataan and Corregidor.

While escapes did not bring about extreme reprisals against other prisoners as they had at Cabanatuan, the Japanese did not take them lightly. One of

Hardee's friends, Major Charles Harrison, apparently attempted escape and was killed by the guards.

By May 1944, American forces were advancing throughout the Pacific. Through a series of victories, they began to close in on the Philippines and Japan. The same day Allied forces on the other side of the world stormed ashore in Normandy, Hardee and his fellow prisoners were blindfolded, roped together, and trucked to Davao to embark on the squalid, dilapidated freighter *Yashu Maru*. Crammed into the ship's holds like sardines, left without adequate sanitation, water, or food, the prisoners were vividly reminded why Americans had deemed these Japanese vessels "hellships."

The ship docked in Cebu, where the prisoners languished a few days before boarding another hellship, *Singoto Maru*, for a miserable voyage to Manila Bay.

The Davao Penal Colony hospital as found in May 1945 by members of the USAFFE Recovered Personnel Field Team and guerrillas of the 1st Battalion, 130th Infantry. When the Japanese closed down the prison farm in June 1944, prisoners too sick to move were left to die. Skeletal and mummified remains were found throughout the hospital and the prisoner barracks. **Source: NARA.**

On June 26, 1944, after sweltering for two days in the holds of the squalid freighter, the prisoners staggered ashore and were marched to Old Bilibid Prison. Hardee, though weaker and more haggard after the trip, had survived two years of Japanese imprisonment, and it seemed the worst was over.

Interior view of the prisoner barracks at Dapecol from May 1945 showing the double tier bunking arrangements. Bedbugs infested the bunks and feasted on the prisoners nightly. **Source: NARA.**

CHAPTER 10

Life at Dapecol

We were handicapped at Dapecol from the start by swaggering, insolent, and high-strung Jap interpreters and noncommissioned officers. They walked around with loaded swagger sticks, whips, and sticks always looking for an opportunity to pounce upon and beat up prisoners for the least infraction of rules or discipline. Chief of these offenders was a little insignificant, black-mustached interpreter by the name of Nishimura, known among the prisoners as "Simon Legree." He wore boots up to his knees and, as was the custom with all of them, a large samurai sword far out of proportion to his small and compact body. His background was that an older brother raised him on a truck farm near Los Angeles, California. He spoke and understood complicated English, even American slang. This background seemed to create in him a burning desire to prove his loyalty to the emperor which he demonstrated daily by beating, sometimes unmercifully and upon slightest provocation, one or more prisoners. He, being a little runt, and the prisoners being unable to defend themselves for fear of immediate torture and execution, caused him to take a great delight in climbing on the biggest American he could find and beating him up publicly by knocking him down with a loaded riding crop which he always carried and then kicking him in unspeakable places.[1]

"Simon" was king for a long number of months, but then the Japs lost confidence in him, relieved him of his interpreter duties, and placed him in charge of the farm tool house. He remarked to me that he was in bad with the Americans and his own people. Certainly he was in bad with us and was regarded as everybody's meat, and in case liberation had come to us at Dapecol with "Simon" still present it would have taken all the self-restraint the prisoners possessed to refrain from tearing him limb from limb.

We had a lieutenant by the name of Hiroshi, who had a face like a horse and a body like an ape. When he was not referred to by the prisoners as "Lieutenant Horseface" he was called the "Five O'Clock Shadow" because he never failed to appear around the main gate of the compound at that time to watch the prisoners check in. He always carried a golf club handle and sometimes used it when a prisoner displeased him. His beatings were mild and reflected his easy-going disposition. He was in charge of truck farm work and while evidently from the lowest classes of Japanese society, strange as it seemed from his appearance, he possessed some intelligence and good common sense.[2]

Major Maeda, our commandant for the larger part of our stay at Dapecol, was an old retired regular army officer who stayed deep in his cups and worried little about our welfare. He had a bungalow built for himself and visiting notables just outside the right of the main gate nestled in a grove of citrus trees. In it he assembled the best of the furniture the colony afforded and had a shower bath installed, the last one in our compound for which use by anyone but the kitchen force was forbidden until torn out for his exclusive use. He used to come sauntering out of his house each morning to the main gate and watch his barefooted, ragged, and half-starved slaves march to their daily toil. A khaki pith helmet always crowned a little round yellow head with intelligent bright eyes. His small, yellow, well-formed body was covered with a white undershirt and khaki shorts. His wooden shoes never failed to scrape along the path as he walked, carrying a short stick in his hand as he peered through a large pair of horned rim glasses that so many Japs wore.

He concerned himself mostly with the general overhead of the camp, and never inspected our mess or seemed to concern himself with our particular welfare. Our dealings with him were few, and then only through the American leader with whom he seemed to chat now and then on general conditions but always through an interpreter. He was good with his sarcastic statements and sadistic torture. On one occasion he announced through our American leader that he had received a sum of money (about ₱2,000–$1,000) from the Pope at Rome to be given to the prisoners. We requested that he buy extra food for us—but we never received the food or the money. As our forces began to push up from the south he had all his stolen furniture packed and shipped to Japan and he disappeared from our lives.

The last to come, but by no means the least of our tormentors, was Sergeant Hashimoto who quickly earned the sobriquet of "Little Caesar." He was a candidate for a commission and seemed to have been sent to us to demonstrate his ability. He must have been satisfactory to the Japs for his commission came through a few months after his arrival. The huskily built, square faced, round headed Jap had double ideas about punishment. "Simon Legree" and the others were strong for strafing the individuals, but "Little Caesar," while never failing to neglect the individuals that came across his path, believed he could convert us to punctuality and docility by mass punishments and lectures. He believed that oratorical proclivities increased his instructional ability—so after each roll call he held us in formation and delivered a long verbose harangue, always only partially translated by an interpreter. These dealt with punctuality, discipline, manners, behavior, and general conduct expected of prisoners. He was strong for bowing and saluting and slapped prisoners right and left when they failed to do so. Whenever he came in sight the word was passed—"Little Caesar"—and whenever any Jap came in our barracks area the word was passed—"High-ho Silver."[3]

It was not uncommon for "Little Caesar" to publicly flog those late at roll call formations—or go through barracks and find a sick, half-starved prisoner and beat him while he ran outdoors to get in formation. He was always beating prisoners while on work details. As a sample of his mentality, some prisoners were trying to plow a young and unbroken carabao. The carabao was giving them trouble as was to be expected. He approached the group, drew his big samurai sword, cut off the carabao's tail and remarked: "That will teach him some sense."[4]

We had about all of "Little Caesar" we could endure when at one roll call he badly flogged three or four men who had dysentery and were running from the latrine to make formation. Most of us had already learned that when a Jap strikes you one should fall to the ground at the first blow. Unless the beast was merciless like "Simon Legree" and began kicking, then your beating was about over. One prisoner did not know this and stood without flinching while "Little Caesar" rained blow after blow on him. Finally, he placed his leg behind the poor helpless prisoner and knocked him over to the ground, injuring his hips and back.

A council of our senior officers sent our American leader to carry a message from us to Major Maeda. The message was oral, but in context about as follows:

> "We are a group of senior officers and were in the service of our country before Hashimoto was born. You are letting this little squirt harass us daily at roll calls with lectures on discipline, conduct, and manners. We

have forgotten more about it than he will ever know. He is always flogging and beating prisoners. We are sure your government at Tokyo will not approve of such conduct. Please keep him out of this compound and assign him to work where he does not come in contact with prisoners. This will save you trouble. This will save us much trouble."

Our leader spoke his piece through an interpreter as we had directed him. Everyone in the Jap office stopped work to listen. Major Maeda called some of his officers around him and asked for a repeat. It was repeated and our leader departed after explaining that this was not of his origin.

We did not expect results but we got them. "Little Caesar" was kept away from the prisoners until a detail was sent to work on the Lasang Airfield. He was sent with them, where according to reports he was worse than ever with his slappings and beatings. He was torpedoed on the Jap hellship off Mindanao in the fall of 1944, where he seems to have killed one of the American officers whom he had often tortured and violently beaten. This he did in order to make good his own escape on a raft upon which Japs and prisoners were climbing. I do not know what his end was or will be, but I am sure that he will be accorded an end suitable to his deeds in the flesh.[5]

Colonel Hunter, the American leader, had chosen me as his executive officer and we used methods of cooperation and persuasion in dealing with the Japs. The cooperation suited them fine but the persuasion in dealing with the Japs was at times too much for them and in a few weeks resulted in our relief. There were many things to be organized in a new camp and we had to worry the Japs a great deal or our prisoners suffered. This of course was more marked than in the administration that followed us who had nothing more to do than keep the organization going. We had to form it. We sought to establish the following principal administration policies:

1. Personnel and detail leaders for all details to be selected daily and changed as necessary by American headquarters.[6]
2. Nature of work would determine age of men to be placed on detail, with hard work details to be performed by young men. Older men to be used on easier details, such as gathering fruits and vegetables, making hats and baskets.
3. The establishment of a store where items not issued and necessary could be purchased by the prisoners.

4. Complete control of administration in the compound by the American headquarters.
5. The organization of a farm planning board composed of American prisoners, Filipinos who knew the farm, and Japanese officers. The board to have from six to ten members.
6. The establishment of a library which was eventually realized after we had been there about eight or nine months. The books were those that had been looted from Philippine public schools.[7]

We had very good luck with the first and second plans. With the aid of Lieutenant Yuki, the Jap in charge of prisoners, we had many older and more dependable details working on the plantation without sentries. They made excuses on the store—they claimed they had no canned goods in Davao like there were in Luzon and that everything had to be brought from Japan where foods and canned meats were scarce. We begged for local goods, chickens, eggs, native products, and fruits. They delayed and delayed and finally after several months permitted the opening of a store, the purchasing to be done by their quartermaster, a son of heaven who was out for his customary oriental squeeze. He purchased tobacco almost entirely with almost no other items ever handled through the store. This tobacco was not manufactured but was sold in hands of one hundred leaves.

Complete control of the administration within the fence was never given to the American commander. If there was anything the Jap loved to do it was to fail to support the officers, cause them to lose face, and then to upbraid them for failure to discipline or control their men. The work of the mess officer and the assistant mess officer was unsatisfactory. There were a number of things Colonel Hunter had tried to have them straighten out in the mess without success. He relieved them. They ran to the Japs and the Japs reinstated them. After this incident, every commander that succeeded Colonel Hunter was afraid to disturb the kitchen set-up and it was never entirely satisfactory to the prisoners. It was always full of big fat cooks and kitchen police when there were men enfeebled or sick to the point of death from starvation. This was condoned by the Japs for under their plan the kitchen and medical forces were to be kept in good physical condition.

The Japs at first thought the farm planning board would be a good plan, but they put us off and finally said that they would do all the planning themselves. In fact they were scared by the advance of our forces from the south and were homesick and wanted to return to Japan. They deliberately planned a crop failure to accomplish these ends and made it most effective in about six months. They tried to blame this on us by saying that the prisoners were no good and would not work.

The Japs did not at first directly order the officers to work but called Colonel Hunter and myself with the detail officer into conference and asked for so many men the next day. This was such a large increase that we replied we could not fill it because of the sick unless we called on about 150 officers to fill the details. They knew this to begin with but evaded the point by ordering us to fill in the details. After the first officers were turned out to work as field hands and the ice was broken they continued to call for more and more men until every officer in the camp was put to work. No respect was paid to rank. It is not customary in any civilized country to turn officers and noncommissioned officers out to do physical labor. This was the last straw in breaking down discipline and morale. Many of the officers had never done manual labor, and did not know how to do it. The enlisted men soon observed this, and often remarked that they wished the "blankety blank officers" would stay at home.

As the demand for more laborers increased the Japanese called on Colonel Hunter for a list of his staff. There is no executive officer in the Japanese organization. They call the position a transmitter of orders, corresponding to our adjutant's position. An executive was disallowed and I joined a detail of men over fifty years of age that had been put to work making hats and baskets until the Jap doctor put me in the hospital, a month or more before the camp was broken up.

I liked this work. It was an occupation and not hard. It entitled me to two worker meals a day. The Japs had heavy chow, workers' chow, and non-workers' chow. The difference in volume just about replaced the energy expended in doing the work. We made baskets, large two handled stout farm or feed baskets, from bejuco vines. They were used on the farm for gathering all types of crops and many other purposes. I was in charge of a department, and it was task work and I had much experience with dead-beats, gold brickers, and passive resisters. I was never in sympathy with it when it was applied to unload one's work on his fellow prisoners. The basket detail was a choice one for the old and the sick men, and was controlled by the American doctors. When we got too many dead-beats a consultation with the doctor resulted in changes. The malingers found themselves on plowing in the fields or some heavy work detail. Weaving hats is a rather complicated thing and by the time I learned it and made about a half dozen hats our first Red Cross shipment arrived. It contained a large number of felt hats so the hat and basket detail was discontinued and a coffee picking detail was organized for us.[8]

The detail was made principally to give the older officers employment, and to get us out in the fields where we could get some native fruits and coconuts to help rebuild our weakened bodies. The coffee we picked and processed would have been a great boon to our mess had the Japs permitted us full use of it. But it was reserved for Sunday morning only and for just a short time. Soon it disappeared from our menu entirely and what the Japs had not otherwise disposed of was permitted to rot in the warehouse.

We had been at Dapecol only a few weeks when the first anniversary of the sneak attack on Pearl Harbor came around. The Japs marched all the American prisoners of war out and placed them in mass formation on their drill ground on the left front of the compound. Everyone was caused to face towards the Imperial Palace in Tokyo and salute the flag of the "red rising sun" in a flag raising ceremony and listen to a reading of the imperial rescript, a proclamation by the emperor amounting to a declaration of war. The flag of the Japanese navy is an ornate and colorful thing but the flag of the army is nothing more than a large red ball printed in the center of a piece of white cotton muslin. This was also the sign used for their airplane markings, and all the prisoners of war had seen enough of it. It was spoken of from the early days of Bataan as a flaming part of the human anatomy that is unprintable. Why they chose to have us hear the imperial rescript read is still a mystery. But why did they choose to do so many things that didn't make sense?[9]

Later in the day, Hunter, Compton, and several others were using our holiday to cook some vegetables and green fruits that we had sneaked in off the farm. Our little fires were on the south side of the barracks where we had a clear view of the sky from our feet to the top of a mountain range, upon which was located the big airfield at Del Monte, now held by the Japs. The field was about 45 miles from us and we could see planes go and come from it when landing or taking off in our direction. Someone remarked that perhaps we might have a token from the south on the day of the first anniversary of war. We stopped our cooking and looked long and wistfully into the sky but there was no sight of an American airplane, nor a motor to be heard.[10]

"By Christmas," someone suggested, "our planes will be coming."

We would have been deeply discouraged had we known and doubted our ability to live through it, but we were to see more anniversaries and Christmases pass before we would be gladdened by the appearance of American airplanes.

Our first Christmas as prisoners found us at Dapecol. Major Larry Prichard had organized and trained a good ensemble of about thirty voices and they sang Christmas carols and other holy week hymns. Men brought in sprigs of green from the farm and all the barracks, kitchen, and hospital wards had a small amount of decorations. It was a holiday and a meat day with a little more to eat than on usual days. The chaplains held special services and this made life a little more livable. One of the officers from Deming, New Mexico, painted a few crayon cards for his friends saying, "I am sorry but it looks like a beriberi Christmas and a Jappy New Year."[11]

Our second Christmas at Dapecol was not so glorious. Under the constant pressure of work Major Prichard's choir had disappeared. There were a few green decorations and the Japs gave us an extra carabao. The chaplains put on special services and we were mindful of the occasion, with thoughts always turned towards home and loved ones.[12]

The Red Cross shipment arrived about March 1, 1943. This was our first shipment and each of us got one Canadian, one British South African, and one-half American package. Additionally, we received an extra issue of corned beef, sugar, and toilet articles that came in bulk shipment. A great many medical supplies and some books and pre–Pearl Harbor magazines were also received. We learned a year or more later that the Canadian and South African packages were meant for the prisoners in Burma but the Japs were mad with them and had diverted their shipment to us.[13]

It was wonderfully good to taste real food again. Our diet had been rice, soup, meat and sometimes dried fish about twice a week. The Red Cross food and medicines stopped the death rate and saved many lives by building up resistance for many months to come. The first thing I ate out of my box was a dried California prune. I have never tasted so good a prune before and never expect to again. Some ate their Red Cross food rapidly but most of the prisoners stretched it as far as possible. We had been prisoners almost a year before the first of it reached us. There had already been such talk of prisoner of war pay but none showed up as yet and most of us were still penniless.

The store was opened up with tobacco, 100 leaves to the hand for sale. It was a well-aged burley type and could be cut up for pipes or cigarettes or rolled into cigars. Many of us learned the art of cigar making. The first proposition the Japs made us was that if we would trade them pound for pound some of our Red Cross white sugar for their brown sugar they would have a soda water plant in Davao make us soda pop. It seems to take refined sugar for this work. It appeared rather childish that a great warlike nation could not afford a few bags of granulated sugar in the midst of a sugar producing country to their own merchants and manufacturers. It was evident that a Jap soft drink maker in Davao was behind it for profit and the Jap supply officer, Lieutenant Shiraji, was in for his squeeze. Believing this would be an entering wedge to procure other much needed items for the store we voted our consent. The result was that about six to ten bottles per man of cheap strawberry and sarsaparilla pop were sold through the store before the scheme played out.[14]

Lieutenant Shiraji, the Jap quartermaster supply officer, had a typical one-track Jap mind. He could never conceive anything more enterprising than the "squeeze" out of our rations and two items at the store. So a two item store it was, often running out of both items for long periods. We could never understand why they did not, after we began to draw pay, put in a store stocked with obtainable local products and really make profit out of us. But the Jap policy was to the contrary.

Tobacco was a staple store product so the next project Lieutenant Shiraji tried was peanuts in the hull once per week, every Friday. With the first issue of peanuts we were allowed one canteen cup per man for 20 centavos. On the second issue money was becoming scarcer and the most fortunate of us could get only two or three cups of nuts. This continued for about six weeks and then the peanuts played out. During the months of June and July the store carried only tobacco and was sometimes out of it for weeks. The tobacco addicts during this period would take part of their food and trade it for tobacco even though the food was scarce and they were on the ragged edge of starvation.[15]

About August 1943, Lieutenant Shiraji added peanut candy as the second store item—once per week, on Friday. A penny slice made with molasses cost ten centavos or five cents in American money. The issue per man was from six to ten slices. On the third week the price was raised to 15 centavos, and the slices were about the thickness of a table knife blade and then the peanut candy project played out entirely.[16]

They were a very inconsistent people. Whatever they started they lacked the follow-through and it soon came to naught. Peanuts are rich in protein and oil and as little as we received and as expensive as they were we hated to see them go. From then to the end of the camp at Dapecol the store handled tobacco only. We begged for other items, such as salt, sugar, and the fruits of the farm and countryside but to no effect. We begged for the fruit of the farm and offered to send details of sick men to go out and gather it daily. The offer was refused. The Japanese would attend to that but they never did to any appreciable extent. Major Maeda said it was better to let the fruit rot on the trees than to give it to the prisoners. Many of our men were suffering from scurvy and pellagra and the fruit was the answer as more than half of us were suffering a dietary deficiency disease.

Dr. Yoshimura, the Jap doctor, was the most humane Jap I came in contact with. He often interceded on our behalf and through his influence a small quantity of fruit such as lemons, limes, coconuts, pineapples, and guavas was brought in for issue to our hospital sick, and sometimes in quantities to allow an occasional issue to each prisoner of war. He often interceded in the matter of food and medical supplies and supported our American doctors who ran the hospital. Often when the command called for more workers than we had well men he would conduct an inspection of the sick and light duty prisoners and put more men on the sick book than our surgeons had on them. He unquestionably saved many American lives. Captain George A. Rader, our hospital adjutant, was very faithful in the performance of his duties and he and Lieutenant Colonel Dwight Deter, C.O. of the hospital, kept very close contact with Dr. "Yosh," as we called him, and this unquestionably kept the death rate at normal.[17]

Chaplain Howden of the 200th Coast Artillery was the first among the officers to die at Dapecol. Lieutenant Colonel Sullivan was the second. He had come with me on the *Coolidge*, leaving a nice family in California. His passing cast a gloom over me. These and several enlisted men were hangovers from Cabanatuan. The Japs furnished some medicines before our Red Cross supplies arrived and by February 1943 the death rate was reduced to normal and remained so for the duration of the camp, but the sick rate was tremendous, due to malaria, poor and too little food, and borderline cases of starvation. When we left after about 17 months of occupation, our cemetery numbered approximately 20 graves, including one murder and two men killed in attempted escapes. This was not bad for 2,000 people and it was the best we did anywhere I was interned.[18]

After we had been at Dapecol about two months we heard news from Cabanatuan, brought through Japanese soldiers that had been our guards there and who had followed us to Dapecol. The death rate had greatly slackened in about six or eight weeks after we left. Like Camp O'Donnell, they had greatly reduced its strength, leaving only the senior officers, the sick, and the working staff. Sanitation, medical, and food conditions had been improved. Gardens and farms had been put in cultivation. It was one of the best camps, but it was high time for improvement.[19]

In the first seven or eight months of our prison life at least half of the Americans who surrendered in Bataan had died and death had made inroads into the Corregidor group. The Corregidor group had not been as weakened as the Bataan group. They had been at the source of the ration supply during combat days and had not been weakened by the Death March. I heard much criticism of the Quartermaster on Bataan and Corregidor, particularly that Corregidor had hoarded the food and surrendered shiploads of sugar and other items of rations. I sought out two of those officers who were in a position to know. We surrendered about 30 days' rations for the garrison of 12,000 men. Had this been divided with the forces in Bataan on the basis of whole, rather than half rations, they would have been consumed in four days after which Corregidor would have been forced to go out with Bataan. It was very good management to keep two days' supplies in Bataan and issue it out to where there was a month's food for 12,000 men when the last surrender took place.[20]

CHAPTER 11

A Hernia Saved My Life

The coffee picking detail was the best one we had during our prison life. We were without a sentry and worked in a large coffee grove about a kilometer from the compound. The detail was composed of older officers, mostly majors and lieutenant colonels. It was contract work in that we picked our allotment for the day and then quit work. We could usually finish our day's task by noon and rest and gather food, coconuts, and fruits in the afternoon. All of us had piles of bananas, guavas, papayas, and coconuts hidden in the grass.

The warming of food for lunch by details was also allowed. We carried our cooked rice out in our mess kits, and the soup and salt we carried out in bulk. We processed and made our own coffee. The place abounded with cassava, talinum, and green papaya and this combination makes excellent soup. Our cook, Colonel Hunter, made us a five gallon can of this each day besides heating up and serving the soup that we brought from our kitchen. Two or three days per week we had two large chickens to put in the soup. These chickens were furnished by Lieutenant Commander Melvyn McCoy and Major Stephen Mellnik, the detail leader and his assistant. They charged up to five pesos per chicken. This pro-rated about 30 centavos per person. They represented to us that they were buying them from a Filipino. We later learned that they were coming from our chicken farm and were being sold to us to raise the money to finance a well-planned escape.[1]

The coffee trees resembled orange trees in size, shape, and likewise had ripe fruit and blossoms at the same time. The fruit looked like large red Michigan cherries but the pulp is nearly tasteless. The center of each berry contains two coffee beans. It is processed by soaking in water, removing the pulp, and sunning the beans. The grove had been neglected since the outbreak of the war and we had to take bolos to clear it out, often removing vines that almost totally covered the trees. The jungle has to be fought incessantly or it will come back and swallow up the labor of man. Coffee was not an item of the Jap ration components so we never knew what became of the bulk of our pickings after it was processed by another detail that worked at the bodega (warehouse). Now and then they gave us enough so all the prisoners had coffee for breakfast about once a week. We guessed that they gave it to the army and civilians in Davao or shipped it to Japan.[2]

Working on the coffee detail gave us excellent opportunities to survey the farm. The Japs would never keep up anything they operated. It was a case of robbery and desecration even of nature. When a bearing banana stalk is cut down to gather its ripening fruit, five or six shoots are already growing up around the mother plant. All but one must be chopped down with a whack of a bolo, or else the crowded interior plants produce no new crop. This was not done and bananas were soon a scarcity. Coconut, guava, papaya, and citrus trees were also chopped down and mutilated in a helter-skelter fashion.

The fine coffee grove was finally mutilated and given to the jungle before we were taken away from the farm. The small sugar cane fields were raped and not replaced. As we had no sugar in our issued rations, the Japs were persuaded to permit us to take down an old sugar mill and bring it into the compound. They did not believe we could do it, but to their disgust we made good cane syrup for our rice until the sugar cane fields were denuded. They would not let us replant. Sugar and sweetening was scarce since they had seized all the sugar output of the islands to make alcohol to run their motors.

The only thing they took care of were the Brahman cattle and carabao herd. They were turned in on the pineapple patches and permitted to destroy them. These herds numbered upwards of a thousand head when we arrived and more when we left. They had preserved them as meat for their own people and armed forces and they were frequently grazed around our compound. As there were abundant rains and ample grass the year round they were kept slick and fat. We were due to have one for butchering twice per week. This would not have absorbed the natural increase of the herd. I suppose we averaged getting three to five per month. When we were given one, it was usually a poor, starved animal that had been sick or worked almost to death. Those having accidents were killed for us and the G.I.s who worked them soon learned how, when Japs were not looking, to cause them to fall into holes and break their legs or neck.

When we were fortunate enough to get one, even the poor starved ones, the Japs took all the good meat, leaving us only about 150 to 200 pounds of carcass, the head, and innards which we called NRA—neck, ribs and, anus. When this was boiled up to feed 2,000 prisoners it made little more than a meat base for one meal or vegetable soup. The common way of eating this was to pour it over a mess kit of steamed rice and count your meat shreds. A hard working G.I. was as hungry after he had eaten as he was before. We were always hungry.[3]

We noticed a few unusual things about Lieutenant Commander McCoy and Major Mellnik and could not understand them at the time. They were Russian and Irish jews and all for themselves and entirely too thick with a couple of enlisted men that were on the detail for getting wood and maintaining camp. We were working without guards, a sort of trustee status that we had worked hard to attain, and every Sunday the Japs permitted them to draw their noon day food and go out to the coffee grove to spend the day and plan the next week's work. Some of the officers they took with them were on the coffee detail, some were not. On Sunday morning, April 4, 1943, after the coffee detail had been running about two months, these officers with eight others passed through the gate as usual to plan their next week's work. I noticed that they carried an unusual amount of baggage.[4]

That night they failed to show up. The Japs locked our gates and began to search, but of course did not search in the jungle before the next morning. This gave them a clear twenty-four hour start. We were sure they would make good their escape and they did. This was the largest single prison break from the Japs to date, and was mostly high ranking officers. It highly incensed the Japs who kept us locked in the compound for several days while they searched in vain. It made it very hard on Lieutenant Yuki, the Jap officer in charge of the prisoners, as he had trusted us without guard against the recommendation of other officers. They relieved him and put him in charge of the worst detail on the farm, the rice fields. Then they proceeded to withdraw all our privileges such as going outside the fence without a guard, bringing food into the compound, individual fires for cooking, and then practically closed the store for two months. Discipline was tightened down and the attitude of the Japs changed from friendliness to hostility. This attitude never changed and many of our privileges were never restored.[5]

The mass punishment dished out consisted in getting all of us who lived in the barracks with any of these escaped men and putting us in isolation in another compound. There were about 500 of us and we were put on rice, salt, and kangkong—camote vine soup for 60 days. Kangkong, or whistle weed, is a wild vine that grows in swamps and rice paddies. Occasionally we had dried fish and through Doctor "Yosh's" intercession after about 30 days, the food was somewhat improved.[6]

We were told that we should be penitent, to make no noise, no laughing, and no singing. Our few newspapers were withheld. During these 60 days I lost all the strength and flesh I had gained during the good days of the coffee detail. Our Red Cross food also had been consumed. My hernia was getting bad and I lay on my back during most of this period and read such books as I could borrow and trade for. Unfortunately, there was not a chaplain to accompany us to our new place of confinement. It so happened that none of them were living in the barracks or bays with any of those who escaped.

When we first arrived in the new compound, as it was called, religious meetings were banned by the Japs just as they had been on several former occasions when we were undergoing mass punishments. As per usual, many of the men turned to small groups for prayer meetings held at irregular intervals and places. These meetings always strengthened the faith and courage of the participants.

After the first Sunday, the Japs gave permission to hold church services in one end of a building that was used for offices, sick call, and general purposes but we had no preacher. It fell to the lot of us line officers to take turns at conducting the services. Lieutenant Colonel Rufus H. "Bill" Rogers of Del Rio, Texas, was in charge and took the first Sunday. Bill's sermon on Christian living was lacking in the pattern of pulpit polish and failed to contain many earmarks of theology, but it was one of the best and most powerful sermons I have ever heard.

Towards the end of our 60 days of penance the Japs permitted some of our chaplains to come over from the other compound and conduct our services. During this time they passed a slip for us to sign that read in effect that our captors had in no ways interfered with our religious beliefs. Certainly they had not tried to convert us to Buddhism or Taoism, but they had at times forbidden and at other times interfered with our opportunities to worship.[7]

Bill Rogers left us several months later to be the American leader on a detail of 650 prisoners of war sent to work on the Lasang Airfield, taking Captain Berg as his adjutant and Lieutenant Colonel Colvard of Deming, New Mexico, as his chief medical officer. All were very fine men and lost their lives with many others in the torpedoing of their boat on September 7, 1944 off the island of Mindanao.[8]

The war situation did not look good. We were fighting back very slowly and Japan was winning in Burma. To one group of prisoners, McCoy and Mellnik and those others who escaped were heroes; to others, they were nothing more than names unprintable. As we marched over to the other compound to go into isolation, an officer on one side of me remarked: "We can take it, and maybe they will do some good and better our conditions." Others were sure they could do no good and vowed vengeance with oaths.[9]

The most optimistic said we would soon get our privileges back—which we never did. Lieutenant Yuki, the Jap officer who was responsible that we were on a trustee status, vowed vengeance and announced that they would be caught, brought back to camp, and that he would personally execute them. Even those who condemned them the most hoped they would never fall back into the hands of the Japs. Some reserved their opinion until it could be seen what their escape would do to ameliorate the general condition of the prisoners. It was my experience that every escape, as well as other breeches of rules under the Japs, brought down the roof on the innocent, among whom were the sick and helpless. I have always doubted that the escapes accomplished enough to overbalance the suffering and misery they caused.[10]

These escapees made it home. Captain William E. Dyess who organized his own McCoy-Mellnik group and joined up with the group as a last subterfuge was a veteran of Bataan, the Death March, and O'Donnell. His splendid series of articles appearing after his death in a large group of syndicated papers throughout the country did great good towards arousing the country and informing them of just what kind of an enemy we were fighting. But knowing the Japs as I do, I do not believe anything could be done to help us in our pitiful plight so far as getting better treatment from our inhumane captors was concerned.

The McCoy-Mellnik escape of ten prisoners eventually received great publicity at home and brought the Death March and our treatment as prisoners home to our people. General MacArthur is said to have told these escapees, "I believe every word you say because I know the Jap, but you will have a hard time persuading the American people to believe it." After arguments back and forth the War Department cleared the story to *Life* magazine and other publications, and the American people not only accepted and believed it but it increased their war determination.[11]

McCoy and Mellnik certainly misjudged the time element when it came to pay. They had resolved to devices to raise money for their escape, and the on the day following it, April 6, 1943, we drew our first prisoner of war pay.

According to the Geneva Conference agreements this was based on the base pay of each grade in the country holding you as a POW. The base pay of a lieutenant colonel was ₱220 per month. It was graduated down the line to the various commissioned and noncommissioned grades. The private was entitled to no pay, but was given ten centavos (5 cents) per day for his slave work. You drew your pay but you didn't draw it. You signed for it all, but were paid a small amount in cash, had certain charges made against your account, and the remainder was placed to your credit in a Japanese Army postal bank with a separate deposit book for each prisoner.

The amount in cash to a lieutenant colonel was ₱40 every other month. At Bilibid it was ₱40, and later ₱45 every month. The charges against an officer for his board, clothes, keep, and other incidentals were all that any civilized country could make against you but these charges were made irrespective of value received. We were charged ₱30 per month for board—one peso per day. We figured if all the goods were bought on the open market they would cost them less than ten cents per day. We were producing most of it on the farm. I put in for every item of clothing that was offered and drew one pair of shoe laces, captured goods that cost me ₱75. Soon thereafter this clothing charge was discontinued.

We paid little attention to these charges for we knew we would never see the money deposited in the bank anyway. At the end of my prison life I had between ₱4,000 to ₱5,000 in the bank deposit but have never seen it, and never expect to. International law provides that your family be paid allotments monthly through neutral countries from your prisoner of war pay. I asked that mine be allotted to my sister Lucy at the Santo Tomas Internment Camp in Manila. Lieutenant Shiraji thought they could do this as she was in an occupied country. If I would put in a letter he would send it to the Manila headquarters for prisoners. I put in a letter every three or four months for a year and a half and was never given any satisfaction as to whether they were allotting the money or not. I learned later that my sister had never heard anything from them about it—nice people, the Japanese.[12]

When our 60 days of penitence were over we moved back into the main compound. I speak of a compound in the sense that it is the enclosure in which prisoners are kept, be it a large one surrounded by a stone wall or a small group of buildings surrounded by a barbed wire fence. The main compound was very crowded. They had caused the prisoners to build a new barracks on the main line. This had been built of rough timber, second hand nails, and used sheet iron roofing. The seven barracks on the line were nothing more than crude one story buildings about 30 feet wide and 175 feet long, covered with sheet iron. They had an aisle lower than the bay floors running from end to end, and the barracks had been built for convicts. The large bays were filled with double decker beds or screened cages, in which the convicts had formerly slept, and were so thick with bed bugs that we could never be rid of them. Like a barn of rats you would have to burn the place down to destroy them. Some of the men had body lice (cooties) but the bed bugs moved in and ate up the lice.[13]

The convicts had been equipped with shower baths near the mess hall. The Japs immediately denied the use of these to the common run of prisoners and reserved it for the use of the cooks and kitchen police. It took diesel oil to pump water so in a short time the shower heads disappeared. Later water was shut off at certain times of day to prevent wastage, usually at the time the prisoners wanted to wash their mess kits. All were forbidden to wash their face and hands at the water spigots. We were supposed to do that at the surface wells that our prisoners had dug in the compound.

Whenever we had a mess hall the Japs always delighted upon one pretext or another in taking it away from us. They wanted us to eat on our beds and be as dirty as possible. At Cabanatuan they made barracks of the mess hall. Here there was a large combination mess hall and chapel built for the use of the convicts. We had used it as a mess hall and chapel, the chaplain's service often being interfered with and religious meetings broken up by the Japs on one pretext or another. Even Sundays were at times taken away from us. The Japs often used this mess hall for showing their pictures. We were invited once to see a movie, the only one I saw during my 34 months under the Japs. This movie had a long news reel showing the fall of Hong Kong, Singapore, Bataan, and Corregidor. It had been our duty to defend the last two places. They wanted us to see them triumphantly victorious. The picture ended with their pulling down the Stars and Stripes that was flying over Corregidor and stomping and spitting upon it.[14]

When we came back from our 60 days of penance, they caused us to bring along our double decker cages and turn our combination mess hall and chapel into living quarters. It was the first time we had been put on dirt floors. The group of lieutenant colonels were placed in the northeast corner on an outside tier, and we barely made ourselves comfortable for our crowded conditions.

While we were on the coffee detail we watched with much interest a grove of avocados and longed for them to get ripe. When they were ripe, Major Maeda had as many saved as the Japs could use and then had the remainder fed to the hogs. In view of our supplication for them and the rich vitamins they contained to cure our scurvy conditions, this was placing the American prisoners of war lower than the swine. They ate the hogs and chickens while we never tasted pork or chicken in our regular prisoner's mess at Davao. While we were in penance, the hens, some 2,000 of them, were laying well. There was great talk one day that tomorrow we would have eggs for breakfast. When the breakfast came the cooks had mixed them in our steamed rice and they neither colored nor flavored it. The issue had been on the basis of one egg per three or four men.

I was a little concerned with my health after the first big escape, for the hernia I had contracted while picking coffee grew more and more acute. I was 70 pounds underweight from my normal of 185 pounds and had beriberi and a mild case of pellagra. One could count every rib as far as they could see me. As I worked on the basket detail my hernia gradually became worse. The beard on my chin used to be red, but is now a silky white. I adopted a long white goatee and wore it for several months. I wore short shorts badly patched, stripped to the waist and wooden shoes without socks. I was a pitiable looking sight and put on all the movement of an old man.

The Jap doctor soon had me on the sick book and soon thereafter I was an in-and-out-of-the-bed hospital case until liberation. The deep facial lines from starvation, and emaciated condition possibly helped influence the Jap doctor to put me in the hospital. This condition caused me in the end to be shipped no further north than Manila, and this undoubtedly saved my life. I was placed in the Dapecol prisoners hospital, remained there until the move north came, and was kept in the sick hospital at Bilibid that saved me from the horrors of the hellships. Otherwise, I would have gone with many others that were lost. There were only about 16 lieutenant colonels of Bataan and Corregidor that made it for home. After they had survived the hardships of the prison camps they were destroyed in the Jap hellships, attempting in the last days of the war to carry them to Japan.

Our dental department set up a little office at Dapecol, just as they did in a part of the hospital in all our main concentration camps in the Philippines. There was always a crying need for dental work as teeth became softer and cavities grew for lack of calcium in our diet. Gums receded, due to scurvy, and teeth loosened in their sockets. Many lost all their teeth, and several who had good complete sets of upper and lower dentures lost the sets to the Japs in many of the "shake downs" and personal robbery inspections we had undergone. These fellows had to survive gumming their food throughout prison life.

The dental officers, Major Perkins and Major Nelson, did what they could to relieve their fellow Americans' suffering but their equipment was meager and the supplies pitiable. An old foot pedal engine instead of electric motors, dull drills, a tiny chest of temporary fillings, and some abrasives and toothache astringents were all they had. All this had been miraculously dragged out of Bataan and Corregidor or saved from the surrender of our forces in the southern islands. The Japs furnished our dental corps nothing and had no dentists or dental supplies for their own forces that served as our jailer detachment. As soon as they learned that we had a little handful of precious supplies they began to demand of our dentists that they do their work and the latter had to accede to their wishes. It was not an uncommon occurrence to see some American officer or enlisted man have to give way in the dental chair to a Jap and this condition prevailed until our supplies were exhausted.[15]

Any portrayal of our life at Dapecol or any of the camps in the Philippines would be incomplete without some understanding of what we called "phonies." These were the people who claimed rank they did not possess. Some were of a mild degree while others were pronounced. When our general officers and full colonels were separated from us, they largely being the recommending and creating authorities on promotion, a person could claim almost any rank he chose and for the period of prison life no one could disprove it, as most everyone had sooner or later been rifled of all their personal papers by our jailers. It was not uncommon to see an officer who served during our war days in one grade put on the insignia of the next higher grade. Many of these cases were deserved and no doubt had "jaw bone" (verbal) authority from the next higher commander or the general officer commanding the sector, but to see officers put on the insignia two or three grades above the grade they had during the fighting days not only seemed farfetched but preposterous.

This condition applied more to those surrendered in the Visayas and Mindanao groups, as the surrenders at Bataan and Corregidor more or less fixed the rank of those who fought there. A first lieutenant came into the Dapecol camp and put on the insignia of a major, another the insignia of a lieutenant colonel.

Their justification would go something like this: "No orders were issued on it, but general so and so told me such and such, or I had a position (usually administrative) for the last few days before we surrendered at such and such a place, in which the tables of organization called for a lieutenant colonel. I showed them to the general and he said he was going to do something about it."

Then there was another almost non-military type of "phony"—the civilian who was caught in the surrender of his town. Possibly he had applied for a commission. He believed he could live in a prisoner of war camp. He was not so certain about the outside with the Japs overrunning and looting the country. The only entrance requirements to a Jap prison camp was an American uniform, and the higher the insignia of rank, the more the prisoner of war pay would be.

The most outstanding case of this I know occurred at Cabanatuan where a civil engineer showed up wearing the insignia of a lieutenant colonel of engineers. He was accepted by an engineer officer in charge of a group of prisoners and made executive officer of the group. This man had a particular knock of ingratiating himself with the Japs and soon he was in command of Cabanatuan. He suited the Japs for a time but doubts arose in the minds of the prisoners. A board of officers conducted a semi-official investigation of his status. He had been "found" at West Point years before. He made a mistake. He did not choose an army serial number in the block of numbers assigned to reserve officers, but had chosen one that belonged with the numbers given his classmates upon graduation at West Point. How could he be working in a civilian capacity in the Philippines for a number of years and have this serial number? So long as he suited the Japs what could the other prisoners do?

Later at Davao, I learned the earlier part of the story from a very reliable officer who had been captured in a town in the southern islands. This man had worked in an army motor pool as a civilian employee. He was charged with some shortages and disappeared just before the surrender and later appeared at Cabanatuan as a lieutenant colonel of engineers. It was a hard life and the "phonies" who got anything out of the Japs have my admiration rather than condemnation.[16]

CHAPTER 12

More Life at Dapecol

The planned crop failure and food scarcity reached its peak at Dapecol about June or July 1943. The prisoners had expected to receive the results of their labors, and they were plenty disgusted when the Japs took the small amount of produce and appropriated it for their own tables. They had our men dress a beef cow and give us the carcass with all the meat taken off and weighed to us our allowance of vegetables, husk and all, but such is the life of a prisoner of war.

Major Maeda solicited statements from us, statements to the effect that if left voluntarily to us we would choose not to work. He flew to the prison office in Manila ostensibly to prove the crop failure, blame it on us, and try to get us moved to Japan. Evidently the Manila office saw through the plot for when he came back he assembled the prisoners, told us the farm would be run on successful lines, and we would work or starve. He promised us all we could produce on the farm. We knew this would never materialize.

The men set in to work and raised a bumper crop, but our table did not benefit materially in quantity. The commanding officer who had made the promise had been transferred. The new one was reminded of it but despite the heavy crop yield we were still on the edge of starvation. He promised to investigate it and did nothing more. They were using the produce to feed the civilians and army in Davao and the ships at sea that made Davao a port of call. The major did at this time admit that their money was no good and that he had to use the farm produce to trade for dried fish but the few trades he made did not last long. We had dried fish mixed with our rice for a few mornings for breakfast.

The story of a prisoner of war in the tropics is the story of food. Hungry men can think of nothing else. Many men talked among the prisoners and made lists of all the good eating houses in the United States, while others compiled books of recipes, and still others made menus. These habits were not confined to Dapecol but were general practices in every prisoner of war camp where I lived. It is a mild form of insanity prevalent among hungry and starving men. I laughed at it for a long time but after more than two years of starvation I succumbed and brought home a month's breakfast menu and some good oriental recipes including a rice meal. They lay at home unopened until a number of housewives asked to see them. They wanted to see what starving men regarded as something good to eat.[1]

As strange as it may seem to those who have never experienced real hunger, our thoughts and conversations rarely went beyond the thoughts of a good breakfast. At least it was the meal most talked of, possibly because this is the meal used to break the night fast. Others have asked me on several occasions if a person's mind weakens or gets cloudy as the body weakens from starvation. The general answer is no. Most men's mental capacities were not weakened in proportion to their bodies but remained clear until the delirium of the last sickness. The loss of flesh was accomplished by a shrinking of all organs, lowered blood pressure, loss of ambition, initiative, and sexual desire. In our extreme desire to live we became selfish, irritable, and each person felt inclined to draw into his own little shell. Of course, grown men enjoyed doing childish things and reading childish literature but this was due more to the monotony of confinement than to any breakdown of mentality. A 1941 copy of a ladies journal came with our first Red Cross shipment. It is a magazine that under normal conditions army officers spend little time reading, but it was the most popular magazine in camp and was thumbed through from page to page until it was worn out by men who poured over it for hours with watery mouths as they looked at the pictures of food platters from the good old days.[2]

The Japs' highest idea of a reward for good work or conduct was to take a party of men out where they could gather bananas, coconuts, and guavas for the Japs' kitchen. They permitted them to fill their stomachs while gathering and permitted them to each bring in a handful to the compound. When escapes increased these trips were discontinued entirely. On the first and only one the basket workers were taken on a major claimed to have lost his class ring. The Japs kindly consented to let him look for it. He tied up a sentry for two days, greatly increased his store of fruits, but failed to find the ring. However a few days later he was wearing it. The Japs were wise. They reacted on the group and prisoners went to gather fruits no more.

A short time after we came out of penance and settled again in the main compound we were treated to our last sight of Japanese newspaper propaganda. Up until this time they had been very good about giving us an occasional copy of a Jap-controlled paper published in English, so long as they were winning. They selected certain copies of the *Manila Bulletin*, the *Tokyo Times*, and the *Japan Advertiser*, and the two copies given us were always posted on the camp bulletin board. The copies selected seemed to have been carefully censored to be sure that they contained nothing of the preparation and advance of our forces to build up our morale, and the Japanese were equally sure that the copy contained blazing accounts of their glorious victories. After our first landings in Italy they had no more victories and the news was so bad for them that they discontinued the occasional issues.[3]

During the 60 days we were in penance we received only two copies of one edition of the *Japan Advertiser*. This edition contained both good news and bad news for their cause. They had overrun and captured an important airfield in the Burma-India theater, their last victory, and their accounts purported to show that this key point was an absolute barrier to any reverse for the Imperial Japanese forces in that theater. This paper carried accounts of the death of one of their leading admirals, Yamamoto, who had been shot down while making a reconnaissance flight in the Southwest Pacific. It carried elaborate accounts of how the Emperor had honored the admiral's young son by having him call at the imperial palace and presenting him with the admiral's samurai sword.[4]

This copy also carried the first news we had of fellow prisoners that had been selected to go from Cabanatuan to Japan and about simultaneously with our selection to go to Davao. A part of these American prisoners of war had been sent to work in a mine in Korea or Manchuria and about half of them had died during the first winter.[5]

The final copies to which we were treated contained the blazing headlines: "Salerno is another Dunkirk for the anti-Axis powers." They devoted columns to prove this and did a good job of it except for the dead giveaway in the last few lines:

"Despite the fact that Salerno is another Dunkirk the audacious Americans have landed at three other points in western Italy and their pretentious allies, the British, have made two landings on the east coast."[6]

This brought back to our minds the claims they formerly made about how our forces had committed a great blunder by landing at Casablanca because the German *Luftwaffe* would absolutely prevent their getting through the mountain passes of Africa and coming into physical contact with General Rommel's forces in Libya. After Rommel's forces had been closed out, they also claimed the anti-Axis powers had made a great mistake in attacking through Africa as this theater has served its purpose in giving their allies time to fortify the great citadel of Europe. This great citadel now before their enemies was a great impregnable wall that would ward off all attacks.[7]

These pompous claims only served to remind us of the great indignation these papers had expressed about how the audacious Americans had bypassed certain well-defended islands in the Gilbert and Marshall groups and gone on to attack islands beyond them that were not so well defended. The Americans were also heralded as very soft and cowardly since, at Attu, they amassed a force of ten to one or even greater before they would attack. Such statements only served to illustrate to us the methods of the operation of our forces. To those of us who were accustomed to evaluating propaganda, to see these statements in print was as childish as the claims of a Jap sentry when General Doolittle staged the token airplane raid on Tokyo. The sentry told some of our men that the people of Tokyo had been sinful and the Emperor had willed that the planes come over and punish them for their sins.[8]

Beards were never a passing fancy with the prisoners of war. They were an economic necessity. At first razors taken from us were given back on a basis of one per squad of ten or twelve men. Later the issues were more liberal and sooner or later most everyone had a razor but blades soon gave out. Some turned out with what we called "grandfather beards" that grew all over their faces and hung down on their chests. Major Charles Dunnagan of Yadkinville, North Carolina refused to have his beard trimmed for a year. He wanted to see how long it would get and it was more than six inches when he had it barbed. Others grew long side burns and shaved their chin and upper lip. The old handlebar moustaches with close shaven chin were rare. It takes too much razor blade to shave the hard whiskers on the chin and throat. A close-clipped moustache with a goatee trimmed to a point with the temple and throat kept closely shaven was the greatest razor blade saver and possibly the most popular type. Lieutenant Colonel Alvin T. Wilson of Bethlehem, Pennsylvania, had one of the most picturesque of the beards—a long red one of the grandfather type that had a cleft trimmed along the center of the chin with the two long points extending down on his chest.[9]

The second Red Cross shipment contained a good many safety razor blades and enough sharpeners to issue about one for every ten men. By using the blades sparingly and the sharpeners often many of us could make one blade last from three to six months. As beards are usually undesirable, especially in crowded and unsanitary quarters, they soon disappeared when the razor blade problem eased. The shortage of safety razor blades at Dapecol created a great demand for the old straight razors. The whetstones for keeping up the farm tools offered opportunities to keep them in condition. One of our corporals had access to a supply in the Japan bodega. He slipped them out of the boxes and for a long time evaded detection in the searches that usually took place at the gate. He built up a lucrative business selling each razor for $50 to $100. Almost everything that anyone could get into the gate was a contribution to the general welfare. The Japs, however, eventually caught him and he served 30 days in the guardhouse for his attempts to help us keep our beards in bounds.

Mail reached Davao with our second Red Cross shipment but we were months from getting it. At first we were told by Mr. Wada, the hunchback interpreter, that there were 8,000 pieces, then 12,000 more were added, and in a few more weeks another shipment was said to have been received. We envisioned a great mail call day with everyone getting a handful of letters. It was about the first of March 1944. We had been prisoners of war for nearly two years and no word from home.[10]

The great mail call day never came. They liked to irritate and plague us in every way possible. Mr. Wada told us that under the regulations of the Japanese army the mail had to be censored at the last rather than at the first office receiving it—the Orient and the reverse way of doing things. There were only two interpreters in camp. They wanted to loaf around and do about a hundred letters per day. It would take them six months to censor the mail on hand at that rate. Then we were told that Mr. Wada's eyes were hurting very badly, etcetera.

I received my first letters on March 26, 1944, one from my beloved wife, one from my mother, and a valentine and short note from my younger daughter. Though my older daughter had also sent a note and valentine, it was months before I was to receive it, yet doubtless it was in the same shipment. The letters were much over a year old, but it was news and warmed my heart that all were living and well a year ago. A most welcome thing in our letters were the Kodak pictures of our families and loved ones. With all the Japs' faults they seemed to love their homes and families, and had a sort of reverence for pictures and let most of them come through that were enclosed in the letters. Pictures of my wife, Elizabeth, and my two daughters, Betty and Mary, showing their growth, of my mother and the little home we had just built in Durham, North Carolina that were sent to show the finishing touches and landscaping were welcome sights and supplemented the few Kodak pictures I had been fortunate enough to carry through the Death March and retain to date. The pictures of our modest brick bungalow with a colonial porch had long been in demand among the prisoners who were always wanting to see them because they brought back fond recollections of civilized living in the United States.

We had our mail calls of a hundred or so letters a day, for 2,000 prisoners, for some weeks. Then the Japs got some additional help and increased the output to four to six hundred letters per day. A few officers who had wives that lived with their mothers and mother's-in-law and had little to do received over a hundred long, unimportant news-less letters before many others received over half dozen. We were out of patience that this sort of thing should go on and have the mail congested by a dozen or more people. I can understand the necessity of the Japanese putting limitations on incoming mail, but did not agree with their 25 word limitations from the home folks. Our cards home were limited to 25 words every two months—maybe they got home, maybe not, but mostly not. My family received three out of fifteen cards. The fourth card came after my arrival home and bore evidence of having been sent through our own postal system after our forces had taken over Japan.The local camp censors were eventually given outside help, and by June 6, 1944, the date of our departure, all mail had been censored and distributed. I had received about 25 letters and cards. Many were missing and some were never received.[11]

I could not believe the news of the second Red Cross shipment. It proved true and showed up the last of February 1944. It arrived at Bilibid, in Manila, in November 1943, and the prisoners there received their distribution about November 23. We each received four individual food packages. All were from the American Red Cross. There were also a large number of extra items of all types of toilet articles, clothing, etcetera, as well as a large shipment of medicines.[12]

By this time we had been reduced to rags, starvation, slavery, and beggary by the Japs, those nice people who charged you full prices for food and clothes without delivering them. Clothing issues had become so scarce that they were always given to those who had the least clothes. That system compelled a person to lie about it or receive nothing. When a little issue of clothing was made to our American supply officer, it was always the same group of men that were naked, had nothing, and had to be taken care of. They were comparable to the man who was in the hospital suffering from scurvy who upon being issued a half a lemon offered to trade it for a cigarette butt.

Lieutenant Shiraji, the Jap supply and quartermaster officer, issued us two of our four Red Cross packages at one time. He was mad, because as he put it, the Americans had sought to depress the morale of the Japanese troops by making up lots of fancy eats and shipping them to us. Their standard of living is so low that we could never make him believe it was nothing fancy, that such items as corned beef, hard bread, and many other items of the canned meats, were too low a grade of food to appear on our daily tables. The Japs did not want us to sell or barter our Red Cross supplies but some people, officers included, have never realized that to obey is better than to sacrifice, so clandestine stores and exchanges flourished. Mr. Wada, seeing the canned meats, recommended that meat and cooking oil be discontinued in our ration issues. So what precious little meat, fish, and oil that was a part of our rations was cut off, and in whole never returned. We went for periods of up to six weeks without a taste of meat of any kind and rice, corn, and vegetable soup without an eye of grease.[13]

Long after the clandestine stores were closed, and the most prodigious were about out of supplies, Lieutenant Shiraji issued the third Red Cross package. He had to get in his spite work, so he reserved the fourth package and issued it to us just after we had loaded on a boat at Lasang for departure. He had chosen to truck these packages ahead and give them to us in a situation that was so crowded that all of us could not lie down and sleep at the same time. There was hardly standing room at the time the issue was made. This condition brought on much stealing as many people were not able to take care of their packages. About the third night while I had gone on deck to the latrine, my package was cleaned out leaving me only soap and toilet articles. I had eaten only the chocolate, one or two small cans of meat, and the can of hard bread.[14]

Our life at Dapecol was always plagued with escapes or pulling off fool tricks by some prisoners that offered the Japs excuses for curtailment of foods, mass punishments, or a tightening of the rules that always resulted in hardships on the innocent. The Japs were always sensitive about the border fences. They had been enlarged from a common cow pasture variety fence to one consisting of three fences of from ten to twelve barbed wire strands each. Each of these was from nine to ten feet high. It was against the rules for prisoners to go within six meters of the inner strands or to throw anything over them. One man was fatally shot by a sentry while in the act of throwing a canteen of water over the fence to a prisoner working on the outside. Another simpleton was shot at by a Jap sentry for gathering kangkong alongside the back fence. He rolled over into a ditch and escaped unhurt. He told his story as if he were a great hero—but what could we do, we had neither authority nor discipline over the prisoners, and such individuals are immune to both.[15]

Some prisoners resorted to the method of placing biblical references on their cards home. Often when the reference was looked up, it was some scathing denunciation of enemies. The Japs permitted one lot of cards to go through, but clamped down on the second lot and put two officers in the guardhouse for thirty days. One was a lieutenant colonel with 26 years of regular army commissioned service, for giving his wife his new address in the latitude and longitude of Davao. They seemed to be perfectly oblivious of the fact that they were dealing with an unknown quantity in the Japanese and were likely to jeopardize the privileges of all prisoners to send cards home. We were very uneasy about them when they served their 30 days, for the Japs caused all who were in the guardhouse to be awakened every hour and to prove that they were awake made them stand on their feet. This badly breaks one's rest. The two officers, however, came through it and were returned to us at the end of their punishment in as good mental and physical condition as could be expected. We scarcely settled down from one disturbance or escape before another began—never a dull moment.[16]

CHAPTER 13

Final Days at Dapecol

We had been returned from penance only a few months when a detail of about 11 men working in the edge of the jungle cutting fence posts became irked with the sentry. Ever since the McCoy-Mellnik escape, the Japs made our officers and men go to work barefooted or in wooden chinelas (sandals). They had the rifles and bayonets, the shoes and clothes and were well fed, but felt unable to guard a handful of ragged and half-starved Americans if equipped in shoes and rags, so off came the shoes. It was not uncommon to see details go out or come in with men and officers' feet bleeding. The sick call was always full of men with bleeding and ulcered feet. Our resistance was so low that the least scratch on the feet, despite careful nursing, produced ulcers. The Japs later consented to some of the harder details wearing shoes.

When Lieutenant Watson of Siloam, near Winston-Salem, North Carolina, who worked on this post cutting detail became irritated with the sentry, he was cautioned by Captain Wohlfeld, an officer on my old regiment, to take care as all the men on the detail did not have on shoes. Watson was quick-tempered and hot headed so all the members of the detail wore shoes from then on. A few days later some irritating situation came up. Watson felt that the Jap sentry was picking on him, and he struck the sentry dead with his shovel while they were resting in the edge of a jungle. Wohlfeld struck the other sentry but not hard enough to kill him. The wounded sentry gave the alarm. The detail leader called for all to come out of the edge of the jungle with their hands above their heads. He and three others did so and were kept in the Jap guardhouse until the investigation was over.[1]

A clash followed. Warrant Officer Boone of the navy was killed, but the other six men made good their escape. It seemed a pity that an old man like Boone, with about 30 years service and probably no intention of making an escape should be caught and killed in such a trap, but such is the fate of prisoners of war. The Japs sounded the alarm, called in all work details, and kept us locked up for three or four days until the search was made. At retreat that night, Mr. Wada made a statement to us that the prisoners had been surrounded, one had been killed, and all would be captured or killed in the next 48 hours.[2]

It seemed so ridiculous that 200 well-equipped and armed Japanese could not close right in on a half dozen unarmed, nearly naked, starved prisoners. We held our peace, except for Major Harrison who sounded off, "Do you expect us to believe that?" The situation was very tense, and we expected trouble from Harrison's remark, but the interpreter pretended not to hear it. Mr. Wada had his faults, but this was not one of them. All interpreters were accused of everything under the shining sun, and none of them, whether Japanese or American, ever remained long in the favor of the prisoners. Treatment in some cases depended more on the Jap interpreter than on the commanding officer for the interpreter stood in a position of influence.

Mr. Wada was a squatty little fellow, weighed about 100 pounds, and with his hunchback, high top boots and long, large samurai sword he looked like a monkey in boots. He was a bright but simple man of the peasant type who sincerely believed in the divinity of the emperor and the all prevailing might of the Japanese empire. He had learned English in an exporting house in Kobe, and was raised in an adjacent province. His aptitude for languages caused his representative in the Diet to recommend that he take up this work. He was specializing in Spanish, and carrying on the correspondence for his house with the South American countries when the war broke out.

His worst fault was to pick out depressing news to give the prisoners of war. He did not possess enough military judgment to weigh propaganda and believed every word published in the Japanese papers. Being weak and deformed, his greatest ambition was to be a man, and to this end he used to take long runs on the race course in front of the compound and earned the sobriquet from the prisoners of "Running Water," a name that suited him well for he was frequently accused of carrying water on both shoulders as well as being a spy and stool pigeon. He was on some occasions kindly to the Americans, was never known to strike one, though he hated the white man with the hate of a cripple, so we were much pleased that he passed over Harrison's remark.

Mr. Wada was quite the opposite of Nishimura, a strutting little mustached interpreter, who so delighted to slap the prisoners around that he earned the well-merited cognomen of "Simon Legree." Captain Rader, the hospital adjutant, has been particularly loyal and faithful in getting medical supplies for the hospital, and was a patient, tolerant, and easy going man who certainly could give no one offense. One day "Simon" became irritated with him and gave him a few slaps publicly. "Simon" was marked as everybody's meat when and if the delivery came, but after this everyone mentally reserved him as being number one for Captain Rader.

The best interpreter was one that worked most of the time with the rice paddy detail and was known as "Pittsburgh." He was intelligent and seemed to have considerable savvy. It was always a matter of extreme irritation to the prisoners that the interpreters, who were civilians, and knew little of military discipline, and most certainly were not responsible for its maintenance among the prisoners, were always slapping them around for what they considered breaches of discipline.[3]

The result of this escape was a tightening up of rules and a shortening of rations. Communications with our detail of 650 men at Lasang and the 100 man detail at Davao were also cut for good and always. The last escape was a sporadic attack without preparation, and they had the same relation to the McCoy-Mellnik escape that manslaughter has to first degree murder. The last escape was not planned and they had no connections with the guerrillas and we were apprehensive lest they be caught, brought back to the camp and executed, but both of these parties made good their purposes and were never taken by the Japs. The McCoy-Mellnik detail made it to Australia. I later talked with Mellnik at Santo Tomas. The Wohlfeld-Watson detail dodged the Japs for a day or so around the camp, took to the jungles and contacted the guerrillas. Watson is now in the states and Wohlfeld was commanding a squadron of the 7th Cavalry in February 1945 and came to visit with me while I was a patient in Evacuation Hospital No. 54. A few days after the event we resumed work, sent a detail to bring in Boone's body, buried it in the American cemetery, and then tried to forget the event.[4]

About this time or a little earlier two enlisted men who worked carabaos in the Mactan rice fields effected an escape. When the train first arrived each morning at the scene of the rice planting activities, the plowboys were allowed to jump off the train and run away for some distance to catch their carabaos that had been permitted to run free and graze during the night. The carabao had wandered off to the edge of the jungle during the night. The men chased them for a few minutes and then jumped into the river and disappeared.

American headquarters tried to persuade the Japs that they had drowned, and they no doubt accounted for them in that manner, but knew better.[5]

Sometime during April or May 1944, after I had been relieved on the basket detail and admitted to the hospital, Major Harrison, whose escape intentions were suspected by his squad at Cabanatuan, got into difficulties with the Japs. He was a member of a rope detail composed of the old and half sick prisoners. These men worked in the shed alongside the basket makers. Harrison had been brooding for some weeks, and spent most of his brooding time sitting in a corner and idling while the remainder of his detail made rope. He evidently was watching his opportunity and when he found that the sentry had leaned his rifle against the wall and had his head turned away from him, Harrison seized a short piece of iron pipe and attacked him. The first blow did not knock him senseless and he gave the alarm.

Major Harrison seized the sentry's rifle, ran towards the main gate, pointed it towards the sentry on the main gate, pulled the trigger and it snapped. He lost his nerve and turned and ran deeper into the compound. He turned again, pointed the rifle a second time at the sentry on the main gate. It snapped a second time—he had put on his fight for an unloaded rifle. He ran still deeper into the compound and upon arrival between barracks one and two called for help. Two or three prisoners who were in the barracks and did not know what had taken place ran to his assistance, but were ignored by the Jap sentries. These sentries took him on to the little guard shed at the main gate where he spent a few minutes and then was carried to the main Japanese guardhouse. He was unhurt when taken to the first guard shed.[6]

Meantime the sentries swarmed around the big work shed where the event had taken place. This was the original big combination chapel and mess hall where we had lived like rats in a barn when first taken out of penance. As they sent details out of the main camp they had made us more comfortable, although just as crowded in the barracks on the main line and had turned this large shed into workshops. As the sentries began to swarm around through the workshops, the leader of the basket detail called *tenko*—assembly and roll call—and the Jap leader of this detail, knowing they were uninvolved, permitted them to be marched through the inner gate to the barracks where they were dismissed. The remainder of the details in the workshops, however, including the rope detail of which Major Harrison was a member, were caused to kneel and were kept in that position from about 10:00 a.m. to 4:30 p.m. If a person moved he was scolded, struck, or threatened with a bayonet. They were so paralyzed at 4:30 p.m. that they had to help each other up and to the barracks.

The gates were closed and matters were very tense for a few hours. At retreat roll call the Japanese commander had it announced that Major Harrison was wounded so badly in capturing him that they doubted that he would live through the night. He was not wounded when he was taken to the first guard shed at the main gate. Some of the prisoners saw him standing docilely between two prisoners at this gate when another Jap sentry plunged a bayonet into him. The next morning at 2:00 a.m., those prisoners of whom Lieutenant Colonel Stubbs was one, who lived in barracks nearest to the main Japanese guardhouse and were awake at that hour, heard Harrison yelling and groaning as if being tortured. At morning roll call it was announced that he had died during the night.[7]

He was a restless type of person, a young West Point graduate who had been in two or more branches of the service. The receipt of mail seemed to disturb him with news of several of his classmates having reached the rank of colonel, and a few rising to general, and it appeared to have added to his unbalanced mental condition. The Japs kept us within the fence for another day, buried him in our cemetery, put us back to work, and treated the incident as the act of a temporarily insane person. Soon after we were taken out of penance it was rumored that the Japs proposed to send out many details to work on other projects and make our camp a base camp for the sick, for supplies, and for the production of farm produce.

The first detail of 100 men went out to work at the Davao motor pool. They were to use this as a secondary base, to drive trucks and cars to various places, and do repair work. The Japs were very poor at motor repairs, and relied on American prisoners to do much of it. The American headquarters followed the policy that we had men who could do anything under the sun, and men were put on at all types of motor, radio, engine, shop and electric repairs. The radio repair men were a good source of news coming into the camp. They kept the radios under repairs and for testing as long as possible and listened to broadcasts *sub rosa*. Our men kept up every Jap radio in every camp I served.[8]

We heard from this Davao detail for some time, as sick men came in and replacements were sent. They were a source of much news being brought into camp. After the McCoy-Mellnik escape, the Japs felt that the Filipino helpers were an aid to the escape and removed all of them from the farm, so news became very scarce. Mr. Acenas, the assistant superintendent, had a good radio and our project supervisor, the old Filipino we called "Pop," would visit there every time there was big news, and would read his short hand notes to us in the coffee grove.[9]

Pop was an unusual Filipino character, a native of Luzon who had been in business in Davao before the war. He was loyal to the Americans to the core and told many stories of Japanese cruelties when they took over Davao. Most of them clustered around how the Japanese civilians had their enemies and competitors shot and bayoneted. His favorite nephew who was a newspaper man was bayoneted before his eyes, and while he temporized with the Japs he was at heart very bitter against them. This move back to Davao from the farm was not to soften his bitterness. He had once owned a car which the Japanese had taken from him, saying that the Americans had built the fine roads so they could sell the Filipinos cars that they did not need. That they did not need such luxuries as electric iceboxes and plumbing, and large houses for large families—he having about 15 children. No! They should learn how to work hard and live miserably. So Pop and his family lost their good house in the prison colony and were moved back to wretchedness in Davao.[10]

The next detail that went out consisted of about 650 men under the leadership of Lieutenant Colonel Rogers. They went to Lasang to help build an airfield. Lasang was thirty kilometers from us and on the road to Davao. It was the saw mill village where we had unloaded from the boat in coming to Dapecol and the place where we finally loaded again when we left. We heard from this detail often for some weeks. Then the Wohlfeld-Watson escape occurred and communications with both details were permanently cut off. The Japs did not care for the other details to learn that we were beginning to assault their sentries. This detail did not have it so easy. The living conditions were miserable. Barracks were crowded, latrines located within a few feet of cooking and living quarters, and all much exposed to bombings that were to come later, in which we heard that some of our men were killed. The men resented being reduced to oriental slavery and moving dirt in buckets and baskets, and no matter how slow this process was it was still aiding the Jap war effort. There was some trouble about it, but the trouble finally calmed down after several men had been cruelly beaten.[11]

A number of my enlisted friends joined the detail, some voluntarily. They asked my advice and I advised as usual, that the greatest safety was in the center of the herd. We were, however, reduced to such a state of nakedness, slavery, and hunger by this time that for the prospect of a little more food some men would volunteer for anything. So they went under the usual bait of more and better food to find conditions worse. My old friend and helper, Corporal Gerken, who had saved my life, and two of Colonel Compton's friends went and were later lost on the Jap hellship that was torpedoed off Mindanao in the fall of 1944.[12]

We left these details of some 750 odd men still on the job when we left Dapecol on June 6, 1944. The Japs told many stories with the prisoners being taken direct to Japan without the usual stop at Manila. This I believe was really ordered, for the mail department at Bilibid, where I later worked, had instructions to sort the mail of these officers and men to go back to Japan. The real end of these details came in September 1944 when the Japs were attempting to carry them to Japan. One of our submarines torpedoed the boat on which they were being transported. It happened off the coast of Sindangan, north of Zamboanga, Mindanao on September 7, 1944. Their boats carrying prisoners of war were never marked.

Our guerrillas controlled the coast line, and our men took to rafts and life boats. As the boat began to sink, the Japs, realizing they were losing the prisoners, threw hand grenades in the hold of the ship and patrolled the waters around the ship machine-gunning, shooting, and clubbing the men who were attempting to get ashore. Out of the 750, only 82 got ashore, nine of them were wounded, and one died from their wounds. Commander Sam Wilson, U.S. Naval Reserve, was in command of the guerrillas. They radioed for a submarine that eventually picked them up. Wilson told me in March 1945 that only 81 reached Australia safely. Here they were treated as great heroes. They were tendered a dance the night before they were to depart for the United States and one man after going through it all unwounded, got too tight and fell down on the ball room floor and broke his arm.[13]

When these details were first separated from us we were still living in the combination chapel and mess hall, and because there were more to go than lived in this old shelter, we had hopes that their going would relieve the crowded and over-congested conditions. But not so with the Japanese. They moved us to just as crowded conditions in the regular barracks on the line. They used one vacant building for our supply, writing, and lounging room and closed the other completely.

Lieutenant Shiraji, the Japanese quartermaster supply officer, we always felt was at the bottom of many of our starvation problems. We always believed that he and Major Maeda, our commandant, were always exercising the "squeeze" on our small ration issue, and converting parts of it as well as our farm products to their own use and benefit by selling or trading them in Davao. Be that as it may, he was a typical example of the middle class Jap and wore an old and well embellished samurai sword. The contacts between him and our American leaders were frequent and close.

An epidemic of rumors and uneasiness passed through the Jap ranks in early 1944 and there was talk among them as well as the prisoners as to what they would do when the American forces arrived. They dug foxholes, machine gun emplacements, and prepared to defend the camp. Fields of fire were cleared and a number of Jap sentries stated their intention of taking to the hills—the sentries being young Formosans. One day this subject came up in a natural discussion at American headquarters in which Lieutenant Shiraji was engaged. This offered him an opportunity to make a sort of off-the-record statement of his intentions. The statement was made by one of our field officers that the Japanese could now surrender and go back to Japan after the war without loss of citizenship or being in disgrace as had formerly been the custom. It was further stated that while we were fighting in Bataan, the emperor had decreed to this effect and it had been announced on Radio Manila, Shanghai, and Tokyo, as well as on KGEI in San Francisco all on the same day. Lieutenant Shiraji admitted that it might be and probably was true, but closed the discussion by saying "I can never surrender. I carry this pistol to commit hari-kari. I shall have to do so. The emperor cannot change that in our generation. My father would kill me when I go home if I surrendered." Things that are taught and inbred for years cannot be suddenly changed in a short time by a declaration of the emperor on paper.[14]

When we moved from Dapecol, Lieutenant Shiraji moved with us and became the supply officer of both Bilibid and Santo Tomas where several thousand civilian Americans and allies were interned. Before his arrival they had fared moderately well, but during his regime they were likewise put through the starvation wringer. On the night that the Yanks and tanks arrived, he took refuge with some 50 other Japs in the Educational Building at Santo Tomas in such a position that to get them out would cost a number of American lives. The American commander negotiated and he and his detachment were permitted to leave with 45 minutes start. Rumors have it that the guerrillas got the detachment soon after they left the main gate. I went through Bilibid twice after the Japs had been completely mopped up in Manila and looked very carefully for Shiraji and others of our guard. I could not find a familiar Jap face. They wanted to die in battle for the emperor, and it gave our combat forces much pleasure to give them their desire. Prisoners of war taken by the Japanese forces were regarded as property of the emperor. In many respects we felt that this was a protection.[15]

CHAPTER 14

A Hellship Trip to Bilibid

It was evident by the spring of 1944 that preparations were underway to move us. A separate list of the sick was prepared and we were made ready to move separately from the healthy ones. There were about 125 of us. I felt then that in the end the hernia would save my life, and would eventually result in my restoration to the flag.

There were many rumors that the sick would be exchanged. At this rumor, and in realization that his opportunities for future promotion were lost because of his long period of internment, Lieutenant Colonel Frank F. "Siki" Carpenter began to show marked symptoms of mental instability. The doctors had no choice and had to put him in the "nut ward" and this about completely unbalanced him. A small number of our fellow prisoners became insane, or mentally unbalanced, under the strain. I did not find the hospital bad. The difference in the quantity of food was not noticeable when you ceased to work and lay on your back several hours a day. Hospitals at O'Donnell and Cabanatuan had been nightmares, places people went to die rather than get well. Though the surgeons often worked heroically at these places there was not enough medicine and equipment to accomplish enough to reward their labors.[1]

Preparation and packing for moving continued and by the first week in May we were ready to go. The Japs as usual began to sell all their surplus equipment and personal belongings in an effort to turn them into American money, wrist watches, and gold jewelry. There was a delay of about a month. Some of the foolish prisoners began bragging that they could never take them out of Dapecol, and proposed to escape into the jungles that lined the roadside.

On the night of June 5, Jap trucks began rolling into camp. Lieutenant Shiraji told the mess officer to feed up everything he had on hand. Extra rice was served to everyone. All persons cooked and ate all the extra food they had gathered from the farms and their little gardens. The ban on individual cooking fires was lifted. No one slept much during the night. At daylight we were loaded, thirty to the truck. Standing, we were roped to each other around the waist and to the truck body, and ordered to tie on blindfolds. We had been told to bring a wide piece of white cloth 36 inches long and have it handy on our person. We had wondered what this was for but soon found out. What irony, after holding us as prisoners for over two years, and issuing us almost no clothes, to ask us to furnish our own blindfolds. A sentry stood in a front corner and another in a back corner of each truck with a large stick, striking anyone over the head or on the hands if they made any noise or gesture. They had the road well-guarded with a sentry every hundred or so yards, and it seemed to use about three or four trucks to pick up sentries behind and post them ahead. We had about three or four short stops for this.[2]

We were unloaded at Lasang and loaded on a boat without the escape of a man. A few big mouths can bring lots of trouble to the weak and innocent, and as is usually the case those who talk the most about escape never attempt it. This was clearly illustrated in the Wohlfeld-Watson escape where navy Warrant Officer Carmichael on the detail had talked constantly about escape, but was among the first to come out of the woods with his hands above his head. He could not do it when the real test came. When loaded on the boat our last Red Cross package was issued to us. What a mess; not even sleeping room, much less room for each to take care of this extra dunnage. It was Lieutenant Shiraji's revenge for having to bother with them at all.[3]

I had a mattress on the floor in the hospital section during the voyage to Cebu. I shared it with another person for a part of two days, and except for the excessive heat and foul air, I was possibly better off than the average person, except that my Red Cross package was looted the second night. The heat and the foul air from the overcrowded conditions was terrible. We remained in Davao waters for two days, and sailed in a convoy of about four or five ships. Our route was around the southern end of Mindanao through the Celebes Sea to Zamboanga. There was quite a collection of Japanese ships in Davao harbor, including a light aircraft carrier for 24 planes, a tanker, several war craft including a cruiser, and a number of cargo vessels.[4]

We stopped the first night in Sarangani Bay, sailed about 4:00 a.m. and stopped the second night in the bay near Cotabato, the famous duck hunting area. We were in Zamboanga harbor for the third night. We were granted free use of the deck over our hold, and this relieved the congestion considerably. This was the rear deck and next to the elevation on the stern upon which their three-inch gun was mounted. A sentry was on the gun most of the time. They would at first not allow a prisoner of war around the elevation, much less the gun. The conditions were so crowded that prisoners sat on the steps and gradually eased their way to the gun. The sentry was off guard and the prisoner tapped the barrel with a piece of metal. There was no sound of metal. He cut a notch in it—it was wood. The same thing happened on a trip we had taken down to Davao. The Japanese, out to conquer the world, were running a war on a shoestring and still believed that they could compete with civilized, well-equipped nations.

A little after dark, while our ship was lying in harbor and close to the piers of Zamboanga, Lieutenant Colonel McGee jumped overboard. There was much shooting but he made good his escape and joined the guerrillas a few days later. He was on duty in Zamboanga when the war began and had many contacts there. The next night when we were a few hours out of Zamboanga and about two miles offshore, a lieutenant who had been assistant librarian at Dapecol also jumped overboard. We never heard of him again. He was an ex-marathon swimmer but had the odds badly against him.[5]

The Japs then ran everyone below deck, closed the hatches and kept us there in insufferable suffocating heat until the end of the voyage to Manila. This resulted in two deaths before we unloaded. Two dead, two escapes, and much suffering by all. Was it worth it? As for any good they did for our cause, I doubt it. Too often when those strong enough to make an escape get the opportunity to do so, they failed to consider the mass punishments and reprisals that would be visited on their fellow prisoners left behind. The Jap officer and the interpreter, Mr. Wada, who were in charge of the prisoners of war on this boat had served with us at Dapecol. These two were again placed in charge of some 1,600 American prisoners of war that sailed from Manila on December 13, 1944. They had the hatches closed this time when the boat sailed. A survivor stated that some forty officers and men died of heat and suffocation in the first day or so, and prior to the time our task force bombed and sank the ship off Subic Bay.[6]

Until we arrived at Cebu we were fed rice and vegetables twice a day. The vegetable soup was from our farm products—mostly squash. At Cebu we changed boats and got nothing more than rice and water twice a day. At Cebu we were hastily unloaded, leaving baggage behind, and marched to an old Spanish fort that had been the headquarters for the Visayan-Mindanao forces in the days of the American control. It had been burned and was in ruins that corresponded with the remainder of the main part of the city. The Japs had built a small sheet iron warehouse in the center of the old walls. Here we were kept for two days. The Jap cavalry posted outside the walls were taking to boots and saddles and preparing to move out as we were marched in. All vessels cleared the port immediately. A general alarm was on. We did not know it at the time, but the Battle of Saipan had just closed and our navy was headed straight for Luzon.[7]

In two days we were loaded into a larger vessel and sailed for Manila. The hatches were kept closed. Two of our number had escaped. We were in the Japanese dog house. To be in any other dog house is bad enough, but here where there was not enough room for all to sit down at once was the worst we had encountered yet.[8]

Section IV
Liberation and Return

> Many of my fellow prisoners were lost en route to the north, and I can never be too thankful to God that I have been spared and returned to the flag. We can always appreciate liberty.
>
> **—David L. Hardee to Elizabeth Hardee, February 23, 1945**

The filthy, exhausted prisoners who disembarked from *Singoto Maru* and marched into Old Bilibid Prison on June 26, 1944, resembled skeletons covered in rags. But Hardee and the other men of Dapecol were grateful to be alive. In Bilibid, they reunited with friends and former associates and exchanged information on the living and the dead, learned what they could of how the war was going, and eagerly absorbed any news at all of the outside world. Hardee, now bedridden from his hernia, found his friend Colonel Louis Hutson still recovering from battle wounds received in January 1942, and the comradely support boosted both men's spirits.

Established by the Spanish in 1865, Old Bilibid Prison was located in central Manila near Santo Tomas University at Azcarraga Street (present-day Recto Avenue) and Quezon Boulevard. The Philippine government had opened a "new" Bilibid Prison in 1940, and in 1942, the Japanese converted the older, abandoned facilities into a prison/hospital for all Allied POWs in the Philippines. The compound was essentially a square, measuring 600 feet on each side, with outer walls 20 feet tall and 4 feet thick topped by electrified wires. From the air, the prison looked like a wheel, with 18 long barracks, measuring 120 by 20 feet, emanating like spokes from a central main guard tower. A 12–foot-high wall bisected the compound. One half served as a prison; the other functioned as a hospital. By 1944, the Japanese had begun using Bilibid as a way station for POWs on Luzon being shipped to Japan.

Old Bilibid Prison, February 1945, as seen from the air. **Source: NARA**

The Japanese administered the entire prison but left the running of the hospital to the prisoners, principally to U.S. Navy medical personnel. Bilibid's crude facilities seemed luxurious to Dapecol's survivors. Solid buildings, practical sanitation, and improved medical resources far surpassed Hardee's previous prison experiences. The food supply was, as always, problematic. In the summer of 1943, the Japanese ordered all available land inside the prison walls be used for prisoner-tended garden plots to augment the prison food supply. As rations shrank, prisoners took to eating everything, including the plants themselves. In July 1944, prisoners received a daily diet of around 1,700 calories; by October, that had dropped to 1,000 calories. In January 1945, prisoners received from seven to ten ounces of rice, corn, and soybeans daily. The men were slowly starving and wondered if they would survive long enough to be liberated.

They knew the invasion was coming. In September 1944, the Americans had begun preparing for the return of U.S. land forces to the Philippines. As part of the preparations for the invasion, over 200 U.S. Navy aircraft from the carriers USS *Hornet*, *Wasp*, *Intrepid*, *Bunker Hill*, and *Lexington* targeted Japanese installations and military forces at Clark, Nielson, and Nichols Fields, the Pandacan oil district, and Japanese shipping installations in Manila Bay. As the raids passed right over Cabanatuan and Bilibid Prisons, spent shell casings and machine gun links rained down inside the compound. The sight of American planes

The hellship *Oryoku Maru* under attack by U.S. Navy aircraft off Olongapo Point, Subic Bay, December 15, 1944. If not for a crippling hernia, Hardee would have been aboard this ship. **Source: U.S. Navy, Naval History and Heritage Command.**

Manila burns as American forces fight their way into the city, February 1945. Bilibid can be seen in the lower left, along with a Japanese roadblock. **Source: NARA.**

downing Japanese aircraft and the fear on the faces of the guards did much to raise prisoner morale. As Filipinos would say to prisoners, "Very soon now, Joe!"

But thousands of prisoners would not live to regain their freedom. They would die aboard Japanese hellships, too frequently the victims of American bombs and torpedoes. In early 1944, officials decided to transport POWs from the Philippines to Japan to work in war industries, thereby freeing up Japanese workers for the army. The Japanese hoped to move the prisoners in advance of Allied forces retaking the Philippines, but American submarines were now on the prowl for Japanese shipping throughout the Pacific. And many of the poor unfortunates confined in the holds of stifling, fetid, unmarked merchant vessels never had a chance. Over 3,000 prisoners, many comrades of Hardee who survived prison life, perished in watery graves when the hellships *Shinyo Maru*, *Arisan Maru*, *Oryoku Maru*, *Brazil Maru*, and *Enoura Maru* went to the bottom. Hardee himself might have joined them had it not been for the hernia that he had incurred at Dapecol.

As prisoners perished at sea, General MacArthur fulfilled his promise to return. Four divisions of the U.S. Sixth Army landed on the island of Leyte on October 20, 1944. Meanwhile, the U.S. Navy and Imperial Japanese Navy fought the largest naval battle in World War II, the Battle of Leyte Gulf. The victory was decisive. After the smoke cleared on October 26, the Americans had effectively destroyed the Japanese navy as a fighting force. Operations on Leyte, however, proved more difficult than expected, and plans to use the island as an airbase for the invasion of Luzon were abandoned after rain turned the ground to mud that made construction of airfields almost impossible. MacArthur thereafter ordered the invasion of the island of Mindoro near Luzon so that it could be used as a site for airfields to support the Luzon invasion. On December 15, 1944, American forces landed on Mindoro. They secured it the next day.

Within a few weeks, approximately 175,000 troops of the U.S. Sixth Army had stormed ashore almost entirely unopposed on the beaches of Lingayen Gulf on Luzon, the same area where General Masaharu Homma's forces disembarked in December 1941. By January 23, American forces had reached Clark Air Base and begun to advance on Manila. MacArthur ordered the 1st Cavalry Division to move on Manila. Two motorized cavalry squadrons raced toward the city on February 3. The flying column lead by the 8th Cavalry reached Manila first, and a tank from the 44th Tank Battalion broke through into Santo Tomas University, liberating civilian internees held there.

The battle was now mere blocks away from Bilibid and the sounds of it could be heard from the prison. The Japanese guards abandoned their posts just after noon on February 4. That evening American infantrymen from the 2nd Battalion, 148th Infantry moved toward Bilibid. One squad entered a long storage room on the west side of the prison. Prying off boards that were covering the windows in the room the soldiers saw prisoners on the other side. Hardee and his comrades were thus freed.

In the days after, Hardee was reunited with his sister and her family at Santo Tomas. He met again with men he had last seen at Bataan and Corregidor and learned they were now generals with MacArthur's forces. But it was one man, a distant cousin, who brought Hardee to tears when he recognized the colonel on a visit to Bilibid: General MacArthur himself. He had indeed returned, and in so doing returned Hardee to freedom and the flag.

The main gate to Old Bilibid Prison after liberation of the POWs by members of the 2nd Battalion, 148th Infantry, 37th Infantry Division on February 4, 1945. **Source: NARA.**

CHAPTER 15

Manila and Bilibid

We looked forward to Manila, but upon arrival after two days sailing we were kept aboard in the ship's holds for five additional days while waiting for pier space. We buried one of our dead in the bay; the second passed just before orders were received to unload and we carried his body to Bilibid for internment. There was a small graveyard at Bilibid where the dead were honored by being placed in small wooden coffins made of rough inch lumber. This burial space was soon to be filled, and when the Japs themselves began to take our dead out to bury them in a Chinese cemetery in Manila, we wondered if the coffins were not a face saving gesture, and believed that they dumped the bodies into graves and used the same coffins over and over again. Meanwhile, the sick were carried in trucks to Bilibid, and the well were marched from Pier 7 where we were all unloaded. Upon arrival at the prison, the sick were assigned to quarters in the hospital. The well were quartered for a day or so and were then sent to Cabanatuan in box cars with ropes tied across the doors.[1]

My baggage and that of the well prisoners was brought up from the boat and piled in the old hospital compound for a day before the Jap sentries would let me go in after it. Colonel Compton then had to spot it for me and help me get it by the sentry at the gate. All that I possessed was in the one barracks bag except for what little I had been able to bring along in a field bag. The barracks bag had been looted by my fellow prisoners who by this time would steal anything not red hot and nailed down. I lost most all of my tobacco and all the canned goods I had denied myself and saved for harder times from the former Red Cross boxes.

I was assigned a bunk in S.O.Q. (sick officers quarters) next to Colonel Hutson. We were old friends together again. He had a bad wound in the hip, still running after two years, and for this reason had not been sent with the generals and other colonels to Japan. There was a toilet and shower at the end of the barracks next to our beds. It was the first one we had seen in over two years. We were dirtier than we could imagine human beings could get. At all the other camps we had bathed from five gallon gasoline tins, stolen from the Japs. In addition to being starved, beaten, and reduced to rags we had been denied the ordinary necessities that all civilized peoples give to their criminals. The inside of a second-class penitentiary looked good. Bilibid was an old and practically abandoned penitentiary, and I heard a dozen officers as they got under the showers exclaim, "this is Heaven." I had a good iron bunk with springs, a mattress, a pillow, a sheet, and a mosquito bar. It really was like heaven.

I was exhausted and nearer to death than I ever had been. I do not believe that I could have stood many more hours in their tortuous hellship. Colonel Hutson had a shot of weak coffee for me. I fell on my bunk, next to his, with a mosquito "T" bar under my mattress and slept for two days. Hutson thought I had died while in the latrine, came to look, and helped me back into bed. I was so near to nervous prostration that it took me several nights to get to normal sleeping. Colonel Hutson's company and help was most comforting. Though he had suffered the tortures of the damned for over two years, he had not lost his sense of humor and he spent much of his time reading and planning houses.

The store was still going very well and items had not gotten excessively high. With limitations placed on purchases we could still supplement our food with mongo beans, sugar, coconuts, coffee, garlic salt, and some other items but they had to be very sparsely used. There was never a time when we were not hungry. Here at Bilibid we were paid the sum of ₱40 per month in cash, and donated another ₱50 per month to the general mess fund to try to hold down the death rate from starvation. The ₱50 per month came from our deposit and not from the cash paid us. For the last two months of the camp, with special permission of the Japs, we donated our entire monthly bank deposits and yet men still continued to die of starvation. At Dapecol we had been paid ₱20 every other month. The Japs' excuse for this small pay was that we had nothing there to spend it on. They were too indifferent to bring in supplies or let the Filipinos do so.[2]

Bilibid was an old Philippine penitentiary, begun by the Spaniards some 300 years ago, and when the war began was being abandoned for the more modern installations at Muntinlupa. It was surrounded by high adobe rock walls that made escape next to impossible. What few escapes as there had been were largely by men who worked on outside details at the time of their escape. The Japs therefore did not inflict mass punishments on the inmates for those escapes, and the feeling here among the prisoners concerning those who had escaped was quite different from the other camps in which I had served.[3]

The outside working details consisted of several hundred prisoners who were able-bodied and were kept there for that purpose. They worked at all sorts of jobs, principally around the piers, and were a source of news and food coming into the compound. They brought in a newspaper almost every day that had been slipped to some of them by a Filipino sympathizer. They frequently operated black markets for such items as they could get that were not procurable through the store; these always helped. Coffee, tea, and tobacco were their most common items. I never understood why the Japs who were great tea users denied it to us as it is cheap, plentiful, and easily transported. About November 1944, these outside details were discontinued and the men shipped on north to Japan or Manchuria, and a fertile source of contact with the outside world was lost.

Cabanatuan was camp number one, Dapecol number two, and Bilibid number three, until Dapecol was discontinued and then Bilibid became number two. Small side camps were given numbers but supplies and mail mostly came from the main camps. Bilibid was never much more than a hospital and a big clearing place for the Manila port for all prisoners of war. In the earlier days it cleared groups going to other places for work in the islands. Now it was clearing them for Japan and other places in the north as the Japs were in the process of closing all places in the Philippines except for the sick.[4]

Small shipments were going often. I recall large sailings as follows:

July 2, 1944—about 1,000 men, Lieutenant Colonel Stubbs, American leader—mostly enlisted men, arrived safely so far as is now known.[5]

August 25, 1944—about 1,030 men and 17 officers, Captains Charles P. Samson and Elmer P. Fleming were the American leaders—arrived safely so far as is now known.[6]

October 11, 1944—about 1,785 men, Lieutenant Colonel Hunter, American leader—about half officers; many field grade—lost except about twelve to fourteen known to have been saved.[7]

December 13, 1944—about 1,660 men, Lieutenant Colonel Brady, American leader—about half officers, many field grade—bombed off Subic Bay, about 1,300 lost.[8]

Bilibid, in its inception as an American prisoner of war camp until just prior to October 11, 1944, had an American naval officer, staff, and a naval organization almost throughout. I have been told that the first naval doctor did good work in organizing the place and obtaining instruments and medical supplies, but he fell into disrepute with the Japs as did most good American leaders because he was always insistent that the prisoners receive decent and humane treatment. In the earlier days of our prison life the Americans often chose their leaders. The choice usually came almost always according to rank, with preference usually falling to the line officers who were accustomed to handling and disciplining men and usually skilled in administrative matters. Most of these never made good with the Japs for very obvious reasons already stated, and the Japs were tremendously scared of leadership among the prisoners. They wanted "yes, sir" men, who would do their bidding, and would not put up a fight for the prisoners as a whole. When an American leader complained that the men were being driven into the fields barefooted and were starved and nearly naked, they could pacify him with a pat on the shoulder, a package of cigarettes, and a promise to investigate, and then they had their man. Leadership was constantly changed until they got what they wanted.[9]

I once advised a young officer that it was no discredit to his military record to be relieved of leadership by the Japs, but that it was to his everlasting discredit if he made good with them to the disgust of the Americans, for this was only a temporary matter, but one he and his fellow Americans would have to live with for the remainder of his life. After the first round of leadership by the senior line officers in the camps where I lived, the leadership was almost constantly on the down grade. The Jap "yes, sir" man policy would not permit it to be otherwise. Too frequently officers deficient in combat records sought to curry favor with the Japs in order to become the G.I. leader hoping such positions would not only give them certain privileges but would bolster their record with our War Department after liberation. From this type of person little could be expected. The Japs, never being satisfied with any leader who insisted too much for betterment of conditions, continued to change until they were satisfied and this was never for any great length of time with anyone.

As a typical example, I once knew a leader who was accused by an eye witness of hogging commissary supplies. On this occasion the delivery of eggs was far short of the orders and not enough to make a general distribution. This leader said he had more money than he had ever had in his life and he was going to eat. He took half of the eggs and sent the other half to the hospital. Each morning for several days he broke about a dozen eggs in his mess kit, went to the kitchen fire where individual cooking was forbidden, and scrambled his eggs for breakfast. This was no help to the morale of the G.I.s.

On another occasion and at a different camp, when the G.I.s and officers were bitterly complaining of having to work with bleeding bare feet all day in the fields and verbal and written complaints were in order from our American leader, he took the opposite course. He and his staff took off their shoes and made a two hour barefooted inspection of the labor details in the fields to show the Jap major that we could take it. When we were taking a vote as to whether or not we would choose to work if work was on a voluntary basis, and the vote was going about one hundred percent against work, one of our staff officers declined to vote.

"It will put me in bad with the Americans or my friends, the Japs," he was quoted as saying. Starvation and slavery put many honest Americans in difficult and embarrassing positions. The decorations this officer held for heroism in action attest to his courage in battle.

From the time I arrived at Bilibid on June 26, 1944 until just prior to October 11, 1944, the naval forces were still in charge of all the works. A medical officer of the navy was the American leader. As the story goes, during the fighting days of Corregidor when the navy was taking wounded and cripples to Australia in submarines, this officer bound his legs in braces and pretended that he could not walk. But when the surrender came he was well and just the type the Japs wanted to head a medical prison.

Bilibid was run by the navy and for the benefit of the navy. If anyone objected to the way in which it was run, they soon found themselves on a list of prisoners to be transferred to Cabanatuan or on a draft to go to Japan. The Asiatic Fleet prior to the war was a small force, far removed from the seat of government, regarded in naval circles as a sacrificial unit and undesirable assignment. The personnel so assigned were often in the Manila clubs beefing and bellyaching about having been sent to this part of the world. The reaction on the civilians was not favorable.[10]

When Admiral Thomas C. Hart withdrew to the Dutch East Indies he carried with him the pick of the flock, except for a few good supply and shop men and some en route to China who were not available and were eventually caught in the surrender. Congress had made them officers. Among those left behind were a few who were real officers and gentlemen. The warrant officers seemed to have run the old navy and except for the hospital part they ran

Bilibid. The naval medical corps men were especially trained in their work, were courteous, accommodating, and on the whole more efficient than our army medical corps men who served us as prisoners of war.[11]

Lieutenant Benjamin Bruce Langdon, a young doctor from Linden, North Carolina was our ward surgeon. He looked after Colonel Hutson and me remarkably well. We were in poor condition, so when the "heavy sick" got extra issues of coconuts and fruits we were well taken care of. The human miseries of Bilibid brought about by the lack of fair and impartial administration by the American staff baffles description, and it is unbelievable by those who never served in prison walls. Yet it was in many respects as good as or better than other prison camps.[12]

CHAPTER 16

Life at Bilibid

Bilibid was in the city of Manila, on the north side of and some distance from the Pasig River, a fact we were to be very glad of later when the Japs chose to defend the river line. Despite the disadvantages of lacking a country atmosphere, space for individual gardens, and the view and air being shut off by a high stone wall surrounding it, most of those who were inmates there did not want to go elsewhere. All dreaded the often and thorough inspections of Lieutenant Naraji Nogi, the Jap doctor in command, who was constantly putting those who were convalescing from their sickness on the list to be shipped to Cabanatuan or Japan. Cabanatuan now was not so bad. There were gardens there and the farm produced good crops, but Japan was the last word in undesired places. The hardships and dangers of travel at sea as a Jap prisoner were understood and everyone felt that the liberation of the Philippines was close at hand.[1]

At the former camps at which I had been, food had been served in mess lines that passed by the containers of rice and soup. The servers used various sized dippers, made from tin cans with handles put on by the carpenter shop. The size of the dipper corresponded to the food status of the individual—heavy, regular, or light chow. There were always complaints and gripes about this system, that there were air pockets in the rice, it wasn't packed tightly in the dipper for one man like it was for another or some fell off and the server refused to replace it. Others complained that the soup was of the wrong consistency, such as when the bottom stirred to the top and this gave the first served advantage over the last, or vice versa. When there was meat soup the complaint was that the kitchen police stirred too little and dipped from the top, thus saving the thick meat on the bottom for themselves. There were always differences about food among starving men.

Here we had a new kind of complaint. The food was brought to our beds and served, with much dissatisfaction that it was not divided evenly and that the servers were leaving too much in the containers. These they carried to the wash racks, scraped, and consumed to the last grain of rice and the last spoon of soup before washing. We persuaded a commander of the navy to supervise the distribution and keep in touch with the kitchen. He agreed, provided we gave him support. He kept elaborate, detailed charts posted in the barracks showing for each meal where the servings were to begin and where the seconds had ended for each classification of food. It worked until we were liberated.[2]

An advantage of Bilibid was the plumbing that permitted the toilet facilities to be near each barracks. Our weakened condition, and the long period of watery food without proteins, had a bad effect on our kidneys and both young and old were forced to get up from three to six times each night. The long walk of a quarter of a mile to and from toilets in other camps so many times each night badly interrupted our rest. As compared to other camps the advantages and miseries of Bilibid were about on par with them. The Japs had set a general pattern of miseries and brutalities fashioned on the very low standard of living and cruelties to which they were daily accustomed. In some respects, Bilibid was better than other camps, in others not so good.

Wherever there are men, there will be differences of opinion and these differences over the procurement and division of food became acute during the long period of planned, systematic, and cruel starvation to which we had been subjected. Cabanatuan had its staff issues and staff purchases, and R.H.I.P. (ranks has its privileges) instead of R.H.I.O. (rank has its obligations) remained, so I am told, until almost the end. Dapecol had its kitchen and hospital food grafts that the ordinary prisoner never quite got to the bottom of. When camp was disbanded there, we had cooks and kitchen police who were fat, healthy, and strong who would chin themselves from 12 to 20 times on a chinning bar when more than half of the prisoners had been badly weakened by starvation. We had plenty of stout, well-kept doctors, and medical corps men who were accused of taking canned milk, corned beef, fruits and other foods issued and intended by the Japs for the use of the patients. The Japs reasoned that if the medical personnel were too weak and could not carry on that the entire prison slave scheme would collapse.

I refused to believe these stories on the doctors so long as we were at Dapecol. But after they had served with us on the 20 day trip to Manila and three or four months at Cabanatuan, where they got the food served to the average prisoner, they were sent back through Bilibid to Japan. Here I saw the old Dapecol medical clique, and with the exception of Captain Rader and one other, they were as thin as the other prisoners. Each had lost from 20 to 30 pounds, and you could count their ribs as you could any other prisoner as far as you could see them. The proof in the pudding is in the eating, and where there is no pudding to eat it shows up very quickly. But to return to the rackets at Bilibid, these were staff issues, messes, and the store that could scarcely escape criticism, as well as the administration of medicines and special diets to favorites, usually of the navy or the medical profession.

Staff issues at Bilibid were complex and offered more opportunities for food procurement than at other camps. The Japanese wanted the staff and the workers to fare better than the average prisoner and gave them heavier issues and sometimes extra items, such as cigarettes, canned milk, and corned beef. They had a special staff mess in which food was received and prepared. The Bilibid staff were in better physical condition than even the Dapecol group. They never felt the horrible pinches of starvation to the extent that they were felt by the average prisoner. Though like the Dapecol group, even including the men of God, they would vow by all that was good and holy that they were getting nothing extra to eat and were living off regular chow.

It only served to increase bitterness when an officer who was a regular patient walked in on a staff officer at mess and found him with coffee, sugar, milk, bananas, or canned meat when the officer making the discovery had not tasted those things for months and months. Nor did it help one's confidence in human nature to see a selected few who had not been moved since the earlier days and who had stored up mongo beans or had access to outside sources throw a handful each day to the wild pigeons that were around the place. This we saw for many days while from one to three men were dying of starvation almost weekly. The beans may have been floor sweepings from storage spaces but they would have been received, washed, and cooked by many of the hungry who would have been grateful for the opportunity.

In the early days of the store at Bilibid, like Cabanatuan and unlike the one at Dapecol, it handled many items. When I arrived on June 26, 1944, many things like canned meats, sugar, flour, dried fish, and fresh meats had become so scarce and so high in price that the Japs had instructed their merchant who supplied us to discontinue them. There was a limited list of items and these soared in price each month. Besides the number of items handled, the other limitations placed on the store by the Japs was that the total amount spent each month should not exceed the total monthly pay roll. The lack of enterprise in the Japs is astounding.[3]

The lieutenant colonels drew ₱40 per month, and this scale was graduated all the way down to the non-working private who drew no pay. Trade authorizations at the store for officers were usually never more than not quite half their pay. The authorization for the non-paid private was ₱6 per month, later, I believe about ₱7.50. All of those authorized to trade in various amounts did not have the money to spend and their friends did not have it to buy for them on halves—a common practice. Each person put in his order for goods during the early part of the month. After the first order had been delivered a second order was permitted and filled, after which the store sometimes had some common items, such as salt and coconuts, that would be sold to the individual to the extent of his authorization, less odd pennies and small change. Unused authorizations were supposed to go to the general mess fund.[4]

All this business was closed by the twenty-fifth of each month. What became of the unused authorizations? Ask the staff, and the reply would be the general mess fund. They were too much for that. The store was run by the naval warrant officer clique—glance into their mess, look at the staff and special messes, look at the supplies of doctors and favorite naval officers and compare them with the mess of the average patient—the answer was too apparent. The store was never audited, as our army or naval regulations require. We had passed beyond the laws governing the armed services of the United States into a topsy-turvy world of the heathen, who in many cases, treated us better than our own leaders who had been set in authority by them.

In the prison camps of O'Donnell, Cabanatuan, and Dapecol, the messes were at once reduced to one common mess and one common level for all. The officers' messes were never established and only two messes existed for the prisoners—a hospital mess with a special diet kitchen, and a general mess for all who were not in the hospital. If any person had extra food of his own he drew his regular food from his mess and supplemented it with the extra food of his own preparation—often cooked on individual or community fires. The navy brought its array of messes to Bilibid, where we had the staff officers mess, the warrant and chief petty officers' mess, the special diet mess, and at the bottom the general mess out of which was fed the bulk of the prisoners, both sick and well.[5]

With so many messes in operation, the general feeling among the prisoners was that by the time all the various messes got their fingers out of the slim issue of Japanese rations there was little left for the general mess. The warrant officers mess was in the end of the sick officers' quarters where I was quartered—opposite end from the end in which Colonel Hutson and I lived, and adjacent to the store operated by the warrant officers.

It was not uncommon that some naval personnel shared in more than one mess. One big fat warrant officer slept about six beds from me. He had been kept in the hospital for the duration of prison life by the naval doctors – "a suspect for tuberculosis." He ate in our general mess and was additionally fed by the warrant officers mess and gave the poorest of his left overs to the closest bed patients. He did not know hunger as we knew it, stayed fat and good natured and remained in the Bilibid hospital section, while numbers of really sick army field officers were sent out to Cabanatuan or to Japan.

The principle of the diet kitchen was well founded provided it was fairly and well administered by the ward and other responsible surgeons. But it was not uncommon to see a naval officer or an army doctor come into the ward with apparently little wrong with him, and soon be favored by special dishes from the diet kitchen, dishes with meat or soup with a meat base and mongo beans while sicker line officers, as was the case of Colonel Hutson, were forced to do without. This officer, shot through the hip and crippled for life, suffered as a weak, starving bed patient for the entire duration of the Bilibid camp. He had many operations from festered bone splinters, many transfusions, and was never for a day put on the special diet but instead was always denied it.

If men living under circumstance of ease and luxury will take advantage of each other for the simple commercial expedient of making a little more money, and members of the armed services will circumvent each other in the matter of getting favorable assignments, what will men do that are being put through a slow systematic course of starvation for an extra cup of rice or a morsel of meat a day when that will stave off the grim reaper, and make return to home and loved ones seem a certainty? Life became so weary that toward the later months at Bilibid it was a common saying among those who disagreed with the practices there that when the Yanks and tanks came it would be as great a relief to get out from under the prison administration as it would be to get out from under the Jap bayonets.

Medical officers were frequently admitted as patients and sent to our ward. Some were really sick, while others were attempting to avoid work or beat the draft to Cabanatuan or Japan. These medical officers often received all sorts of attention with consultation after consultation from their fellow medics, blood and saline transfusions, and vitamins and special diets, for what appeared to be trivial complaints while deathly sick line officers of the army received only passing notice from the corpsmen and doctors. In the earlier days of Bilibid, Colonel Hutson saw some line officers of field grade die from pure neglect while a great to do was made over half sick medics next to them.

One naval doctor of the Mormon religion came into Bilibid for a second time with claims of arthritis in the muscles of his legs that almost prevented him from walking. He was in to beat the draft to Japan. On his former visit he claimed stomach trouble, but was soon proved a faker and returned to duty. This time he had an ironclad alibi, but in the dark of the nights, every time he hobbled to the toilet door, and after looking around to see that he was not under observation, he would straighten up and step right along. Colonel Hutson and I were where we could see him and he did not know it. He succeeded in not being sent to Japan, was put on special diets, and remained with us until the rescue.

There were from three to five other unfortunate doctors who played the hospital because they were dope addicts. The ward surgeon one day became impatient with one of them and bawled him out in the presence of others, refusing him dope on the ground that he was an addict. The addict complained to the American in charge and the ward surgeon instead of receiving support was transferred to an enlisted man's ward.[6]

The Japs were anxious for sulphathiasol. It seemed to be a recent product that had not been supplied to their army. It is said to be especially good for treatment of venereal diseases. They would trade all types of food for it. The average patient soon traded his hoardings of a dozen or so tablets to the Japs, but a heavy traffic between some of the medical personnel continued for some time. It was a matter of general knowledge that the Jap market was so fruitful for this product, and it was said that clever counterfeiters profited greatly by making a perfect imitation mold of a popular brand. In this they molded sodium bicarbonate in perfect imitation, and passed it to the Jap soldiers in exchange for much sought after mongo beans, meat, tobacco, and fruits.[7]

There were many good, hard-working, conscientious doctors, but the poor characterless ones were a bad advertisement for the profession. At all the camps I served, the heart of many a good medical officer was broken because they had to attempt to practice medicine without drugs. The Japs had almost completely robbed us of our medicines on the Death March, and the

Red Cross supply was slow coming and had to be used sparingly. We used leaves from trees to make bitter tea and also charcoal to help stop diarrhea and dysentery. At O'Donnell, the doctors and corps men had been weakened and starved by the Death March, just as had all the others. All civilized armies provide for the commanders, staff, and medics to ride in order that they take care of the men and sick at the end of the journey, but not so with the Japs in handling the prisoners of war.[8]

Of all the doctors I met in prison life I rate Colonel James W. Duckworth, Captain Rader, and Lieutenant Langdon as some of the most unselfish and the most trustworthy people I have ever seen. They would conscientiously do all they could in an unselfish way for the prisoner and did great good. Colonel Duckworth and Captain Rader were in positions to persuade the Japs into issuing us more food and medicines. I feel that these two should be awarded the Distinguished Service Medal, if our War Department ever makes any awards for prison service.[9]

Colonel Duckworth was the clean-up man. He cleaned up the hospitals in Bataan, then talked the Japs into permitting him to take his instruments and medicines to Camp O'Donnell where he commanded and cleaned up that death hole. He had a superior way with the Japs and got many things for prisoners. The decrease in the death rate attests to it. He was an old friend, and I shook hands with him when he came on the *President Coolidge* as a member of the boarding party. I never saw him but once on this tour in the Far East, but my heart was warmed when I learned he had reached his family in San Francisco. I am saddened over Captain Rader. He was on the boat torpedoed on October 24, 1944, of which only a handful were saved.

The word *quan* seemed to grow into popular use in all prison camps. It seemed to come from some native dialect meaning how, when, where, or such like, but it was applied liberally to eats, cooking utensils, clothes and almost every phase of prisoner of war life. Individual cooking, authorized by the Geneva agreements, was forbidden at Dapecol but was always authorized at Bilibid. We had in our sick ward five electric grills on which we could boil pots. They were run on schedule, the men being assigned to the stoves in groups and the groups given hours for cooking. We had in our group a navy commander who had put in many years service in the U.S. Geodetic Survey. He worked the garbage cans at the Jap kitchens for edibles that he kept in various pots and rusty tin cans which he was always trying to keep warm on the stove to prevent spoilage. He wanted to cook all the time. When he exhausted my patience, I would get Hutson to chase him off, and vice versa. He was more frequently a trial on our quick tempers.[10]

We held in and I do not believe ever lost our balance. It was very easy to lose one's balance in prison life when you were thrown directly into close contact with men of all types, many of whose language was very foul. This foul language is very contagious in prison and grates deeply on a person's sense of refinement. Fights between prisoners were frequent. I suppose that if I owe my life to any one characteristic it was that of remaining calm. I never permitted myself to get stirred up, to worry, to become angry, or to rely too much on rumors that left one flat a few days later.

Rumors began the day we started on the Death March and continued during our prison life. The reasons often were the lack of newspapers, broadcasts, and outside contact. The first rumors related to prisoner exchanges and to where we were going. Someone had heard an item in the news where the British made the Japs offers in gold for the prisoners taken at Singapore. Soon rumors had us all redeemed by the United States for 30 dollars in gold per head. After arrival at camp rumors concerned everything. At one time during the early days at Cabanatuan they had 250,000 Americans landing at Lingayan Gulf and 120,000 on the east coast of Luzon. Slogans, mottos and meaningless slang words were also bandied about: "Home alive in '45," "The Golden Gate in '48," "Christmas Turkey in Albuquerque"—these were the most common ones.[11]

They were good to keep up interest and pass the time away, but very bad for the extreme optimist who experienced a considerable let-down when they proved untrue. One prisoner kept a catalogue of rumors and had over 2,000 in the first six months of our internment. Some were repeated dozens of times. "We have bombed the Celebes" was circulated at Dapecol until it became a joke. The Japs always started a favorite rumor that we were to be exchanged when morale was low, the death rate excessive, and further living seemed unbearable.

It would be unfair to close this picture of prison life without paying tribute to the egotist, the optimist, and the pessimist. I do not mean the egotist who breaks under the strain of dementia praecox (premature dementia) or enjoys so many hallucinations of grandeur that he has to be locked up. We had several of them. I speak of the everyday "I" man who thinks considerably of himself and his own accomplishments. Prison life is full of them. Removal from the practical, every day hard knocks of life into an atmosphere where sensible people will sacrifice deeply to get along, so much so that they will converse only on agreeable subjects, tends to develop this trait of character so rapidly that the egotist soon becomes a nuisance to his fellow prisoners. Some could not bear to see two officers engaged in a private conservation without intruding with some humorous remark intended to draw attention to themselves. Others broke into private conversations with such remarks as "Well, now, let me tell you a few things." At times the "butinsky" seemed insufferable.

Most of the "egos" were entirely inconsiderate of others. I saw a lieutenant colonel with 26 years of regular service do his washing and spread his clothes on his shelter half to dry, and put the whole array in the middle of a path alongside the barracks. This path during the noon hour was used by at least 150 men going or coming back from the latrine. He would have corrected his child for doing such a thing yet he expected everyone to walk around his clothes for the reason that they were his. "The king can do no wrong" was too often the attitude of the egotist.

The optimist always had a lag in the news and he would have us out of prison from two weeks to two months; the pessimist from one to two years. All lived on optimism, and many of the worst pessimists died. They were like the bulls and the bears on the stock market. Be it as it may, we had lived for three years on faith and hope but the greatest of these was charity, I also being chief among the sinners. It is hard to forgive and forget, but that is what must take place and these memoirs of our sufferings are written not to keep them alive, but with the hopes that our people will not fall again into the old ruts of pacifism and unpreparedness lest these sufferings be repeated. It is a marvelous trait of the human mind that it so easily forgets the hardships and clings to the pleasantries of the past. If this were not true most of the war veterans would soon be raving maniacs.

It is the constitutional privilege of every G.I. to gripe. It is bad enough when things are going well and even when the army is victorious. Even in Germany in 1919, when we were sitting on top of the world, the grumblers and gripers had their day in court. If it was this bad in a victorious army, try to imagine it is a defeated one. We had them of all types and calibers. I once listened very patiently to a long tirade of an officer recently returned from civil life, an inexperienced officer from a small town in a sparsely populated community. Everything in Bataan was wrong, we shouldn't have surrendered, General King would have made a very good "old so and so," Wainwright was a "this and that," and MacArthur was called "Dugout Doug."

I told him very mildly and kindly that I liked to think that everyone in Bataan did their best according to the talents with which God had endowed them, some had ten talents, some of us possibly not a half one, and that I had known King and Wainwright for a number of years and they were very able men and that I had been several times cited for gallantry in action. Also, that General MacArthur was the only man among the quick or the dead that had ever run me to cover, and related a little incident that happened at the command post during the bombings of Manila. I then closed by mildly suggesting that possibly we could have done better in Bataan had you been in command. I lived with this officer for many more months during my prison life, and we became good friends, but I never heard him criticize anything else that happened in Bataan. Had it been later I could have told him about General MacArthur making me cry, not through harshness but through kindness after we were liberated.

CHAPTER 17

Final Days of Imprisonment

During our entire prison life we became well-acquainted with every state and many cities and towns across the United States. All that was required was to say to a fellow prisoner that you believed his was a good community and you considered settling there after the war. You would be immediately treated without obligation to a good chamber of commerce lecture on the virtues of the town and section.

We lived in Florida, California, the great Northwest, and the magic valley of Texas. We spent our summers touring the Ozarks, Great Smokies, and New England. If you fancied trout fishing, the virtues of the Yellowstone National Park were not neglected. Big game hunting in the Rockies was a favorite, and an old sour dough had us in high mind to hunt with him on the last American frontier—Alaska—the last big resort of fish and game. Had most of us survived we would have had friends in all parts of the country. When maps were available, they were well worn by people planning trips and there were many discussions between the trailer enthusiast and the cabin-camp supporters. Aside from food, nothing to a man in confinement is more attractive than the thought of your own motor car and the freedom of the great open roads of America.

As monotonous as our life was, Colonel Hutson often remarked "How long! How Long!" Still, we were not in Shangri Lai and time was marching on. Each day seemed an eternity within itself, but to look backwards a month, a year, or more things seemed to have passed rapidly. We sat out in front of our barracks and the Jap anti-aircraft was practicing. A few Jap planes were in the air. We had sat there the night before and on many previous nights watching the twelve Jap searchlights drill.

The hand of the clocks moved toward 9:30 a.m.; it was September 21, 1944. As the Japs said in their propaganda pictures of the bombing of Pearl Harbor until they were almost on their target, “They are still dancing at the Royal Hawaiian Hotel,” so our naval commanders were saying as our task force planes approached: “Radio Manila is still broadcasting.” Their anti-aircraft guns continued to practice, and then suddenly the sky thickened with planes very high in the air. Someone counted 24 to the north, and someone counted 48 to the south.

“They are Japs. I have counted as many as ninety in the air at one time in Bataan,” a pessimist declared.

“God Almighty,” someone shouted, “look out there to the west, just under that big cloud. There are hundreds; you can’t count them fast enough, the sky is black with ‘em.”

We sat in muted silence for the briefest of moments. Then the dive bombers began to peel off from their formations and start into dives as straight as arrows, with a machine-like precision far beyond the competency of the Jap fliers. The Yanks were here—overhead, at least, but they had not brought rations.

The alarm was sounded, the sentries ran us in and locked the doors, but through the windows we could see small segments of sky. We could see the planes dive, the bombs released, and the explosions were the sweetest music we had ever heard. They rained down on the airfields, port area, piers, and ships in the harbor twice that day. Next day, with the Jap air supremacy being broken, they came in small formations and bombed almost all day. I later saw the navy’s estimate of damage. It was entirely too small. Fires burned flagrantly day and night and explosions shook the earth for two days after the planes were gone. The surprise was complete, the damage immense. From then on Jap air power was on the wane, and supplies were moved from the Manila area as fast and as successfully as they could do so.[1]

Our outside details had been discontinued but some radio experts built a small set and hid it in the store. Those who listened in had to be discreet as to how they put out the news but we had the general picture of the march of events. We knew of the landings at Leyte and Mindoro and something of the great sea battles.

We hated to see the group go out on October 11, 1944. Our forces were closing in on the Japanese life line and we had a dark foreboding of danger for them. The men going felt it also, and numbers of them came by my bunk and asked me to write their people should I get home first. Others left letters of instruction to be sent to their people, some not realizing that these were to take the force of last wills and testaments. Colonel Hunter, the senior officer and American leader felt it. Colonel Deter, our Dapecol medical officer, and Captain Rader felt it, so did many others that went on the boat.[2]

Many rumors came back to us regarding this shipment. The news was so bad I refused to believe it. We had heard that every boat taking prisoners had been sunk, but never received confirmation. But persistent rumors were usually in the end confirmed. They had kept this group around a long time waiting a favorable opportunity to get them out. The old Bilibid medical staff was included. They finally began the trip on October 11, 1944, and were torpedoed and sunk somewhere off Formosa on October 24, 1944. There were about 1,785 on board.

Five enlisted men were saved and made it to the coast of China and back home. Robert S. Overbeck of Baltimore, Maryland was one of the survivors. He reached home and wrote his people in Santo Tomas before we left Manila. He knew of no other survivors. It seems too absolute to be true. Seven or eight others were later reported by the Japs as having been landed in Formosa where one died. After the surrender of Japan, the press carried a statement that seven prisoners, torpedoed on October 24, 1944, were liberated from Japanese prison camps in Japan. If these are the seven previously reported in Formosa, then only 12 survived. If these seven are additional, still less than 20 survived out of over 1,800. The horrors of the sinking and how the Japs drowned those who clung to rafts and attempted to get on the lifeboats is told in the April 1945 *Cosmopolitan* article, "We Prayed to Die," by Sergeant Calvin Graef, who escaped with Overbeck to China.[3]

The change of administration at Bilibid from the navy to the army was an innovation but conditions changed very little. The practices previously discussed had become so deeply engrained in the life of the place that a young army major, taken from his practice at Los Angeles, California just before the outbreak of the war, and with little administrative experience, could do little to improve conditions, but he made a good effort. The store by this time handled few items and was practically closed, prices were soaring, and the food situation was becoming worse and worse if such a thing was possible.[4]

The draft to Japan of December 13, 1944, carried many friends, including Compton, Dencker, Edmands, Brady, "Zero" Wilson, Tom Tarpley, "Dinty"

Moore, and many others. They were going out in the face of death and knew it. Commander Warner P. Portz, the senior naval officer at Bilibid, was on the shipment. He made a written protest to the Japanese but it did no good. He and the remainder were sent away. The Japanese had him at their office a few times to question him about his protest. Their discussions, however, did not cluster around the central theme of how they were evading international law and rules of land warfare by moving prisoners of war through waters that were in the combat zone without marking the boat, but instead dealt with the silly and superficial matters as to how he knew it was dangerous, a combat zone, and the boats were unmarked, etcetera. Many came by my bunk to leave messages to their loved ones, as had the previous group. "On some fond breast the parting soul relies."[5]

The work of our task forces and other forces were closing in all too well for the Japanese. Numerous air raids on Manila had taken place. An air alarm was sounded when they had been gone from Bilibid long enough to soon be loaded on the boat, but it was not followed by the customary raid. Ill omens from this boat soon appeared. The Japs soon began to collect mess kits and load some of our Red Cross medicines, blankets, clothing, and barbed wire on trucks to carry to Bataan to a group from a shipwreck. They admitted that the boat had been bombed on the 14th and bombed again and sunk on the 15th, and that they had all the rescued prisoners on a beach somewhere in Bataan.

In a few days the reports of the dead and missing began to come to the Japanese prison office headquarters. Our Americans working there as clerks began to pass small lists around and to look for their friends, and upon request to look for our friends. Lieutenant Colonel Brady, the American leader, was the first one reported dead, then came Compton, Dencker, Major John Turner and others. I made a copy of the 15 dead and 181 missing and it did not include all the G.I.s. The total dead and missing was estimated at about 225. Later the Japs reported 1,001, and in the end less than 300 of this shipment survived and returned to their flag and country. From the way the reports of the dead came in we believed they had died ashore, or their bodies washed ashore and were identified, and that all the missing were lost on the ship. These death reports came in fragmentarily until December 22, when those rescued were loaded on other boats at San Fernando, La Union, and sailed again to Japan. Some of these boats went through safely while others were torpedoed.[6]

On the boats of October 11 and December 13 was a small group of British prisoners whose saga is still sadder than any Americans. They had been captured in the fall of Singapore, and were used to build a railroad in the jungles of Burma and Indochina, where the death rate was so fearful that they claimed a human life for every crosstie. Their senior officers would not permit them to bow to Orientals as required of prisoners by Japanese army regulations. They found the Japs just as we did. They bluffed about the Geneva conference, but in a tight place they would say that they were not signatories and they were running the prison camps on Japanese army regulations. The punishment they received for refusing to bow was the loss of their first Red Cross Christmas packages that were sent to the Americans. This is possibly the explanation of why our first shipment was composed of American, Canadian and South African packages.

The boat on which these prisoners were loaded in a far port of the south had engine trouble. They stopped at various ports, including one or two in Borneo, and took over three months to reach Manila where they lay in the bay for about six weeks. Beriberi, dysentery and starvation were so bad that many men had to crawl on their hands and knees. They were too weak to help each other up the ladders to go on deck for fresh air. They prayed for death and buried about 75 of their number in Manila Bay, not to mention those buried at sea for the three months they were en route to Manila. When they did finally sail from Manila our task force raid of September 21–22, 1944 bombed and sank their boat. About 150 survivors were brought into Bilibid and a similar number sent to Cabanatuan. They had many cases of amoebic dysentery among them. They stayed with us for a few weeks and were reshipped on October 11 and December 13 with our men only to repeat their disastrous experiences.[7]

I never kept a diary for fear of its falling into Japanese hands and the truth resulting in personal disaster. About Christmas 1944, however, it became evident that we would die or be rescued at Bilibid. So long as we remained there little danger was in evidence of a search, so I made a record of a few outstanding days. Here are a few of them.

CHRISTMAS DAY, 1944

Two hundred, sixty-four individual Red Cross packages, undelivered to the addressees and over 14 months old, were divided among the 429 prisoners of Bilibid. All food was put into the general mess. This gave us some sugar, prunes, and raisins to put in our breakfast lugao, and a cup of hot chocolate, without milk, for each person. We drew lots for the remaining goods. I drew one pair of socks, one large cake of Ivory soap, two packages of chewing gum, one lead pencil, eight razor blades, two handkerchiefs, one bath towel, one pair of shorts (drawers), two undershirts, half a can of Dr. Lyon's Toothpowder, ten cigarettes (five Camels, five Luckies), one wash cloth, and one stick of caramel candy. Supper at 3:30 p.m.: hot chocolate, a large issue of steamed rice, a small portion of soup made of greens, soy meal, garlic and cornmeal, camote pudding with coconut sauce. We were cut to two meals per day in October 1944. Reason given was the shortage of firewood. Every stick of firewood was weighed and charged to the United States, just as food was weighed and charged. This was the best Christmas dinner I have had since 1942 when I ate at my own table. There were no Christmas carols and no decorations. There was no opportunity for either.[8]

TUESDAY, DECEMBER 26, 1944

We have lived so close to the bed rocks of human existence for so long that a little makes us very happy, both the increased food and the Red Cross issue of yesterday, and especially the bath towel of which I am as proud as a child with new shoes. It is the first and only bath towel I have possessed since becoming a prisoner of war. An air alarm is on. A detail is preparing to move the kitchen from the other compound to this one. It seems to be in preparation to clear our prisoner of war activities out of the other division of the compound so, as rumors have it, they can occupy it with civilian internees from Baguio. Breakfast 8:00 a.m.: lugao with toasted coconut. Supper at 3:30 p.m.: steamed rice, steamed camotes with a very thin soup. We are making up for our half decent food of yesterday.[9]

THURSDAY, DECEMBER 28, 1944

The old year is about to go. We are very hopeful of the new one—trusting that in 1945 we will be restored to home and loved ones. Breakfast: plain lugao. It is remarkable what the human body when put to the test can exist on, particularly when no exercise is taken. Some of the calorie experts say that we are down to about one thousand calories per day. My weight is 123.5 pounds. I have been down to as low as 119, or a loss of 71 pounds from my normal 190. I do not know if I ever was lower than 119 or not. It does not help a starving person to weigh too often or to count their calories. We should be thankful for what we are getting. Rumors have it that many Filipinos are starving and dying very rapidly, that rice issues include 440,000 people, or the entire population of

Manila. Supper: (2 meals per day) steamed rice, steamed camotes, soup made of chayotes, camotes, greens, corn, and soy meal.

THURSDAY, JANUARY 9, 1945

A bright cheerful morning, the fourth successive day of air raids. We are cheerful about the future. Breakfast: lugao with some little dried fruit, sugar and coconuts—it was good. Two hundred men came in a few days ago from Fort McKinley bringing our total numbers to 628. Fifty-four undelivered individual Red Cross packages were given to them. This was the source of better lugao for two breakfasts. Supper last night: lugao made of an equal mixture of rice and cracked corn flavored with soup bullion from Red Cross packages. Reports of losses from vessels coming in. Dead: Jasper Brady, Irving Compton, Walter Dencker (all lieutenant colonels) and Majors Howard Cavender, John Turner and Captain Tom Powell. Missing: Lieutenant Colonels Francis Conaty, Tom Powell, Majors John Neiger, Thompson Maurey, and John Heil of the Marine Corps.[10]

MONDAY AND TUESDAY, JANUARY 28, 29, 1945

Completed 27 years of service and began to draw another $15.00 per month "Foggie." Unless promoted I will get only one more increase in pay no matter how long I remain in the service. My deposit with the Japanese for prisoner of war pay is over ₱5,000. I never expect to see this money. We signed the Jap pay roll for January on the twenty-ninth. My undrawn pay accumulated with the Chief of Finance is about $4,348.00 unless there has been a new pay bill passed or increase in rations and rental allowances. The food situation has been so acute that we donated all of our last month's Jap pay (December 1944) to the general mess fund. It bought two packages of picadura (cigarette rolling) smoking tobacco per man, and 2,400 coconuts for use by 628 prisoners. Rations: 50 grams of soy beans, 50 grams of rice flour, 100 grams of white corn meal, plus a small cup of soup made from camote vine tops with a slight fish flavor. Rations on the twenty-ninth are the same less the fish flavor. This is less than one half pound of starch and carbohydrate food per day per man.

WEDNESDAY, JANUARY 30, 1945

We were issued rations for the month of February during the last few days. They are locked in our store room. This is an innovation for the Japs. It appears that they expect a siege. The basis is 200 grams per day per man of rice, corn, and such vegetables as may be brought in daily for soup. Less than one half pound per day to exist on. Can we do it? I think not. The death rate will soar again. This was cut about one-third, and everyone except the chosen few have gotten very hungry since the 26th when the cut went into effect. Yesterday a number of sacks (100 pounds each) of dried cassava were brought into our store room. Everyone was very expectant of it for breakfast. It did not show up, but instead we had the usual amount of cracked corn mush. It was not well cooked and very watery. Disappointment and disgust with our mess officers and kitchen force—morale very low. I hope everyone keeps their temper and no one starts a fight with the big fat Jew mess officer or any member of the staff. If they do it will embroil so many mad people that it will result in a riot and will have to be settled by a Jap firing squad or by Jap bayonets. Dinner 4:00 p.m.: cassava has been added, about 50 grams, making a better meal.

THURSDAY, JANUARY 31, 1945

We were heartened last night by the issue of nine extra sacks of cracked corn, about half meal and half bran. We were glad to see the addition. It looks like we will have about 300 grams of rice, cracked corn and cassava per man per day. When cooked the water expansion brings it to a weight of about 1,800 grams. For breakfast we have 800 grams of cracked corn. This is a little more than one good helping of hominy grits—no meat, no bread, no sweets, no coffee, nor grease.

FRIDAY, FEBRUARY 1, 1945

One twelfth of the year is gone. We wonder what the month will bring forth. January has brought a good deal. Many explosions in the city, many fires, our planes flying low and in complete mastery of the air. We know of the landings on Luzon. We have heard General MacArthur's statement that the Japs had lost their last natural defense of Manila when they failed to defend the Pampanga River line. The sound of artillery fire is very audible and getting louder each day. We can see flashes at night. The food situation is little changed. Five small tubs of miso, 50 kilos (110 pounds) dried fish, greens, a soup made of pineapples, some soy beans, and rice were brought in this morning. Some soy beans have been added to our menu and to our stores. Breakfast: the usual amount of cracked corn mush. Dinner 4:00 p.m.: rice lugao, cracked corn, cassava, and soy meal all cooked together, green soup with the strong flavor of dried fish.[11]

SATURDAY, FEBRUARY 2, 1945

Breakfast: 800 grams of lugao, made of cracked corn, cracked rice, and ground coconuts. Dinner yesterday was 100 grams of grain, cassava, and soy beans, plus camote vine soup, and 45 grams of dried and ground fish. Note that this 45 grams is about two heaping tablespoons full. This fish is very strong, flavors well but smells like a fertilizer factory. It is made of dried fish heads, deep fried and run through a meat grinder. In this way all the fish is eaten except the lens in the eyes which does not grind up in the teeth or dissolve in the digestive fluids. The coconuts were purchased for the general mess by the store with our entire January Jap pay. This was to supplement the food issued us. Six hundred, fifty nuts for about ₱12,000 ($6,000) or about ₱2.80 ($1.40) per nut in bulk lots. Quite a contrast to the prewar price of three centavos (1 ½ cents). In June 1944, when I came to Bilibid, they were 80 centavos (40 cents) each. It takes 70 for each breakfast so the entire month's payroll purchased a nine day breakfast supply, each breakfast averaged about one sixth of a coconut per man.

End Diary.

CHAPTER 18

Liberation

Events moved on with little change for us until the night of February 3, all except the noise of the guns becoming louder and louder. At roll call on that night, the Jap sentries taking it were in a hurry to finish and told our American assistants that it was their last *tenko* as they had orders to leave during the early part of the night.

We sat outside as usual until just before dark, when the heavy rumble of tanks and much cannonading caused the Japs to run us in and close the doors. They brought in some extra troops, filled their previously prepared foxholes, and formed a skirmish line where part of our barracks would be in the direct line of fire should our troops storm the front gate. At first we were dubious as to what was happening, but when the steady crack, crack, crack of our .50 caliber machine guns came to our ears we knew that our men and tanks were shooting in the streets around us and running the Japs to cover. The Far Eastern University (Jap headquarters) received a double amount of fire. The sky was red in that direction and we judged it to be burning. Then came millions of small explosions caused by the burning of a small arms ammunition dump. The cannonading was continuous. It sounded like a large group of the Fourth of July rowdies shooting up the town. We wondered what targets they had found to draw so much fire, and if the Americans were not shooting at every Jap that showed himself in order to run them all to cover. That is exactly what they were doing. The shooting lasted during the night and increased at daylight, while fires still raged.[1]

Next morning about 8:00 a.m., after taking a hurried roll call, all the Japs assembled at and behind the gate in full field marching equipment. At 10:30 a.m., a bombastic proclamation was read to us, to the effect that the Japs were freeing us of their own free will and accord, but for us not to venture on the streets for fear of snipers. At 11:00 a.m. they marched through the gates and we went on three meals a day.[2]

When the Japs announced that we were free a great delight filled our hearts, but they were still in the compound and for fear of retribution we made little outward demonstration. I took stock of the prisoners and there were only three that had made the long trek with me in all places and were in Bilibid to be liberated. These were like myself lieutenant colonels: Wallace E. Durst of the quartermaster corps, Memory B. Cain, anti-aircraft artillery, and Halstead C. Fowler of the field artillery. Our saga had been the same—the fall of Bataan, the Death March, Camps O'Donnell, Cabanatuan, Dapecol, and the liberation at Bilibid.[3]

All four of us were walking skeletons and had you asked any of us what had brought us through, the answer would have been the same—our time had not yet come. We had gotten some lucky breaks, the best being that our ailments had saved us being shipped to Japan. All vowed that with God continuing to be our helper, we would never be hungry again. Colonel Durst had been the victim of many diseases, but none of them that good food would not cure. Cain had in the early days of imprisonment been struck over the head by a Jap interpreter with a loaded swagger stick, rendering him temporarily insensible, and causing a concussion from which he suffered excruciatingly at frequent periods during his entire imprisonment. Fowler had suffered much, and beriberi had almost totally paralyzed his optical nerves. We had all been left behind by the Japs to die.[4]

No one left the compound, and everything was quiet with us until about dark. No contact was made with the outside to my knowledge. About dark some of our men observed the planks that had been used to board up a door in the west wall being knocked into the compound by someone on the opposite side. These men went to the place to see what was happening and more planks fell into the inside of the compound. They called to know who it was and what the party was doing.

"Just knocking these planks out to get some air. It is damned hot in here. Too damned hot for men to try to sleep. But why are you asking? Who are you to know?"

"We are prisoners of war."

"Prisoners of war, Hell! There are no prisoners of war around here but the Japs."

"Says who? We have been prisoners of war for three years under the Japs."

"The Hell you say! Did they treat you good?"

"No, pretty rough, beat and starved us to death."

"The dirty bastards, and we had to run them to death before we could kill them."[5]

Major Wendt, commanding a battalion of the 37th Division, soon ended the conversation by asking the name of the place, how many prisoners there were, and where the entrance was located. Ten minutes later he marched a guard through the main gate. We were in the arms of a regiment bivouacked about us. The planes had been over us for months, the tanks had surrounded us for about 24 hours, but when the white foot soldiers marched in we knew that we were again under the stars and stripes.[6]

Good grew out of Valley Forge which has become a synonym of hunger and suffering in the American army. Here General Washington quartered about 11,000 men for less than four months, beginning about December 17, 1777. At first 2,898, or about 26 percent, were "unfit for duty because they are bare foot and otherwise naked." Here, he and General Von Steuben emerged with a hardened and revitalized force. Their losses from deaths were less than 27.2 percent.[7]

We had been under the red rising sun for 33 months and 25 days. The Corregidor group for 27 days less. In round numbers, about 70,000 Filipinos and about 15,000 Americans prisoners surrendered between Bataan and Corregidor. The Filipinos had been forced to take or sign an oath at Camp O'Donnell in the summer of 1942, when they were liberated, but not until death made great inroads into their numbers. About 50 percent of the Americans were dead by the end of their first year's imprisonment. Unburied bodies littered the route of the Death March, and lay unshrouded and uncoffined in graves at O'Donnell, Cabanatuan, and wherever the Americans worked. About 15 percent are known to have died in Formosa, Manchukuo, or have been lost at sea, and these returns are incomplete. About 5 percent—about 1,100 of us—were liberated by the advance of forces at Cabanatuan and Bilibid. Summarizing: 50 percent dead by the end of the first year, 15 percent believed dead or lost at sea, and five percent rescued, leaving 30 percent of the American prisoners taken in Bataan and Corregidor still in the hands of the enemy at the time of our rescue. May God bless and preserve them. When final figures of our losses are available they will be even more appalling. The Japanese have done us much harm, and may God reward them according to their works.[8]

CHAPTER 19

Homeward Bound

We were no longer prisoners of war. It was wonderful to be a free American but circumstances kept us closely pinned to our environment for a few days. The Battle of Manila raged around us. We were weak, sick, unarmed, and it was unsafe to go outside of the compound. Its high stone walls stopped flying bullets.

Our forces were about 150 miles from bases up in Lingayen Gulf and were being supplied by transportation operating over one narrow rough road, studded with temporary bridges. The supply of front line units with ammunition and food was of first importance. All released prisoners were patient. There was not a grumble from anyone, for we were too glad to be away from the Japs and back under the flag.[1]

All next day, and for two or three more days, our officers came through our barracks. Old friends to clasp hands, talk, and bring news of the world from which we had been shut off for so long. They divided among us good American cigarettes, money, clothes, bits of food, and wanted to know what else they could do. It was a joy to us, and we were a shock to them in our ragged, weakened, and emaciated condition. Our American food could not get to us at once, but we had what we had dreamed of for many months. Our own food service went through the barracks three times a day with heaping boxes of rice, and thick soup made meaty with mongo and soy beans, calling "seconds! Plenty of them. Can't you eat anymore?" It hurt us then and always will hurt us to see food go to waste. We had many ways of civilization to brush up on. I put on my socks and shoes as soon as the Japs left to become accustomed to wearing them.[2]

On the second night, and we will always date things from Liberation Day, the fires from the battle raged heavier than ever. Our troops were fighting a mean house-to-house and room-to-room battle down towards the Pasig River.

The fires lit up the whole area like day as the giant sparks were suspended thousands of feet in the air. It was as picturesque as any man-made fireworks could be, but sickeningly repulsive because so many lives, homes, and businesses were going up in flames.

Suddenly, as we stood in the yard of our old jail and watched it the wind changed direction, blowing everything towards us. Word was passed to get such baggage as one could carry and form in marching order. Litter cases were carried out and loaded into trucks. Those able to walk only a few hundred yards sat down by the road to wait for more trucks. Everything was heading north out of the city.[3]

My old friend Dr. Brown marched beside me. We marched about 1,000 yards. His ankles began to swell and his heart began to act up. My strength also began to play out. I proposed we go over by the side of the road and sit down.

"No, no," he quickly retorted, "We'll get hit over the head."

"You are not a slave any longer, Doc, you are a free man. I am a colonel and you are a captain in this army."

I led him protestingly to the side of the road, spoke to an MP, and he flagged down a truck and put us aboard.[4]

We unloaded at the Ang Tibay shoe factory in the northern outskirts of the city where the liberated prisoners from Bilibid were kept for a couple of days while the fire raged. Here we tasted our first chocolate, and a taste of sauerkraut and weenies was better then than delicacies are now.[5]

Again my old friends who had not gotten to Bilibid came in. Dick Marshall, Paul Stivers, and Charles Willoughby were now major generals. Oscar Griswold and Charles Hall were corps commanders and soon to be lieutenant generals. Bob Burns was the chemical officer of an army, and Dick Walk a division chief of staff. They all came to sit on our bunks, talk, and offer us anything they had. To them we seemed to appear as a voice from a tomb or as ones resurrected from the dead.[6]

"I am hungry," I said to Marshall, and he led me to his jeep and gave me a large carton box containing ten K-rations. I carried it back inside and passed most of it out. I can still see those bony outstretched hands and haggard, hungry faces as they begged me not to forget them.[7]

Colonel Hutson, several other senior officers, and I were called in to conference with the high command, told of the situation, and asked where we thought our group should be sent until we could be routed towards home. As strange as it may seem, we chose our old prison wards where the last of our rags and a bunk awaited us. The fires in Manila passed the danger point for Bilibid and we went back to our old haunt for a few days until our transportation could carry us to places for shipment by water for home. The bed cases were sent to our hospital at Santo Tomas instead of Bilibid; Hutson went along with the bed cases.

We had scarcely arrived at Bilibid and straightened out our belongings that had been thrown into the middle of the floor by looters when General MacArthur came through the barracks.

"Hardee," he said as he clasped my hand, "the last time I saw you I was sending you to make infantry of the Air Corps."

"By the way, I have just had a letter, in fact a couple of them from Mrs. Hardee. All are well at your home. I told her I believed you were here about Manila and I would soon come up to see you."

At the mention of my family from whom I had no word for over a year and a half I began to cry. General MacArthur passed on and one of his assistants, General Bonner Fellers, whom I had not seen for years, came along with his joyous "Hello, Dave," and soon restored my emotional balance.[8]

It seemed for a long time after we first returned to good American food that we would starve to death before the next meal. There were not enough cheese and chocolates. All of us craved them, but our doctors and dieticians knew best. I tried to get in touch with my sister and her family at Santo Tomas, but was strongly advised against going there because the battle still raged nearby. I learned of news through a young lady who had been interned at Santo Tomas and was helping our forces register us. Lucy, Carl, and Roberta were well, but my younger niece, little Esten, about eight years of age, had died from cerebral meningitis about three or four months ago.[9]

Our Red Cross worker came in that afternoon bringing mail, stationary, and pencils for our first letters home. I received one of the great joys of liberation: two letters from my beloved wife and my daughters and one letter from mother. They were just a few weeks old and had come up to me through our forces in the south. I was given the courtesy of a 25 word radio message home, but before it could get out of the city the work of our broadcasting systems had heralded the good news of my rescue to my loved ones at home.

It was a big moment for my family as they were ready to go to church when the telephone rang.

"Turn on our radio. Your husband is in Manila."

It was too late, but during the day friends called and telephoned to repeat the words of Mrs. Mary M. Harries who had been interviewed by a broadcaster at Santo Tomas. She mentioned my name as an old friend better known as "Pop Hardee" who had walked into Manila today and was with her.[10]

That night Santo Tomas was shelled by the Japs. My thoughts turned to my people there. I rushed to see the young lady the first thing next morning who had told me of them the day before. I met her as she arrived at Bilibid. She believed them to be safe, and had seen a list of 35 dead but their names were not on it. I felt easier and went back to the barracks and packed up Hutson's things and gave them to a Red Cross man to be carried to him at Santo Tomas. The Red Cross worker put them on his jeep, reached in his pocket and dug out a note from Louis.[11]

"Lucy had a slight accident last night. She wants you to come over here and be with her. Am doing all I can from this end to get you transferred to this hospital."

Our headquarters had just been turned down on a similar request for Chaplain Wilcox, whose daughter and family were there. They believed they could do something for me due to my sister's accident and the recent loss of her younger daughter, but their attempts by phone were fruitless. I went back to the barracks in despair, but no sooner had I arrived than an orderly came from headquarters.[12]

"Colonel Hardee and Chaplain Wilcox will be at the east gate with their baggage for transfer to Santo Tomas in ten minutes. Remaining personnel will pack and be ready to move north by trucks at daylight."

The chaplain and I took off quickly and it was the last time we were to see our fellows from Bilibid together again. It was a welcome change. Santo Tomas was crowded with civilian internees, many my old friends whom I had not seen since the war began. Lucy's accident was more than slight. Louis had broken the news gently. A piece of Jap high explosive had instantly killed the woman with whom she was talking and carried away the calf of Lucy's left leg and five inches of the small bone. She was emaciated and suffering, but it was an unspeakable joy to be with her and her little family.

There was some doubt as to whether we should inform mother of Lucy's injury. She was in the high seventies, had five sons in the armed service, and we felt that she had been worried a great deal about us in the Philippines. We were afraid the news would precede us in some exaggerated form. She had always met the problems of life courageously so we decided to write her. Sure enough, the bad news preceded our letter by those who arrived at home before the mail, but it did not reach her in a shocking or exaggerated form as we had feared. In a day or two we were sent over to an evacuation hospital in the Quezon Memorial Hospital that had been left standing by the Japs who had torn out its plumbing and metal installations.

The Battle of Manila was still raging. The Japs were strongly defending the walled city (Intramuros) and were fighting desperately along the line of Taft Avenue. Our guns were constantly shelling strong points that had been located in big well-constructed public buildings. Our hospital was shelled the night after our arrival by Jap guns. Why couldn't the destroyers get on out of the city and fight it out with our forces in the open? They should know that they could only bring destruction on themselves, on thousands of innocent men, women and children, and the city itself. If this is what they wanted they succeeded admirably.

The city that had been burning for days continued to billow great columns of smoke to the sky. Tales of numerous atrocities came back to us by our wounded. We knew the inhabitants were being trapped and killed like rats.[13]

We were uneasy about Auntie Florence Margaret Olsen, my brother-in-law's old aunt. She had been a patient for a long time in the Philippine General Hospital that was located on Taft Avenue about the line of fighting. I located the surgeon of the 37th Division, described her and asked that his men bring her in to me as soon as they located her. Next afternoon they brought her in on a litter. She was dazed, half-conscious, and did not know any of us for hours. She was up in the seventies, the widow of one of our fine Spanish-American veterans who had made his home in Manila after the American occupation at the beginning of the century and had died there. The Japs had by starvation reduced her to a living skeleton, with long thick gray flowing hair. It was days before we could get her story.

While they were fighting through the hospital, she had attempted to get out of the way of bullets, flying debris, and traffic by lying on the floor and rolling under a bed. A Jap brutally kicked her with a large hob-nailed shoe on her hip. This caused her leg to wither and break out with a terrible case of shingles. She was a bed patient for some time after arrival at San Francisco.

Soon after the brutal kicking, G.I.s picked her up on a litter and while carrying her to the ambulance she spotted three Japs in civilian clothes standing in the yard by the walk. They could not deceive her. She had lived in the Orient too long for that. She pointed them out to the litter carriers, including the one she believed had kicked her.

"Excuse us, lady, but you wouldn't mind if we killed them?"

"By all means."

So they lowered her litter to the walk, drew their automatics and after calmly finishing off the Japs, loaded her in the ambulance and proceeded. It seemed stranger than fiction that it should happen to her.

Colonel Hutson and the other liberated sick prisoners of war left to be flown to Leyte and come home by boat. I didn't feel able to fly and requested that my family be kept together and that all sail on the first hospital ship to leave Manila Bay. The request was honored and we were soon transferred back to Santo Tomas where the Fifth Field Hospital had been set up.

As the fighting was moving further away each day, our nerves began to settle, we were partly relaxed, and I began to put on a pound per day to make up for my 70 pound loss, but we were always hungry and craved chocolates and cheese. My pellagra had disappeared; the beriberi was disappearing. I was gaining strength and could walk very well. I went down to visit the advance supply base just established in the city and met many old friends, including the executive officer who had waved us good bye at San Francisco on November 1, 1941. He asked if I had been promoted. I replied in the affirmative but stated I had no insignia and no place to buy it as exchanges had not yet opened. He plucked off his and he and General Frink seemed to get quite a kick out of pinning on my eagles.[14]

I thought with my eagles flying I would see if they would talk, so I visited the mess officer at the LUBSEC and told my story about my family wanting cheese and chocolates. I caught a *calesa* (little pony cart) back to Santo Tomas and went directly to the nipa shack of my brother-in-law where he, Roberta, and Bill and Jane Wolfe were eating lunch.[15]

"I see you have your eagles flying," said Carl.

"And talking too," I replied as I set a carton box on the chair beside him.

"I've made a raid, you see."

"No, your eagles are not talking, Dave," said Jane Wolfe. "If you asked me I'd say they had been screaming," for my niece Roberta was pulling a carton of chewing gum, a carton of cigarettes, a carton of chocolate, and an eight-pound can of American cheese out of the box I had presented them. They put on the smile that doesn't wear off, for they had been hungry for these things for so long.

One afternoon, while at the Fifth Field Hospital dreaming of home and awaiting transportation, an aide came into the ward and inquired for me. Mrs. MacArthur wished to see me. She had recently come up from Australia, and was making the rounds of the hospitals talking to old friends and cheering the sick—a noble and brave woman. It was a very great delight to talk to an American lady whose smiling countenance did not show the strain and pinch of starvation that marked the faces of all our liberated women at Santo Tomas.[16]

It was also a great joy to see a lady neatly and tastily dressed in varied colors, just as I was soon to see my wife, daughters, and others when we finally got out of the war zone. All of our women who had been interned by the Japanese were forced to dress themselves and their children in pillow covers and bed sheets that they had ingeniously fashioned into clothes, too often without the dyes necessary to effect any tasty combination of colors. We chatted at length of the old days of retreat from Manila, the hard days of Corregidor, the whereabouts of old friends and the joy that awaited me in my homecoming. She took her leave to call on my sister whom she told not to worry over me as the old devilish twinkle had come back into my eyes.

Our ward surgeon carried Chaplain Wilcox and me to look over Manila. The Pearl of the Orient was a desecrated and sad wreck. The three bridges across the Pasig River had been blown by the Japs. Everything on the north side of the river from a couple of blocks from the water's edge including Escolta, the main business and financial section, had been burned; the mass of blackened ruins came to the very doors of Bilibid where we had been jailed. On the south side of the river that contained the old and historic walled city, the public buildings, piers, and beautiful residences of Dewey Boulevard were a massive wreck and ruined beyond replacement. Only a few buildings could ever be repaired without tearing them down to their foundations. Most of them were already down to their foundations.[17]

The beautiful legislative building made of reinforced concrete and the new treasury building were unrecognizable. The massive steel reinforcements hung down the sides like naked chicken wire. Everything on Taft Avenue, another beautiful residential street, lay in ruins. Even the city streets were a series of holes which the jeep climbed slowly into and out of. Thousands of lives and millions in property had been wiped out. The picturesque old Fort Santiago at the end of the walled city that commanded the mouth of the river was a massive and unrecognizable pit of rock, brick, and mortar. The stench of death filled our nostrils at almost every place.[18]

The Japs in their fanatical suicidal stand had accomplished with their passing the greatest possible loss of lives and property. I went twice through Bilibid—now a Jap prison camp. Before we were marched away this conversion began. We derived great pleasure in seeing our forces march the captives in. Now I was looking for some of my old jailers. I had some good recipes of burned half-cooked rice and thin sweet potato vine soup to recommend, but there was not a familiar face there among all the prisoners. Our combat troops had done a fine job of helping them to die for their emperor.

Santo Tomas was the scene of much activity on the morning of April 9. Baggage had been crated and loaded the afternoon and night before. By mid-afternoon, we were on the *Cape Meares*, anchored out in north Manila Bay. We sailed early the next day, passed the old wrecks of Jap ships in the bay, and were soon cruising by Corregidor, the rock of tragic memory. In some of its few remaining trees hung white parachutes, grim reminders of our paratroopers' work in taking the island a few weeks before. Soon we were in the open sea—ten ships in the convoy. Manila was to our backs, a place of sad and tragic memories, a great scar on our hearts that will go with many who loved it so well to their graves.[19]

We broke from the convoy at Leyte and lay there in the gulf for a few days awaiting another to form. *Cape Meares* was a small troop transport ship, ill-adapted for hospital missions. It had an extra hospital medical team aboard. The crew gave up their staterooms to the sick. There were not many bed cases. I shared the troop commander's cabin and bath with him. My cot was comfortable, but the heat at night during the blackouts was almost insufferable. The crew did everything that willing hands and loving hearts could do to make our trip pleasant. The food was good. We had been through so much that everything delighted us.

We were soon away from Leyte on a week's voyage to Eniwetok in the Marshalls. We bucked an equatorial current all the way and this cooled down the boat. At Eniwetok many ships lay in the atoll-surrounded bay. We took on oil and some complained that there was not time to go ashore, while others consoled them with the thought that had one never been here it would be nothing out of his life. We had less than a day at Honolulu without opportunity to go ashore.

By noon on May 12 we were passing the islands that lay a few miles out of San Francisco Bay. I began to feel relieved. I was the senior officer aboard.

The transport officer and the ship's captain had given me certain limitations because we would have to function together in case of disaster. We had passed through two submarine actions and an alarm. It seems that tragedy had stalked us to the Golden Gate. Soon we were standing on the forward deck. The fog was beginning to raise. The voice of the transport chaplain was coming through the boat's loud speakers.

"On the right you will see the Cliff House. Over behind it are the radio towers for the Presidio of San Francisco. The fog is now breaking, so look straight ahead and you will see the Golden Gate Bridge."

"Your troubles are now behind you."

We looked ahead and bowed our heads with reverence and thanked God for our lives and America.

"Where slaves once more their native lands behold."

There was no tongue able to utter, and no voice capable to pitch or even hum the tune "California Here We Come, Right Back Where We Started From"—a tune so often heard in Jap concentration camps—for those whose eyes were not blinded with tears were using all the composure they possessed to hold them back. We should not have been ashamed of them for they were neither tears of sorrow or anger but the kind everyone should love to shed. As we passed under the great arch of the bridge, the sun broke through the thinning clouds and illuminated the gigantic structure. We looked up. It was home sweet home. It could have been no more beautiful a sight to us if it were gold-plated.

Appendix

Military Decorations and Medal Citations

MILITARY DECORATIONS OF COLONEL DAVID L. HARDEE

- Distinguished Service Cross
- Silver Star with three Bronze Oak Leaf Clusters
- Bronze Star Medal
- Purple Heart with one Bronze Oak Leaf Cluster
- Prisoner of War Medal
- World War I Victory Medal with five Battle Clasps, (France Service Clasp, Aisne-Marne, Montidier-Noyon, Meuse-Argonne, and Defensive Sector)
- Army of Occupation of Germany Medal
- Yangtze Service Medal
- American Defense Service Medal with Foreign Service Clasp
- American Campaign Medal
- Asiatic-Pacific Campaign Medal with two Bronze Service Stars
- World War II Victory Medal
- Presidential Unit Citation with two Bronze Oak Leaf Clusters
- Combat Infantryman Badge
- Philippine Presidential Unit Citation
- Philippine Defense Medal with one Bronze Service Star
- Philippine Liberation Medal with one Bronze Service Star
- Philippine Independence Medal

DISTINGUISHED SERVICE CROSS

The President of the United States of America, authorized by Act of Congress July 9, 1918, takes pleasure in presenting the Distinguished Service Cross to Colonel (Infantry), [then Lieutenant Colonel] David Lyddall Hardee (ASN: O-11903), United States Army, for extraordinary heroism in action at Orion and Limay, Bataan, Philippine Islands, on April 7–8, 1942. Colonel Hardee was serving in the capacity of Executive Officer of a Provisional Air Corps Regiment, operating as Infantry. Although suffering from disease and so weak he could scarcely walk, he had remained on front-line duty for 73 days, refusing evacuation. On April 7, 1942, Colonel Hardee's regiment was attacked on its front, left flank, and left rear by a superior enemy ground force supported by heavy artillery fire and by numerous enemy bombers. During the two days conflict which followed, Colonel Hardee, continually under enemy fire, visited and rallied the troops, directing them to new positions, personally leading convoys and supervising the maintenance of communications. The resolute, calm and determined leadership of this officer while under hostile fire was in a large measure responsible for the regiment's fighting six delaying actions in two days, throughout which it preserved its combat integrity and was still fighting astride the main approach to our rear area when the final action of the Bataan operation terminated. The courage, heroism, and personal example displayed by Colonel Hardee upheld the highest tradition of the military service.

General Orders: Headquarters, U.S. Army Forces in the Far East, General Orders No. 69 (April 7, 1945)
Action Date: April 7–8, 1942
Service: Army
Rank: Colonel

SILVER STAR

The President of the United States of America, authorized by Act of Congress July 9, 1918, takes pleasure in presenting the Silver Star to First Lieutenant (Infantry) David Lyddall Hardee (ASN: O-11903), United States Army, for gallantry in action while serving with the 28th Infantry Regiment, 1st Division, American Expeditionary Forces. A soldier with splendid qualities of courage and bravery, during the Meuse-Argonne Operation, October 4–12, 1918, he displayed great gallantry and devotion to duty.

General Orders: Headquarters, 2d Infantry Brigade, American Forces in Germany, General Orders No. 6 (July 12, 1919)
Action Date: October 4–12, 1918
Service: Army
Rank: First Lieutenant
Regiment: 28th Infantry Regiment
Division: 1st Division, American Expeditionary Forces

SILVER STAR

The President of the United States of America, authorized by Act of Congress July 9, 1918, takes pleasure in presenting a Bronze Oak Leaf Cluster in lieu of a Second Award of the Silver Star to First Lieutenant (Infantry), [then Second Lieutenant] David Lyddall Hardee (ASN: O-11903), United States Army, for gallantry in action while serving with the 3d Battalion, 28th Infantry Regiment, 1st Division, American Expeditionary Forces, in action near Exermont, France, October 9, 1918. In the advance of 9 October he aided the progress of his battalion by his aggressiveness and was instrumental in the capture and holding of Hill 263. In the assault on the hill he fearlessly led his men through more than 100 yards of dense, shoulder-high underbrush which was impregnated with a persistent type of powdered gas, across the bottom of a ravine on which enemy machine guns were concentrating their fire. This fire caused severe losses, which would have held up the advance and had not his heroic example inspired his men to follow instead of holding on in the woods where there was cover.

General Orders: War Department, General Orders No. 15 (April 5, 1923)
Action Date: October 9, 1918
Service: Army
Rank: First Lieutenant
Battalion: 3d Battalion
Regiment: 28th Infantry Regiment
Division: 1st Division, American Expeditionary Forces

SILVER STAR

The President of the United States of America, authorized by Act of Congress July 9, 1918, takes pleasure in presenting a Second Bronze Oak Leaf Cluster in lieu of a Third Award of the Silver Star to First Lieutenant (Infantry), [then Second Lieutenant] David Lyddall Hardee (ASN: O-11903), United States Army, for gallantry in action while serving with the 3d Battalion, 28th Infantry Regiment, 1st Division, American Expeditionary Forces, in action at Cheveuges, France, November 7, 1918, while engaged with the enemy near the heights of Sedan. The battalion being halted temporarily by intense machine gun and artillery fire from both front and flanks delivered from the heights above the town, he moved the battalion forward by the use of whistle and visual signals, transmitted in the face of terrific enemy fire. His indifference to danger and his devotion to duty were by force of example largely responsible for the success of the battalion in this operation.

General Orders: War Department, General Orders No. 13 (March 31, 1923)
Action Date: November 7, 1918
Service: Army
Rank: First Lieutenant
Battalion: 3d Battalion
Regiment: 28th Infantry Regiment
Division: 1st Division, American Expeditionary Forces

SILVER STAR

The President of the United States of America, authorized by Act of Congress July 9, 1918, takes pleasure in presenting a Third Bronze Oak Leaf Cluster in lieu of a Fourth Award of the Silver Star to Lieutenant Colonel (Infantry) David Lyddall Hardee (ASN: O-11903), United States Army, for gallantry in action on the afternoon of April 8, 1942, when the enemy was bombing and strafing our position south of Limay, Philippine Islands, and were infiltrating to within a few hundred yards in preparation for an attack. This officer voluntarily went forward and organized the main line of resistance, when bombed and strafed by a formation of nine hostile bombers. His presence and example was an inspiration to all the men of his regiment.

General Orders: Headquarters, II Philippine Corps in the Field, General Orders No. 46 (April 9, 1942)
Action Date: April 8, 1942
Service: Army
Rank: Lieutenant Colonel

BRONZE STAR

By direction of the President, under the provisions of Executive Order 9419, February 4, 1944 (Sec. II, WD Bul. 3, 1944), a Bronze Star is awarded to Colonel (Infantry), [then Lieutenant Colonel] David Lyddall Hardee (ASN: O-11903), Provisional Air Corps Regiment, operating as Infantry, for exemplary conduct in ground combat against the armed enemy in January 1942, in the Pacific Theater of Operations.

General Orders: Department of the Army, Letter Orders (October 12, 1949)
Action Date: January 1942
Service: Army
Rank: Colonel

Notes

EDITOR'S INTRODUCTION

1. William S. Powell, *North Carolina Lives: The Tar Heel Who's Who* (Hopkinsville, KY: Historical Record Association, 1962), 543; Hugh T. Leffler, *History of North Carolina: Family and Personal History,* vol. 3 (New York: Lewis Historical Publishing Co., Inc., 1956), 43; David L. Hardee, *The Eastern North Carolina Hardy—Hardee Family in the South and Southwest* (Raleigh, NC: David L. Hardee, 1966), 160; "Synopsis of the Work of Colonel David L. Hardee," undated, in possession of Mrs. Mary Hardee Stutz, Havelock, NC.

2. Officer's Record Book for David L. Hardee, David L. Hardee Papers (DLHP), Military Collection, Miscellaneous Papers, Various Dates, Box 79, State Archives of North Carolina, Raleigh, NC (NCA); "Another Tar Heel in First Division Parade," *Wilmington Morning Star,* September 20, 1919, 6; Leffler, *History,* 43.

3. Commendation for Recruiting Work from Commanding General, 1st Division, Camp Zackary Taylor to 1st Lieutenant David L. Hardee, April 25, 1920, Box 79, DLHP, NCA; "Salisbury is Scene of Pretty Marriage," *Greensboro Daily News,* October 8, 1922, 10; Robert T. Finney, *History of the Air Corps Tactical School, 1920–1940* (1955; reprint, Washington, DC: Air Force History and Museums Program, 1998), 116; David L. Hardee to Willis Smith, May 28, 1951, Carl Thomas Durham Papers, #3507, Box 61, Southern Historical Collection, Wilson Library, University of North Carolina at Chapel Hill, NC.

4. David L. Hardee to Willis Smith, May 28, 1951, Carl Thomas Durham Papers, #3507, Box 61, Southern Historical Collection, Wilson Library, University of North Carolina at Chapel Hill, NC; "Army Orders and Assignments," *NYT,* November 29, 1924, 27; "Fort Benning Aerial Demonstration is Underway Today," *Thomasville* (GA) *Times-Enterprise,* May 3, 1927, 7; David L. Hardee, "Infantry's Defense Against Combat Aviation," *Infantry Journal* 29 (July 1926): 50–55; David L. Hardee, "The Air Corps and the Infantry," *Infantry Journal* 30 (March

1927): 265–74; David L. Hardee, "Recent Developments on Protection of Infantry Against Aircraft," *Infantry Journal* 32 (March 1928): 249–56.

5. Leffler, *History,* 43; Powell, *Lives,* 543; "Army Captain Given Yangtze Service Medal," *Winston-Salem Journal,* March 14, 1935, 12; Army Orders and Assignments," *NYT,* September 12, 1934, 46; "Synopsis of the Work of Colonel David L. Hardee," undated, in possession of Mrs. Mary Hardee Stutz, Havelock, NC; "To Leave City," *Twin-City* (Winston-Salem, NC) *Sentinel,* March 5, 1938, 3; "Army Orders and Assignments," *NYT,* March 4, 1938, 38; Department of War, Adjutant General's Office, *Official Army Register,* 1 January 1943 (Washington, DC: Government Printing Office [GPO], 1943), 375.

6. "Army Orders and Assignments," *NYT,* March 26, 1941, 44; telegram from David L. Hardee to Mrs. Elizabeth Hardee, September 18, 1941, DLHP, Box 79, NCA.

7. Special Orders No. 24, January 26, 1942, Headquarters, USAFFE, Record Group (RG)496, Records of General Headquarters, Southwest Pacific Area and United States Army Forces, Pacific, USAFFE, Box 54, National Archives and Records Administration at College Park, MD (NARA).

8. Stanley L. Falk, *Bataan: The March of Death* (New York: W.W. Norton, 1962), 11.

9. Office of the Adjutant General, Army *Battle Casualties and Nonbattle Deaths in World War II: Final Report, 7 December 1941–31 December 1946* (Washington, DC: Department of the Army, 1953), 95; Mary Ellen Condon-Rall and Albert E. Cowdrey, *The Medical Department: Medical Service in the War Against Japan* (Washington, DC: U.S. Army Center of Military History [CMH], 1998), 383.

10. Robert C. Doyle, *A Prisoner's Duty: Great Escapes in U.S. Military History* (Annapolis, MD: Naval Institute Press, 1997), 150–55; Robert C. Doyle, *Voices from Captivity: Interpreting the American POW Narrative* (Lawrence, KS: University Press of Kansas, 1994), 47–53; Linda Goetz Holmes, *Unjust Enrichment: American POWs Under the Rising Sun* (Old Saybrook, CT: Konecky and Konecky, 2001), 10–21; Yuki Tanaka, *Hidden Horrors: Japanese War Crimes in World War II* (Boulder, CO: Westview Press, 1996), 16–18, 37–40, 73–74, 198–208; S. P. MacKenzie, "The Treatment of Prisoners of War in World War II," *Journal of Modern History* 66, no. 3 (September 1994): 512–18; Philip A. Towle, "Japanese Treatment of Prisoners in 1904–05—Foreign Officers' Reports," *Military Affairs* 39, no. 3 (October 1975): 115–18; John E. Olson, *O'Donnell: Andersonville of the Pacific* (John E. Olson, 1985), 163–75; Gavan Daws, *Prisoners of the Japanese: POWs of World War II in the Pacific* (New York: William Morrow, 1994), 96–99; U.S. Department of State, *Foreign Relations of the United States: Diplomatic Papers, 1942,* vol. 1

(Washington, DC: Government Printing Office [GPO], 1960), 796–800; International Committee of the Red Cross (ICRC), *Convention Relative to the Treatment of Prisoners of War,* Geneva, July 27, 1929.

11. Wartime POW memoirs: William E. Dyess, *The Dyess Story: The Eye-Witness Account of the Death March from Bataan and the Narrative of Experiences in Japanese Prison Camps and of Eventual Escape,* ed. Charles Leavelle (New York: G. P. Putnam's Sons, 1944); Melvin H. McCoy, Stephen M. Mellnik, and Welbourn Kelley, *Ten Escape from Tojo* (New York: Farrar and Rinehart, 1944). Postwar accounts: Jonathan M. Wainwright, *General Wainwright's Story: The Account of Four Years of Humiliating Defeat, Surrender, and Captivity,* ed. Robert Considine (Garden City, NY: Doubleday, 1946); Calvin Ellsworth Chunn, ed., *Of Rice and Men: The Story of Americans Under the Rising Sun* (Tulsa, OK: Veterans' Publishing Co., 1946); Alan McCracken, *Very Soon Now, Joe* (New York: Hobson Book Press, 1947); Robert Reynolds, *Of Rice and Men* (Philadelphia: Dorrance, 1947).

12. Memoirs from decades removed: Paul L. Ashton, *Bataan Diary* and *And Somebody Gives a Damn!* (Santa Barbara, CA: Ashton, 1984; 1990); William A. Berry with James Edwin Alexander, *Prisoner of the Rising Sun* (Norman, OK: University of Oklahoma Press, 1993); John R. Bumgarner, *Parade of the Dead: A U.S. Army Physician's Memoir of Imprisonment by the Japanese, 1942–1945* (Jefferson, NC: McFarland and Co., 1995); Eugene C. Jacobs, *Blood Brothers: A Medic's Sketch Book* (New York: Carlton Press, 1985); Gene S. Jacobsen, *We Refused to Die: My Time as a Prisoner of War in Bataan and Japan, 1942–1945* (Salt Lake City, UT: University of Utah Press, 2004); Manny Lawton, *Some Survived: An Eyewitness Account of the Bataan Death March and the Men Who Lived Through It* (Chapel Hill: Algonquin Books, 2004); Carl S. Nordin, *We Were Next to Nothing: An American POW's Account of Japanese Prison Camps and Deliverance in World War II* (Jefferson, NC: McFarland and Co., 1997). Scholarly works: E. Bartlett Kerr, *Surrender and Survival: The Experience of American POWs in the Pacific, 1941–1945 (New York: William Morrow, 1985);* Donald Knox, *Death March: The Survivors of Bataan* (New York: Harcourt Brace Jovanovich, 1981); Gavan Daws, *Prisoners;* Brian MacArthur, *Surviving the Sword: Prisoners of the Japanese in the Far East, 1942–45.* New York: Random House, 2005); Gregory F. Michno, *Death on the Hellships: Prisoners at Sea in the Pacific War* (Annapolis, MD: Naval Institute Press, 2001); Tanaka, *Horrors.* Journalistic histories or accounts: John D. Lukacs, *Escape from Davao: The Forgotten Story of the Most Daring Prison Break of the Pacific War* (New York: Simon and Schuster, 2010); Bill Sloan, *Undefeated: America's Heroic Fight for Bataan and Corregidor* (New York: Simon and Schuster, 2012); John A. Glusman, *Conduct Under Fire: Four*

American Doctors and Their Fight for Life as Prisoners of the Japanese, 1941–1945 (New York: Penguin, 2005); Duane Heisinger, *Father Found* (Longwood, FL: Xulon Press, 2003). Previously unpublished memoirs: Damon Gause, *The War Journal of Major Damon "Rocky" Gause* (New York: Hyperion, 1999); Thomas Hayes, *Bilibid Diary: The Secret Notebooks of Commander Thomas Hayes, POW, the Philippines, 1942–45,* ed. A. B. Feuer (Hamden, CT: Archon Books, 1987); Irvin Alexander, *Surviving Bataan and Beyond: Colonel Irvin Alexander's Odyssey as a Japanese Prisoner of War,* ed. Dominic J. Caraccilo (Mechanicsburg, PA: Stackpole, 1999); Lewis Beebe, *Prisoner of the Rising Sun: The Lost Diary of Brig. Gen. Lewis Beebe,* ed. John M. Beebe (College Station, TX: Texas A&M University Press, 2006).

13 Edgar A. Quinn to David L. Hardee, May 11, 1945, letter in possession of Mrs. Mary Hardee Stutz, Havelock, NC.

14. Doyle, *Voices,* 3–5, 81–85.

15. "Col. Hardee Says Death Preferable to Jap Camp," *News and Observer* (Raleigh, NC), August 14, 1945, 5; "Horrors of Jap Prisons Related by Col. Hardee," *News and Observer,* August 19, 1945, 3, 6; "Invasion by 'Heathens' Worse Than Sherman's 'Hell'—Hardee," *Twin-City Sentinel,* July 3, 1945, 1; House Committee on Interstate and Foreign Commerce, *Enemy Property Commission Hearings,* 80th Cong., 1st sess., 1947, 365–70; Mary Hardee Stutz, interview by author, Havelock, NC, September 11, 2013; David L. Hardee, "Memoirs of a Jap Prisoner of War" (Unpublished memoir, 1946, in possession of United States Military Academy Library, West Point, NY), inscription on cover.

16. Military Record and Report of Separation Certificate of Service for David L. Hardee (DD-214) in possession of Mrs. Mary Hardee Stutz, Havelock, NC; "CD Chief Named for Wake," *News and Observer,* February 16, 1954; "Col. Hardee Will Retire," *News and Observer,* May 9, 1961, 24; Mary Hardee Stutz, interview by author, Havelock, NC, September 11, 2013; "Col. Hardee is Named to National Position," *Raleigh Times,* August 1, 1957, 2; "Legion of Valor Members Meet," *Fayetteville* (NC) *Observer,* January 12, 1958; "The Last Retreat," *General Orders—Legion of Valor,* Nov-Dec 1969, 10; "Col. David L. Hardee Dies Here at Age 79," *News and Observer,* November 25, 1969, 10; "Former CD Head Dies Here," *Raleigh Times,* November 24, 1969, 1.

FOREWORD

1. The Battle of Bladensburg occurred in the War of 1812 on August 24, 1814, where a large force of untrained American troops were routed and defeated by a small force of British veterans. This defeat resulted in the capture of Washington, DC, and the burning of many public buildings. The first Battle of Bull Run on July 21,

1861, in the American Civil War again witnessed Federal forces routed and defeated by Confederates. Washington, DC, was not attacked, but its defense threatened.

2. Major General Charles E. Kilbourne, Jr., of Virginia received the Medal of Honor for his actions in the Philippine-American War. Postwar, in the late 1920s, he initiated the development of what became the Malinta Tunnel on Corregidor. Charles M. Hubbard and Collis H. Davis, Jr., *Corregidor in Peace and War* (Columbia: University of Missouri Press, 2006), 63–66; "Gen. Charles E. Kilbourne Dies; Medal of Honor Holder Was 90," *New York Times*, November 13, 1963, 41.

CHAPTER 1 THE WAR IS ON

1. South Dakota native Arthur W. Wermuth, Jr., of the 1st Battalion, 57th Infantry (PS), gained fame for leading small scouting units behind enemy lines. He was liberated in August 1945 from a prison camp in Mukden, Manchuria. Clark Lee, *The Call it Pacific* (New York: Viking Press, 1943), 234–36; "'One-Man Army,' Capt. Wermuth of Bataan, Freed," *Los Angeles Times* (*LAT*), August 30, 1945, 1, 2; Donald J. Young, *The Battle of Bataan: A Complete History*, 2d ed. (Jefferson, NC: McFarland and Co., 2009), 29, 118.

2. Originally the Department Hospital, Manila, Philippines, the hospital served as the general hospital for the Philippine Department. In 1920 the army renamed in honor of Army Medical Corps founder Brigadier General George Miller Sternberg.

3. 31st Infantry: U.S. Army, 31st Infantry Regiment, "History of the 31st Infantry Regiment" (Carlisle, PA: U.S. Army Military History Institute, 1958), 1–2; John W. Whitman, *Bataan: Our Last Ditch: The Bataan Campaign, 1942* (New York: Hippocrene Books, 1990), 180. Shanghai Incident: Herbert P. Bix, *Hirohito and the Making of Modern Japan* (New York: Harper Collins Pub., 2000), 250–51; Meirion Harries and Susie Harries, *Soldiers of the Sun: The Rise and Fall of the Imperial Japanese Army* (New York: Random House, 1991), 159–62; Donald A. Jordan, *China's Trial by Fire: The Shanghai War of 1932* (Ann Arbor, MI: University of Michigan Press, 2001). Open Door Policy: Walter LaFeber, *The New Empire: An Interpretation of American Expansion, 1860–1898* (Ithaca, NY: Cornell University Press, 1963), 30, 43–44; Michael H. Hunt, *Ideology and U.S. Foreign Policy* (New Haven, CT: Yale University Press, 1987), 4–11.

4. Training of Philippine divisions: Louis Morton, *The Fall of the Philippines* (1953; reprint, Washington, DC: CMH, 1989), 25–30; Mellnick, *Philippine*, 19–32; Whitman, *Ditch*, 16–38. Camp Wheeler, located near Macon, Georgia was in existence from 1917–19 and 1940–46. For the latter period, it served as an infantry replacement center to provide army recruits with basic and advanced individual training. Louis D. Hutson of South Carolina commanded the 33rd Infantry (PA)

until being severely wounded on January 19, 1942 when he took a machine gun bullet in his right hip which hit his pelvis and exited through his intestines. He miraculously survived the wound and was liberated from Bilibid Prison on February 4, 1945. David L. Hardee to Elizabeth Hardee, February 14, 1942, Box 79, DLHP, NCA; "Relatives Receive Word of Col. Hutson," *Aiken* (SC) *Standard and Review,* July 24, 1942, 1; "Hutson Wounded in Philippines," *Aiken Standard and Review,* February 4, 1942, 1; "Back from Jap Prison, Has Joyous Reunion," *Aiken Standard and Review,* March 16, 1945, 1; "Col. Louis Hutson Brings News of Aiken Men Held by Japs," *Aiken Standard and Review,* March 14, 1945, 1.

5. The luxury liner SS *President Coolidge* was built for the Dollar Steamship Lines before being transferred to the American President Lines in 1938 and converted into a troopship in 1941. On October 26, 1942, while ferrying the bulk of the 43rd Infantry Division to the island of Espiritu Santo in the Republic of Vanuatu, she accidentally struck two American mines and sank. David Doubilet, "Wreck of the Coolidge," *National Geographic* 173, no. 4 (April 1988): 458–67. North Dakota native Lough commanded the Philippine Division. Chynoweth of Wyoming and Vachon of Maine were promoted to brigadier general on December 20, 1941. Chynoweth commanded the 61st Division (PA), and Vachon the 101st Division (PA). In March, Chynoweth assumed command of the Visayan Force, and Vachon the Cotabato-Davao sector forces. Steel of Maryland commanded the 31st Infantry (U.S.) but on March 1, 1942 became chief of staff for II Corps. All four men were liberated in Mukden, Manchuria, in August 1945. Whitman, *Ditch,* 71, 180; "Gen. Lough in New Post: He is Appointed to Command Philippines Department," *NYT,* November 29, 1941, 4; "Ten U.S. and Six Philippine Generals Captured on Bataan," *Washington Post* (*WP*), April 18, 1942, 3; "Gen. Chynoweth Awarded D.S.M.," *WP,* November 17, 1942, 3; Marshall Andrews, "4 Brigadiers, 12 Colonels are Advanced," *WP,* December 20, 1941, 5; "New Experience," *WP,* October 1, 1945, 6; Morton, *Philippines,* 69n29, 360, 501, 512–13; D. Clayton James, ed., *South to Bataan, North to Mukden: The Prison Diary of Brigadier General W. E. Brougher* (Athens, GA: University of Georgia Press, 1971), 58, 68.

6. See note 24.

7. Lieutenant Colonel Irving Compton of Colorado served at the II Philippine Corps headquarters. He died on December 15, 1944, in the sinking of *Oryoku Maru.* Michno, *Hellships,* 258–62; "Widow Gets Medal for Husband's Courage," *Lodi* (CA) *News-Sentinel,* September 26, 1987, 5; Compton, Irving, RG389, Records of the Office of the Provost Marshal General, (POW-PGM) Electronic and Special Media Records Services Division, NARA.

8. Established in 1908 adjacent to the town of Wahiawa on Oahu, the barracks remain the home of the 25th Infantry Division since 1941. They are named in

honor of Lieutenant General John M. Schofield, a Medal of Honor recipient and former Commanding General of the United State Army.

9. The SS *President Pierce* of the Dollar Steamship Lines was commandeered by the army on July 31, 1941 and renamed the USAT *Hugh L. Scott*. On August 14, 1942, the U.S. Navy acquired the vessel and commissioned her as the USS *Hugh L. Scott* (AP-43) on September 7, 1942. The German submarine *U-130* sank the *Scott* at Fedala Bay, Morocco, on November 12, 1942. "Hugh L. Scott (AP-13)," Dictionary of American Naval Fighting Ships (DANFS) online; USS *Louisville:* "Louisville (CA-28)," DANFS online.

10. Built in the 1920s at a cost of 12 million pesos, the concrete and steel pier was 1,400 feet long and 240 feet wide and was designed to accommodate luxury ocean liners. C. W. Geiger, "Oil Handling Facilities at the Port of Manila," *Oil and Fat Industries* 7, no. 2 (February 1930): 52.

11. The U.S. Army Corps of Engineers built the Manila Army and Navy Club in 1911, open only to officers. It became a social meeting point and site of business for American military leaders stationed in the Philippines. Fort William McKinley, established in 1901 (permanent land acquired in 1902), served as the headquarters for the United States Army Forces in the Far East's Philippine Division and Philippine Department. On May 15, 1949, the U.S. government turned possession of the fort over to the Philippine government who renamed the installation Fort Andres Bonifacio. While awaiting orders, Hardee was assigned to Headquarters of the Philippine Department. Special Orders No. 87, December 4, 1941, Headquarters, USAFFE, December 4, 1941, RG496, Records of General Headquarters, Southwest Pacific Area and United States Army Forces, Pacific, USAAF, Box 54, NARA.

12. Senator Robert Rice Reynolds was a Democrat from Asheville, North Carolina, who served in the U.S. Senate from 1932 to 1945. A staunch isolationist and nationalist, he opposed the Neutrality Acts and garnered considerable controversy with remarks perceived as pro-fascist and anti-Semitic. Julian M. Pleasants, *Buncombe Bob: The Life and Times of Robert Rice Reynolds* (Chapel Hill: University of North Carolina Press, 2000). Faddis, a Pennsylvania Democrat, resigned his seat in December 1942 to return to active army service. "Faddis, Charles Isiah, (1890–1972)," Biographical Directory of the United States Congress online.

13. Hardee and MacArthur were distant cousins. Hardee, *Hardee Family*, 86–89.

14. Colonel Charles P. Stivers of Illinois was the G-1 under MacArthur. German-born Colonel Charles A. Willoughby served as MacArthur's G-2 throughout the war. A Virginia-native, Major General Richard J. Marshall served as deputy and later outright chief of staff for MacArthur. Lieutenant Colonel LeGrande Diller, a New York native, was MacArthur's press relations advisor. All four men evacuated with MacArthur to Australia in March 1942. Hiroshi Masuda, *MacArthur in Asia: The*

General and His Staff in the Philippines, Japan, and Korea, trans. Reiko Yamamoto (Ithaca, NY: Cornell University Press, 2012), 10–21. Colonel Lewis C. Beebe of Iowa served as MacArthur's G-4 until MacArthur left for Australia, whereupon he was promoted to flag rank and made deputy chief of staff of USAFFE. He was liberated from a prison in Mukden, Manchuria, in August 1945. Beebe, *Rising,* 13–16.

15. Hardee was detailed on temporary duty at USAFFE's Headquarters. Special Orders No. 87, December 4, 1941, RG496, Records of General Headquarters, Southwest Pacific Area and United States Army Forces, Pacific, USAAF, Box 54, NARA. Colonel Lorenzo D. Gasser of Ohio commanded the 31st Infantry from June 1931 to March 1934 while Hardee was a first lieutenant during the Shanghai Incident. "Gen. Lorenzo Gasser, Veteran of 3 Wars," *Washington Post,* October 30, 1955, A14; "Maj. Gen. Gasser, Served in 3 Wars," *NYT,* October 31, 1955, 25.

16. The General Luna, previously the Calle Real del Palacio, is the main thoroughfare in the Intramuros, the walled historic center of Manila built by the Spanish. The Cuartel de Espana served as the military headquarters for the 31st Infantry and MacArthur's command post until his evacuation to Australia in March 1942. The buildings today house the University of the City of Manila (*Pamantasan ng Lungsod ng Maynila*). The Santa Lucia Barracks in 1941 was home to the 31st Infantry. The fighting in Manila in 1945 destroyed the barracks, although postwar the Philippine government used the original walls when rebuilding the structure.

17. Although speculative, this is probably Lieutenant Robert W. Weil of Ohio who died in the Osaka Main Camp, Chikko Osaka, Japan, in August 1943. Lieutenant Short is either Robert E. Short or Edward L. Short. The former was liberated from the Tokyo POW Camp Branch #2 (Kawasaki) in August 1945, and the latter died on *Enoura Maru.* Short, Robert E., and Short, Edward L., War Department, Adjutant General's Office, Records of World War II Prisoners of War, created 1942–1947, RG389, POW-PGM, NARA.

18. The Philippine Scouts in the 45th and 57th Infantry (PS) were the elite of the Filipino troops, totaling over 4,000 men. Young, *Bataan,* 6; Morton, *Philippines,* 21–22, 71.

19. A Maine native, Doane was executive officer of the 31st Infantry (U.S.) prior to the Japanese attacks in December 1941. On January 26, 1942, he was promoted to colonel and placed in command of the Provisional Air Corps Regiment. He was liberated from a prison camp in Mukden, Manchuria, in August 1945. Karl H. Lowe, *America's Foreign Legion: The 31st Infantry Regiment at War and Peace* (book manuscript in progress), Chapter 6, 5, 31stinfantry.org; Sheldon H. Mendelson, "Operations of the Provisional Air Corps Regiment in the Defense of Bataan Peninsula, P.I., 8 January–10 April 1942" (Fort Benning, GA: U.S. Army Infantry School, 1946–1947), 15; "List of Americans Sent from Formosa," *NYT,*

February 10, 1945, 5; Special Orders No. 24, January 26, 1942, Headquarters, USAFFE, RG496, Box 54, NARA.

20. Then-Lieutenant Colonel Clear was a military observer of the Imperial Japanese Army (IJA) prior to the outbreak of hostilities. In July 1941, the U.S. Army assistant chief of staff, G-2, ordered Clear to Singapore to investigate and report "on the advisability and practicality of establishing a system of secret intelligence in the Far East." Caught in Manila at the start of hostilities, he left the country by submarine on February 3, 1942. He spent the remainder of the war at the U.S. Army Command and General Staff School lecturing about the IJA. John G. Doll, *The Battling Bastards of Bataan: A Chronology of the First Days of World War II in the Philippines,* 6th ed. (Bennington, VT: Merriman Press, 2008), 50; "Corregidor Called Bull's Eye for Foe," *NYT,* April 13, 1942, 3; "Honors Two Colonels for Pacific Heroism," *NYT,* July 23, 1942, 12; "Officer Doubts Early End of Japanese War," *LAT,* June 19, 1945, A12; Warren J. Clear, "Close-Up of the Jap Fighting-Man," U.S. Army Command and General Staff School, Fort Leavenworth, KS, October 1942; Warren J. Clear, *Far Eastern Survey Report* (Washington, DC: GPO, 1942), i.

21. Lieutenant Colonel Francis H. Wilson of Virginia was a military aide for MacArthur and joined the general in Australia, later serving on the general's staff in Japan as the chief of the historical section. Masuda, *Asia,* 19–20. Lieutenant Colonel Roy C. Hilton of South Carolina was the assistant chief of staff, G-4, for the Luzon Force at Bataan. He was liberated from a prison camp in Mukden, Manchuria, in August 1945. The Citadel Newsroom, "Cadets Trade Spring Break for Bataan Memorial Death March," *The Citadel,* March 4, 2011, online. Baguio was the summer capital for the Philippine Commonwealth and home to the barracks and military installations, notably Camp John Hay, of the Philippine Army. The Luneta Park (today Rizal Park) is an urban park adjacent to the Intramuros and Manila Bay. December 8, 1941 air attacks: William H. Bartsch, *December 8, 1941: MacArthur's Pearl Harbor* (College Station, TX: Texas A&M University Press, 2003), 267–407; Morton, *Philippines,* 79–90; Wesley Frank Craven and James Lea Cate, *Plans and Early Operations, January 1939 to August 1942,* vol. 1 of *The Army Air Forces in World War II* (1949; reprint, Washington, DC: Office of Air Force History, GPO, 1983), 201–13; John Burton, *Fortnight of Infamy: The Collapse of Allied Airpower West of Pearl Harbor* (Annapolis, MD: Naval Institute Press, 2006), 118–48; Adrian R. Martin and Larry W. Stephenson, *Operation Plum: The Ill-fated 27th Bombardment Group and the Fight for the Western Pacific* (College Station, TX: Texas A&M University Press, 2008), 51–64.

22. Japanese bombers: Mark R. Peattie, *Sunburst: The Rise of Japanese Naval Air Power, 1909–1941* (Annapolis, MD: Naval Institute Press, 2001), 161, 166; Bartsch, *December,* 266–74, 288–90.

23. The Cavite Navy Yard located at Sangley Point, Canacao Point, Cavite, on the eastern half of Manila Bay south of the capital, was home of the U.S. Navy Asiatic Fleet. Nichols Field was home to the 20th Air Base Group and the 17th and 21st Pursuit Squadrons, with the field located south of Manila in Pasay City, Luzon. Craven and Cate, *Plans,* 177, 203; Glusman, *Conduct,* 39–40. December 10, 1941 attacks: Morton, *Philippines,* 94–95; Glusman, *Conduct,* 55–59; Burton, *Fortnight,* 190–96.

24. Gillahan managed to escape the island of Corregidor with a group of 12 nurses (11 army, one navy) aboard the submarine USS *Spearfish* on May 3, 1942, which arrived in Australia by the third week of May. Gillahan returned to the United States with ten of the nurses on July 2, 1942. Whitlow left Corregidor aboard a navy PBY seaplane on the night of April 29, 1942, but it suffered irreparable damage while attempting to take off from Lake Lanao on Mindanao. The passengers surrendered to the Japanese on May 11, 1942 and Whitlow remained at the Santo Tomas Internment Camp in Manila until its liberation in February 1945. Elizabeth M. Norman, *We Band of Angels: The Untold Story of American Nurses Trapped on Bataan by the Japanese* (New York: Random House, 1999), 104–121, 301–303, n1,2,3,14; "Survivors Depict Battles in Pacific," *NYT,* July 3, 1942, 1; "Miss Whitlow Suffered Many Perils of War: Danville Nurse Still Missing," *The Bee* (Danville, VA), August 27, 1942, 1; "Lt. Whitlow Tells About Liberation: She Gives Vivid Description of Life as Prisoner," *The Bee,* March 14, 1945, 3.

25. Morse of Montana commanded the 102nd Division (PA) and the Cagayan Sector during the fight for the island of Mindanao. Captured in May 1942, he was liberated from a prison camp in Mukden, Manchuria, in August 1945. Morton, *Philippines,* 516–18; "Japanese Move Wainwright and Other Captives," *LAT,* February 10, 1945, 5; Morse, William P., RG389, POW-PGM, NARA.

26. WPO-3, War Plan Orange No. 3: Morton, *Philippines,* 61–71; Ronald H. Spector, *Eagle Against the Sun: The American War with Japan* (New York: Free Press, 1985), 54–59; Edward S. Miller, *War Plan Orange: The U.S. Strategy to Defeat Japan, 1897–1945* (Annapolis, MD: Naval Institute Press, 1991), 60–63.

27. Major General Sutherland of Maryland was MacArthur's most senior aide and escaped with MacArthur to Australia, where he remained general's right hand man during the Pacific War. Masuda, *Asia,* 10–11. Muzzey, of South Berwick, Maine, before the war he was an assistant professor of education at Temple University. He died aboard *Oryoku Maru* on December 15, 1944. Stephen Mellnik, *Philippine Diary, 1939–1945* (New York: Van Nostrand Reinhold Co., 1969), 166; "Wife Gets Letter from Corregidor," *Indiana* (PA) *Evening Gazette,* June 18,

1942, 16; "So. Berwick Man Dies in Ship Sinking," *Portsmouth* (NH) *Herald,* August 14, 1945, 2. Captain Kelly of Madison, Florida became one of America's first heroes of World War II on December 10, 1941, when he and his crew bombed the Japanese cruiser *Natori.* Returning to base, a flight of Japanese A6M Zero fighters attacked his B-17. Kelly kept the bomber level for his crew to bail out but the bomber exploded before his exit and he died on impact. General Orders No. 48, December 21, 1941, RG496, Records of General Headquarters, Southwest Pacific Area and United States Army Forces, Pacific, USAAF, Box 53, NARA; Burton, *Fortnight,* 196–99; Saburo Sakai with Martin Caidin and Fred Saito, *Samurai!* (New York: E. P. Dutton and Co., Inc., 1957), 76–80; Allison Ind, *Bataan: The Judgement Seat: The Saga of the Philippine Command of the United States Army Air Force, May 1941 to May 1942* (New York: Macmillan Co., 1944), 117–18.

CHAPTER 2 THE BILLION DOLLAR CHRISTMAS TREE

1. Japanese advance: Morton, *Philippines,* 121–44, 161–64. In October 1941, the U.S. Army chartered the German-built inter-island vessel USAT *Don Esteban* to transport personnel and supplies in the Philippines. She was lost off Mindoro on March 2, 1942. David Hubert Grover, *U.S. Army Ships and Watercraft of World War II* (Annapolis, MD: Naval Institute Press, 1987), 13.

2. MacArthur and risk: William Manchester, *American Caesar: Douglas MacArthur, 1880–1964* (Boston: Little, Brown and Co., 1978), 212–13; Masuda, *Asia,* 53.

3. Pandacan is a district in Manila and remains a location of several major oil depots. A native of Brooklyn, New York, Casey, of the Army Corps of Engineers, joined MacArthur's staff in November 1941. Evacuated with MacArthur to Australia, Casey served with MacArthur through to the Japanese Occupation. Masuda, *Asia,* 12–14; Hugh John Casey, *Engineer Memoirs: Major General Hugh J. Casey, US Army* (Washington, DC: Office of History, U.S. Army Corps of Engineers, 1993), 161–72. WPO-3 plans in effect: Morton, *Philippines,* 163–65; Beebe, *Rising,* 28; Whitman, *Ditch,* 45–50. Manila as Open City: Manuel Luis Quezon, *The Good Fight* (New York: D. Appleton-Century Co., Inc., 1946), 197–98, 208; Douglas MacArthur, *The Campaigns of MacArthur in the Pacific,* vol. 1 of *Reports of General MacArthur* (1966; reprint, Washington, DC: CMH, 1994), 15; Morton, *Philippines,* 232–34.

4. Major General Moore commanded the harbor defenses of Manila and Subic Bays, including the Philippine Coast Artillery during the Battle of Bataan. When MacArthur left Corregidor, he designated Moore as commander of the garrison with orders to defend the island until the last. He was liberated from a prison camp in Mukden, Manchuria, in August 1945. Morton, *Philippines,* 22, 44–45, 360–61;

Beebe, *Rising,* 228n4. Constructed from 1922–1932 beneath Malinta Hill on Corregidor, the tunnel's main east-to-west passage measured 836 feet long and 24 feet wide with 24 lateral shafts, each approximately 400 feet long branching off from the main passage. Morton, *Philippines,* 474–75; Mellnik, *Philippine,* 54–55; Sloan, *Undefeated,* 150–51.

5. Colonel Carl H. Seals served as the Adjutant General for the USAFFE under MacArthur and later General Jonathan M. Wainwright before leaving with his wife, Margaret Byroade Seals, in a navy PBY on the night of April 29, 1942. After the aircraft sustained irreparable damage, Colonel and Mrs. Seals surrendered to the Japanese on May 11, 1942. General Seals was liberated from a prison camp in Mukden, Manchuria, in August 1945, and Mrs. Seals in Manila in February 1945. Norman, *Angels,* 104–21, 301–3, n1, 2, 3; Beebe, *Rising,* 50, 79–80, 108, 229; Victor L. Mapes with Scott A. Mills, *The Butchers, The Baker: The World War II Memoir of a United States Army Air Corps Soldier Captured by the Japanese in the Philippines* (Jefferson, NC: McFarland and Co., 2000), 99–101; Mellnik, *Philippine,* 308.

6. Gold and Silver bullion: Mellnik, *Philippine,* 116; Whitman, *Ditch,* 409–10; Ashton, *Somebody,* 236–45; William B. Breuer, *MacArthur's Undercover War: Spies, Saboteurs, Guerrillas and Secret Missions* (Edison, NJ: Castle Books, 2005), 67–71.

7. Manuel Luis Quezón y Molina served as president of the Commonwealth of the Philippines from 1935 until 1944. The first Filipino head of state, he fled the country and established a government in exile in Washington, DC, until dying from tuberculosis on August 1, 1944. Quezon, *Fight.* Beds: Lee, *Pacific,* 165.

8. Funk, from Portland, Oregon, was promoted to brigadier general on February 1, 1942. He briefly commanded the 57th Infantry (PS) before becoming the chief of staff for Major General Edward P. King, commander of the Luzon Force, on March 11, 1942. He was liberated from a camp in Mukden, Manchuria, in August 1945. Chief of Staff Office Diary, 51, RG2, Box 2, MM; Special Orders No. 66, March 11, 1942, Headquarters, USAFFE, RG496, Box 54, NARA; Morton, *Philippines,* 455–56; Beebe, *Rising,* 40, 44, 50, 63, 69, 229n7; "Roosevelt Names 4 Major Generals: Also Sends Senate Nominations of Twenty Brigadiers," *NYT,* January 29, 1942, 4; Whitman, *Ditch,* 152–53.

9. Established on December 23, 1941 at Limay, General Hospital No. 1 processed all battlefield surgical cases. With the withdrawal in January 1942, it relocated to Little Baguio by the ammunition and quartermaster depots. By April 9, 1942, the open-air facility held approximately 1,800 patients. Morton, *Philippines,* 258, 380–81; Norman, *Angels,* 94.

10. Signal Hill is located to the east of Trail 7, approximately at the intersection of lines drawn due north of Kilometer Post 188 and due west of Kilometer Post

199. Trail Map, Bataan Peninsula, prepared by Engineer, USAAF, February 18, 1942, RG496, Records of General Headquarters, Southwest Pacific Area and United States Army Forces, Pacific, USAAF, Box 40, NARA. Hardee held the title as advance command post commandant until January 26, 1942. Chief of Staff Office Diary, 51, RG2, Box 2, MM; Special Orders No. 24, January 26, 1942, Headquarters, USAFFWE, RG496, Box 54, NARA.

11. Troops went on half rations beginning on January 5, 1942. Morton, *Philippines,* 256–57; Beebe, *Rising,* 35; Whitman, *Ditch,* 48–49.

12. Battle of the Points: Morton, *Philippines,* 296–312; Whitman, *Ditch,* 249–323.

13. The command post by fighting's end was just east of Kilometer Post 168 on the East Road. Road and Trail Map, Bataan Peninsula, Department Engineer, USAFFE, January 4, 1942, RG496, Records of General Headquarters, Southwest Pacific Area and United States Army Forces, Pacific, USAAF, Box 40, NARA. 57th Infantry (PS) fighting: Morton, *Philippines,* 251, 266–72; Whitman, *Ditch,* 128–54.

14. On January 13, 1942, Funk relieved Colonel George S. Clarke as commander of the 57th Infantry (PS). Regarding fighting: Morton, *Philippines,* 273–78, 285–95, 325; Whitman, *Ditch,* 152–53.

15. Visit by Sutherland, not MacArthur: Morton, *Philippines,* 290; Young, *Bataan,* 63; Whitman, *Ditch,* 227.

16. Special Orders No. 24, January 26, 1942, Headquarters, USAFFE, RG496, Records of General Headquarters, Southwest Pacific Area and United States Army Forces, Pacific, USAFFE, Box 54, NARA.

17. Inspector General Colonel Milton A. Hill of Michigan left Corregidor aboard the submarine USS *Spearfish* on May 3, 1942. Morton, *Philippines,* 548; Norman, *Angels,* 108; "Colonel Sees Long, Tough War," *LAT,* August 23, 1942, A6. Major General George M. Parker, Jr., of Iowa commanded the South Luzon Force, composed of the 41st and 51st Divisions (PA), assigned to protect the area south and east of Manila. Later, he was placed in command of the Bataan Defense Force to prepare defensive positions on Bataan. On January 7, 1942, he assumed command of the East Sector of the Bataan peninsula, re-designated the II Philippine Corps. Morton, *Philippines,* 69, 141, 165, 247; Whitman, *Ditch,* 89–91.

CHAPTER 3 MANY PILOTS AND NO AIRPLANES

1. The Provisional Air Corps Regiment organized as a unit on January 8–9, 1942, initially under the command of Colonel Harrison H.C. Richards, MacArthur's senior air corps officer (whom Doane replaced). By March 31, 1942, the regiment consisted of 90 officers, 1,408 enlisted men, and 17 Filipino scouts. Morton, *Philippines,* 327; Young, *Bataan,* 7; Mendelson, "Provisional," 8–10; Whitman,

Ditch, 454–55; John S. Coleman, Jr., *Bataan and Beyond: Memories of an American POW* (College Station, TX: Texas A&M University Press, 1978), 20–25; Leslie F. Zimmerman, "Diary of Lieutenant Colonel Leslie F. Zimmerman, POW in Philippines, World War II" (Unpublished memoir, transcribed by U.S. Air Force Historical Research Agency, December 1989), 49–93.

2. These guns, eight 75mm and four 2.95-inch guns, came from the 1st Battalion, 24th Field Artillery (PA). Tank defenses and artillery: Mendelson, "Provisional," 7, 15; Whitman, *Ditch,* 454; Ashton, *Diary,* 137; Coleman, *Bataan and Beyond,* 21.

3. A member of the 27th Bombardment Group, Captain Mark M. Wohlfeld of New York survived a year and a half of imprisonment until on March 27, 1944 he and five other prisoners escaped from the Davao Penal Colony. He later fought with Filipino guerrillas until October 1944 when he linked up with the American invasion forces at Leyte. Knox, *Death,* 275–92; Kerr, *Surrender,* 195; "Prisoners in Jap Camp Reunited After 22 Years," *Titusville* (PA) *Herald,* May 5, 1966, 5. On the Provisional Air Corps Regiment's left flank in Sector C was the 32nd Infantry Regiment of the 31st Infantry (PA) and the remains of the 51st Infantry (PA) reorganized into the 51st Regimental Combat Team (PA) under the command of Brigadier General Clifford Bluemel. Whitman, *Ditch,* 456.

4. Japanese plans and actions: Morton, *Philippines,* 261–62, 347–50. Training airmen: Zimmerman, "Diary," 91–93; Whitman, *Ditch,* 455–56; Coleman, *Bataan and Beyond,* 19–20; Gause, *Journal,* 9. Wainwright visit: Young, *Bataan,* 169–77; Morton, *Philippines,* 360–66.

5. Lieutenant Colonel Ovid O. "Zero" Wilson of Texas served as General Wainwright's aide before the war and as G-1 for II Philippine Corps. He was liberated from a prison camp in Mukden, Manchuria, in August 1945. James, *Mukden,* 169–70; Chris Schaefer, *Bataan Diary: An American Family in World War II, 1941–1945* (Houston: Riverview Publishing, 2004), 9; memorials, Ovid O. Wilson 1924, West Point Association of Graduates, online.

6. Without a third battalion, the regiment could not effectively man the reserve line. Whitman, *Ditch,* 455; Mendelson, "Operations," 16–17. Commanding the 32nd Infantry (PA), Colonel Edwin H. Johnson of the District of Columbia fought alongside the Provisional Air Corps Regiment. In August 1945, he was liberated from a prison camp in Mukden, Manchuria. "Col. Johnson Retires After Long Service," *Star and Sentinel* (Gettysburg, PA), August 15, 1953, 1; Whitman, *Ditch,* 165.

7. Shanghai: Jordan, *China's,* 46–47, 63. Remaining American airpower: Craven and Cates, *Plans,* 224, 404–6; Maurer, *Combat,* 75. Dive bombers: Gause, *Journal,* 9; Mendelson, "Provisional," 17–18; Coleman, *Bataan and Beyond,* 35–36.

8. Hunger: Morton, *Philippines,* 367–76; Mendelson, "Provisional," 18–20;

Gause, *Journal,* 16–17; Coleman, *Bataan and Beyond,* 32–41; Zimmerman, "Diary," 74–78; Young, *Bataan,* 156–59.

9. Captain Marion Lawton witnessed the death Colonel Irwin of Ohio, who was shot by a Japanese guard after repeatedly lagging behind on the Death March. Irwin, John W., RG389, POW-PGM, NARA; Knox, *Death,* 122; Lawton, *Some,* 17–19. Brigadier General Mateo Capinpin commanded the 21st Division (PA). He survived the Death March, and the Japanese released him in late 1942; afterward he became involved with guerrilla activities. "Brigadier General Capinpin: Monumental Deeds," Camp Mateo Capinpin, Philippine Army online; Morton, *Philippines,* 422–23.

10. Aircraft machine guns: Mendelson, "Provisional," 10; Gause, *Journal,* 9; Knox, *Death,* 95; Coleman, *Bataan and Beyond,* 43; Zimmerman, "Diary," 66.

11. Evacuation of MacArthur: Masuda, *Asia,* 93–119; Manchester, *Caesar,* 241–76; Morton, *Philippines,* 353–60; George W. Smith, *MacArthur's Escape: John "Wild Man" Buckeley and the Rescue of an American Hero* (St. Paul, MN: Zenith Press, 2005), 163–208. Stowell of New Jersey was liberated from a prison camp in Mukden, Manchuria, in August 1945. "List of Americans Sent from Formosa," *NYT,* February 10, 1945, 5; "Rotary Club Members Hear of Death March," *Zanesville* (OH) *Signal,* October 28, 1948, 2. Wainwright assumed command of the West Sector of the Bataan Defense Force, later I Philippine Corps, on January 7, 1942, when the Battle of Bataan began. On March 10, 1942, MacArthur named Wainwright commander of all forces on Luzon. By March 20, now Lieutenant General Wainwright assumed command of U.S. Forces in the Philippines (USFIP). For the post of commander of the Luzon Force, Wainwright would tap Major General Edward P. King, Jr., Wainwright, *General,* 1–5; Morton, *Philippines,* 247, 360–66; Young, *Bataan,* 169–77.

12. President Franklin D. Roosevelt's fireside chat, "On Progress of the War," aired on February 23, 1942. Franklin D. Roosevelt, "On Progress of the War," February 23, 1942, The American Presidency Project online; Morton, *Philippines,* 387–88; Mapes, *Butchers,* 46; Zimmerman, "Diary," 102.

13. Mosquitoes and malaria: Morton, *Philippines,* 376–79; Mendelson, "Provisional," 19; Glusman, *Conduct,* 135–36; Zimmerman, "Diary," 81–84. A carabao, also known as a water buffalo, is the national animal of the Philippines and are frequently used as draft animals.

14. Eating carabao: Morton, *Philippines,* 370; Samuel C. Grashio and Bernard Norling, *Return to Freedom: The War Memoirs of Col. Samuel C. Grashio USAF (Ret.)* (Tulsa, OK: MCN Press, 1982), 14–15; Dyess, *Story,* 47; Coleman, *Bataan and Beyond,* 29.

15. The Japanese shelling commenced on Good Friday, April 3. Morton,

Philippines, 421–29; Whitman, *Ditch,* 475–92.

16. Attack of April 5, 1942: Morton, *Philippines,* 429–41; Whitman, *Ditch,* 493–517.

17. Bluemel: Morton, *Philippines,* 438–440; Young, *Bataan,* 202–3; Whitman, *Ditch,* 514–15. By April 7, 1942, the remnants of the 32nd and 51st Infantry Regiments (PA) were located to the left flank of the Provisional Air Corps Regiment.

18. Colonel Edwin H. Johnson, from Pennsylvania, was liberated from a prison camp in Mukden, Manchuria, in August 1945. "Col. Johnson Alive in Jap Prison Camp," *Gettysburg Compiler,* September 1, 1945, 1; "Col. Johnson Tells Clubmen of Prison Days," *Gettysburg Times,* January 22, 1946, 1, 4; "Ex-Prisoner of War at Fort Sill," *Gettysburg Times,* September 26, 1946, 1. Japanese attack on 32nd Infantry (PA): Morton, *Philippines,* 444; Whitman, *Ditch,* 528–29.

19. Tanks: Mendelson, "Provisional," 21–22; Morton, *Philippines,* 444; Whitman, *Ditch,* 529–31; Coleman, *Bataan and Beyond,* 45–47.

20. Corporal Gerken of Kings County, New York, served with the 28th Materiel Squadron, 20th Air Base Group originally stationed at Nichols Field before merging into the Provisional Air Corps Regiment. He died on September 7, 1944, on *Shinyo Maru.* Gerken, Edward, RG389, POW-PGM, NARA. Collapse of line along San Vincente River: Morton, *Philippines,* 445; Whitman, *Ditch,* 532–34; Young, *Bataan,* 212–15; Coleman, *Bataan and Beyond,* 47–49.

21. First Lieutenant Damon "Rocky" Gause of Georgia wrote his memoir in 1944, although it was not published until 1999. Gause, *Journal,* x–xii. On November 28, 1942, a letter from Gause to Elizabeth Hardee informed her that David was alive and well at the time of his escape. "Col. D.L. Hardee is Prisoner of Japanese on Philippine Island: Army Official Who Escaped from Japs Says Hardee Alive," *Durham Herald-Sun,* November 29, 1942; Elizabeth Hardee to David L. Hardee, September 26, 1943, DLHP, Box 79, NCA.

22. Lawton published his own account of the war. Lawton, *Some.*

23. Morehouse of New York served as MacArthur's family doctor and accompanied the general to Australia in March 1942. Masuda, *Asia,* 22; Morton, *Philippines,* 359n26.

24. First Lieutenant George W. Kane, Jr., of Georgia was liberated from the prison camp at Cabanatuan on January 30, 1945, during a raid by members of the 6th Ranger Battalion. Kane, George W. Jr., RG389, POW-PGM, NARA. First Lieutenant Bert Schwarz of New York survived the sinking of *Shinyo Maru* and was rescued by the submarine USS *Narwhal* on September 29, 1944. Michno, *Hellships,* 226–322; Schwarz, Bert, RG389, POW-PGM, NARA.

25. Dive bombers and withdrawal: Morton, *Philippines,* 446–50; Mendelson,

"Provisional," 22; Whitman, *Ditch,* 546–61; Coleman, *Bataan and Beyond,* 48–53.

CHAPTER 4 THE LAST DAYS IN BATAAN

1. C-ration: Jerold E. Brown, ed., *Historical Dictionary of the U.S. Army* (Westport, CT: Greenwood Press, 2001), 133–34.

2. Bombing: Knox, *Death,* 100–101; Young, *Bataan,* 219; Whitman, *Ditch,* 559–60; Coleman, *Bataan and Beyond,* 52–53.

3. These were units of the Nagano Detachment and the Japanese 4th Division. By 1800 hours, the Japanese had breached the Alangan line on the east (right flank). Young, *Bataan,* 220; Whitman, *Ditch,* 562. Morton, *Philippines,* 451. Lieutenant Colonel William H. Maverick of Texas commanded the 20th Air Base Group. On January 8, 1942, he assembled personnel for the Provisional Air Corps Regiment. He died on *Brazil Maru* on January 28, 1945. Mendelson, "Provisional," 8–9; Maverick, William H., RG389, POW-PGM, NARA.

4. On the evening of April 8, the regiment bivouacked near Trail 20, on the south side of the Lamao River. Morton, *Philippines,* 451–52; Knox, *Death,* 101; Gause, *Journal,* 21. Taylor's identity remains unknown.

5. Both battalions withdrew in confusion. Aside from Colonel Doane, Hardee and other command elements relocated to the final defensive line south of a branch of Trail 20 and north of Cabcaben. Knox, *Death,* 101; Coleman, *Bataan and Beyond,* 54–59; Whitman, *Ditch,* 568–69.

6. Major Emmert C. Lentz of Ohio was a medical officer in the Army Air Corps. He was liberated in August 1945 from the Zentsuji POW Camp (Hiroshima No. 1) in Japan. Lentz, Emmert C., RG389, POW-PGM, NARA; "Dr. (Col.) Emmert C. Lentz," *The Quan* (Pittsburgh, PA), June 1974, 9. Earthquake: Morton, *Philippines,* 459; Young, *Bataan,* 228–29; Whitman, *Ditch,* 570; Lester I. Tenney, *My Hitch in Hell: The Bataan Death March* (Washington, DC: Brassey's, Inc., 2000), 35.

7. General King attempted to form a defensive line with the Provisional Coast Artillery Brigade (AA) (PCAB) and the 1st Philippine Constabulary. The PCAB consisted of the 200th Coast Artillery (AA) and the 515th Coast Artillery (AA), numbering 1,816 men from the New Mexico National Guard. Morton, *Philippines,* 451, 451n28; "New Mexico National Guard's Involvement in the Bataan Death March," New Mexico National Guard Bataan Memorial Museum online. Colonel Charles G. Sage of New Mexico commanded the provisional brigade and the 200th Coast Artillery (AA). He was liberated in August 1945 from a prison camp in Mukden, Manchuria. "Deming Men Liberated from Jap Prison Camp," *Deming* (NM) *Headlight,* August 31, 1945; "New Mexico Guard Honors Gen. Sage," *El Paso Herald-Post,* August 20, 1957, 1, 4.

8. Hospitals No. 1 and No. 2: Norman, *Angels,* 84–95; Glusman, *Conduct,* 158; Knox, *Death,* 103–8.

9. Collapse of II Corps: Morton, *Philippines,* 452–53; Young, *Bataan,* 225–27; Whitman, *Ditch,* 536–38, 544–47.

10. Ammunition dumps were detonated around 0200 hours. Morton, *Philippines,* 460; Whitman, *Ditch,* 572–73.

11. General King surrender decision: Morton, *Philippines,* 458–59; Falk, *Bataan,* 18–20; Chunn, *Rice,* 1–8.

12. American surrender: Chunn, *Rice,* 8–12; Morton, *Philippines,* 463–67; Falk, *Bataan,* 21–25; Wainwright, *General,* 81–83.

13. This was just east of Kilometer Post 168, where both King and Parker co-located their headquarters by April 9. Morton, *Philippines,* 459; Whitman, *Ditch,* 513, 547.

14. Filipino training: see chapter 1, note 4.

15. Colonel Garfinkle of Colorado was the II Corps inspector general. He was liberated from a prison camp in Mukden, Manchuria, in August 1945. Knox, *Death,* 141; Garfinkle, Abraham, RG389, POW-PGM, NARA; "Garfinkle, Abraham 'Abe' #1654," Mukden Prisoner of War Remembrance Society online. Colonel Gempachi Sato commanded the Japanese 61st Infantry and as field commander captured Corregidor on May 6, 1942. Falk, *Bataan,* 79–80; Morton, *Philippines,* 443, 553, 571–72.

16. Shakedown references are ubiquitous in memoirs. Examples: Knox, *Death,* 113–16; Falk, *Bataan,* 82–83, 96; Kerr, *Surrender,* 52–53; Lawton, *Some,* 15; Grashio, *Freedom,* 32.

17. Lieutenant Colonel Dennis M. Moore of Texas served as General Parker's G-2 and was liberated from the Kiejo prison camp in Seoul, Korea, in August 1945. Moore, Dennis M., RG389, POW-PGM, NARA; "Chinese Fighting Better Than in Japanese War," *Pacific Stars and Stripes,* February 13, 1951, 2.

CHAPTER 5 THE DEATH MARCH

1. Colonel James W. "Pat" Callahan, Jr., of Kansas was the Provost Marshal for II Corps. He was liberated in August 1945 from a prison camp in Mukden, Manchuria. Callahan, James W., RG389, POW-PGM, NARA.

2. Hardee's distance is off if he was eight to ten kilometers from Cabcaben. His march more likely began in the vicinity of Kilometer Post 168, near II Corps headquarters. Road and Trail Map, Bataan Peninsula, Department Engineer, USAFFE, January 4, 1942, RG496, Records of General Headquarters, Southwest Pacific Area and United States Army Forces, Pacific, USAAF, Box 40, NARA; Morton,

Philippines, 282n40. Bodies run over: Knox, *Death,* 121, 125; Richard M. Gordon with Benjamin S. Llamzon, *Horyo: Memoirs of an American POW* (St. Paul, MN: Paragon House, 1999), 97; Gene Boyt with David L. Burch, *Bataan: A Survivor's Story* (Norman, OK: University of Oklahoma Press, 2004), 125.

3. Water: Falk, *Bataan,* 131–36; Reynolds, *Rice and Men,* 59–60; Boyt, *Survivor's Story,* 131–32; Knox, *Death,* 127–35; Robert W. Levering, *Horror Trek: A True Story of Bataan, the Death March and Three and One-Half Years in Japanese Prison Camps* (Dayton, OH: Horstman Printing Co., 1948), 65, 75–76. Shakedowns: Falk, *Bataan,* 127–29; Tony Bilek in collaboration with Gene O'Connell, *No Uncle Sam: The Forgotten of Bataan* (Kent, OH: Kent State University Press, 2003), 50–52.

4. This may be Warrant Officer Junior Grade Charles Moore of the 19th Bombardment Group, who died on January 9, 1945, on *Enoura Maru,* or possibly Captain Paul E. Moore of the field artillery who also died on *Enoura Maru,* January 12, 1945. Moore, Charles and Moore, Paul E., RG389, POW-PGM, NARA.

5. Captain John H. Spigler from Oregon served as the acting G-1 for the Air Warning Service, Fifth Interceptor Command in the early part of the Philippine Campaign until being assigned on February 22, 1942, to the Fire Director Center, II Philippine Corps. His official date of death is listed as April 16, 1942. Technical Sergeant Lee, 31st Infantry is possibly Master Sergeant Odell B. Lee of Texas, assigned to the 75th Ordnance Company. His date of death is recorded as April 30, 1942. Both men remain listed as missing in action. Perpetuation of testimony of David L. Hardee, September 18, 1946, RG331, Allied Operational and Occupation Headquarters, World War II, Supreme Commander for the Allied Powers (SCAP), Legal Section, Administrative Division, Prisoner of War File, 1945–1947, Box 1095, NARA; Ind, Judgment, 67; Special Orders No. 50, February 22, 1942, Headquarters, USAFFE, RG496, Box 54, NARA; John H. Spigler and Odell B. Lee, American Battle Monuments Commission, World War II database online. Japanese money: Falk, *Bataan,* 130–31; Knox, *Death,* 116; Dyess, *Story,* 69–70; Olson, *O'Donnell,* 150–54.

6. Dougherty of Texas commanded the Provisional Field Artillery Brigade of the Philippine Division. He was liberated from a prison camp in Mukden, Manchuria, in August 1945. "Colonel Louis R. Dougherty, Now Prisoner of Japs, is Ranked Among Texas' Outstanding Heroes of War," *Reporter-Telegram* (Midland, TX), May 20, 1943, 4; "Texans Among POW Moved by Japs," *Laredo Times,* February 11, 1945, 6; "Midland Colonel, Captured on Bataan, in Frisco Hospital," *Abilene Reporter-News,* September 17, 1945, 7.

7. José Protasio Rizal Mercado y Alonso Realonda was a Filipino nationalist and is a national hero of the Philippines. The Spanish executed him on December 30,

1896, a date now celebrated as a national holiday. Rizal's execution served to spark the Philippine Revolution. Gregorio F. Zaide and Sonia M. Zaide, *Jose Rizal: Life, Works and Writings of a Genius, Writer, Scientist and National Hero* (Quezon City, Philippines: All-Nations Publishing Co., Inc., 1999); Austin Coates, *Rizal: Philippine Nationalist and Martyr* (New York: Oxford University Press, 1968).

8. Drummond, from California, died on December 15, 1944, on *Oryoku Maru.* "Lt. Col. Hinton Drummond is Japanese Prisoner," *Spirit Lake Beacon* (IA), March 4, 1942, 1; Chunn, *Rice,* 46; Drummond, W. Hinton, RG389, POW-PGM, NARA.

9. Burying prisoners alive: Perpetuation of testimony of David L. Hardee, September 18, 1946, RG331, SCAP, Box 1095, NARA; Falk, *Bataan,* 146–47; Knox, *Death,* 144.

10. The American canteen with the chained cap proved superior to the Japanese design. Falk, *Bataan,* 148; Bilek, *Uncle,* 64.

11. Captain William Avery of New York served on Colonel Steel's staff in the 31st Infantry (U.S.). He died at Camp O'Donnell on May 10, 1942. Avery, William, RG389, POW-PGM, NARA.

12. This is possibly First Lieutenant Homer Joseph Martin who listed his home of record as the Philippines and served in the 202nd Engineer Battalion (PA). He was liberated from prison camp in Japan in August 1945. Martin, Homer J., RG389, POW-PMG, NARA.

13. Orani holding area: Falk, *Bataan,* 162–66; Dyess, *Story,* 84–85.

14. The Culo River Bridge near Layac was a steel and concrete highway bridge blown up on January 6, 1942 after the last American and Filipino forces crossed into Bataan. Whitman, *Ditch,* 6–7; Morton, *Philippines,* 223, 225.

15. Filipino generosity: Falk, *Bataan,* 158–59, 171; Dyess, *Story,* 90; Grashio, *Freedom,* 42–43; Boyt, *Survivor's Story,* 135.

16. No location has been found corresponding to this name. This is probably San Roque Arbol, a *barangay* (suburb) of Lubao between the Culo River and Gumain River, south of Lubao.

17. Rural background in Japanese army: Robert J.C. Butow, *Tojo and the Coming of the War* (Stanford, CA: Stanford University Press, 1961), 16, 22; Edward J. Drea, *In the Service of the Emperor: Essays on the Imperial Japanese Army* (Lincoln, NE: University of Nebraska Press, 2003), 78–80; Richard J. Smethurst, *A Social Basis for Prewar Japanese Militarism: The Army and the Rural Community* (Berkeley, CA: University of California Press, 1974), xiv–xix; Harries and Harries, *Soldiers,* 127–28, 168, 178.

18. Filipino guerrillas fought with Americans to liberate the country and far outnumbered collaborators. David Joel Steinberg, *Philippine Collaboration in*

World War II (Ann Arbor, MI: University of Michigan Press, 1967), 55–60, 92–95; Spector, *Eagle,* 466–68; Mellnik, *Philippine,* 241–312; M. Hamlin Cannon, *Leyte: The Return to the Philippines* (1953; reprint, Washington, DC: CMH, 1993), 14–20; Robert Ross Smith, *Triumph in the Philippines* (1963; reprint, Washington, DC: CMH, 1993), 26–27, 53–54, 313–15, 591–96.

19. The National Rice and Corn Corporation owned the warehouse, measuring 150 by 70 feet. Falk, *Bataan,* 171–75; Grashio, *Freedom,* 44.

20. "The Black Hole of Calcutta" was a dungeon at Fort William in Calcutta, India where prisoners were allegedly confined in 1756 in cramped, suffocating conditions. John Holwell Zephaniah, *A Genuine Narrative of the Deplorable Deaths of the English Gentlemen, and Others, who were Suffocated in the Black-Hole in Fort-William, at Calcutta, in the Kingdom of Bengal; in the Night succeeding the 20th Day of June, 1756* (London: A Millar, 1758).

21. Food by San Fernando: Dyess, *Story,* 90; Falk, *Bataan,* 177–78; Gordon, *Horyo,* 97–98; Bilek, *Uncle,* 63–65.

22. Japanese comfort women: Maria Rosa Henson, *Comfort Woman: A Filipina's Story of Prostitution and Slavery Under the Japanese Military* (New York: Rowman and Littlefield Publishers, Inc., 1999); Yuki Tanaka, *Japan's Comfort Women: Sexual Slavery and Prostitution During World War II and the U.S. Occupation* (New York: Routledge, 2002); Margaret Stetz and Bonnie B.C. Oh, eds., *Legacies of the Comfort Women of World War II* (Armonk, NY: M.E. Sharpe, Inc., 2001); George Hicks, *The Comfort Women: Japan's Brutal Regime of Enforced Prostitution in the Second World War* (New York: W.W. Norton and Co., 1995).

23. Co-Prosperity Sphere: John W. Dower, *War Without Mercy: Race and Power in the Pacific War* (New York: Pantheon Books, 1986), 7, 262–90; Steinberg, *Collaboration,* 44–70; Saburō Ienaga, *The Pacific War: World War II and the Japanese, 1931–1945* (New York: Pantheon Books, 1978), 153–80; Andrew Gordon, *A Modern History of Japan: From Tokugawa Times to the Present,* 2d ed. (New York: Oxford University Press, 2009), 208–9.

24. The Japanese moved prisoners by rail from San Fernando to the town of Capas, 25 miles north. The prisoners rode in steel or wooden boxcars measuring 33 by 8 by 7 feet and 16 by 8 by 6 feet, respectively. Falk, *Bataan,* 176–89; Knox, *Death,* 150–52; Gordon, *Horyo,* 98–101.

25. The actual distance from the rail station to the camp was six kilometers, just under four miles. Olson, *O'Donnell,* 27. Captain Yoshio Tsuneyoshi was a 50-year old reserve officer sent to Camp O'Donnell in mid-April 1942 to run the camp. He was relieved of command in late May 1942. A U.S. Eighth Army war crimes tribunal sentenced him to life imprisonment with hard labor for the deaths of

American POWs at Camp O'Donnell. Kerr, *Surrender,* 60–61, 65; "Life Term for Japanese: 8th Army Tribunal Convicts the Head of Camp O'Donnell," *NYT,* November 22, 1947, 2; Glusman, *Conduct,* 226; Olson, *O'Donnell,* 41, 44, 171; *United States of America v. Yoshio Tsuneyoshi,* Headquarters U.S. Eighth Army, Yokohama, Japan, May 24, 1949, Research and Documentation Center for War Crimes Trials, Far East Yokohama Trials, Philipp University of Marburg, Germany (RDCWCT); assorted testimony and statements, RG331, SCAP, Box 1086, NARA.

26. Anti-Japanese racist sentiment: Dower, *Mercy,* 81–93. Tsyneyoshi's rant is prevalent in memoirs. Examples: Dyess, *Story,* 98–100; Gordon, *Horyo,* 108–9; Bilek, *Uncle,* 69–70; Olson, *O'Donnell,* 44–46; Levering, *Horror Trek,* 80–82; Boyt, *Survivor's Story,* 142–43.

27. Tsuneyoshi claimed an appointment as the military governor of Legazpi but instead returned to Japan. Olson, *O'Donnell,* 174.

28. Tsuneyoshi placed King in charge of all prisoners, ordering him to inform the new POWs of the Japanese orders and the need to obey them. Olson, *O'Donnell,* 46–47; Kerr, *Surrender,* 63; testimony by Edward P. King, January 14, 1946, RG 331, SCAP, Box 1086, NARA.

29. Technically, Hardee's party lost two men, Spigler and Lee, although it is not clear if he considered them part of his II Corp group or of another body of men near his group on the march.

30. The approximate distances for Hardee's journey totals 25 miles by rail and 60 miles by foot. Historian Stanley Falk estimates American deaths at between 600 and 650 and Filipino deaths from 5,000 to 10,000. Falk, *Bataan,* 194, 197–98.

CHAPTER 6 CAMP O'DONNELL

1. Camp O'Donnell description: Olson, *O'Donnell,* 9, 31–39. 93–103; Heisinger, *Father,* 189–90; Grashio, *Freedom,* 53–54; Dyess, *Story,* 98–106; Lawton, *Some,* 25; Jacobsen, *Refused,* 94–96.

2. A Winston-Salem native, Smothers commanded the 3rd Battalion, 45th Infantry (PS). He died on April 26, 1945, aboard a ferry destined for a POW camp in Korea. Major Smothers's two sons, Thomas and Richard, who would go on to host *The Smothers Brothers Comedy Hour,* a highly controversial program during the height of the Vietnam War. David Bianculli, *Dangerously Funny: The Uncensored Story of The Smothers Brothers Comedy Hour* (New York: Simon and Schuster, 2009), 2–4; Smothers, Thomas B., Jr., RG389, POW-PGM, NARA; John Hinton, "City Council Approves Compassionate City Designation," *Winston-Salem Journal,* July 15, 2013. Chief Warrant Officer John M. Curry of Mississippi, a member of USAFFE's Adjutant Generals Department, died at Cabanatuan Prison Camp on June 28, 1942. Curry, John M., RG389, POW-PGM, NARA.

3. Roemer of Delaware served in the chemical warfare service with the Philippine Scouts. He died on January 22, 1945, on *Brazil Maru.* Roemer, Louis E., RG389, POW-PGM, NARA. Fort Howard is a former army installation in the town of Edgemere, Maryland. Lack of medicine, flies and sanitation: Gordon, *Horyo,* 111–14; Olson, *O'Donnell,* 53, 117–27; Kerr, *Surrender,* 61–63; Preston John Hubbard, *Apocalypse Undone: My Survival of Japanese Imprisonment During World War II* (Nashville: Vanderbilt University Press, 1990), 96–100; Knox, *Death,* 161–62, 169–70.

4. Major Samuel E. Donald of Virginia was the Protestant chaplain for the 2nd Battalion, Provisional Air Corps Regiment. He was liberated from the Fukuoka POW Camp No. 3, Yawata, Kyushu Island in August 1945. Richard S. Roper, *Brothers of Paul: Activities of Prisoner of War Chaplains in the Philippines During WWII* (Odenton, MD: Revere Printing, 2003), 105–8; Chunn, *Rice,* 89, 93; Olson, *O'Donnell,* 137. Donald, Samuel E., RG389, POW-PGM, NARA. Reverend Robert Marion Hardee was Donald's classmate. From April 11, 1942, to January 20, 1943, from 1,564 to 1,567 Americans and approximately 20,000 Filipinos died at O'Donnell. Olson, *O'Donnell,* 155–159; Dyess, *Story,* 101; Tenney, *Hitch,* 69; Grashio, *Freedom,* 55–56; U.S. Department of War, Office of the Provost Marshal General, *American Prisoners of War in the Philippines* (Washington, DC: Office of the Provost Marshal General, November 19, 1945).

5. Prisoner perspective on survival of older men: Feuer, *Bilibid,* 144; Caraccilo, *Beyond,* 34; Olson, *O'Donnell,* 157.

6. Propaganda leaflets: Morton, *Philippines,* 384–87, 418; Levering, *Trek,* 49–50; Zimmerman, "Diary," 104–5; John Toland, *But Not in Shame: The Six Months After Pearl Harbor* (New York: Random House, 1961), 267–68, photo page 8.

7. Colonel Ralph Hirsch of Arkansas served in the field artillery assigned to the Luzon Force headquarters. The Japanese executed other Americans for possession of Japanese money or objects. Perpetuation of testimony of David L. Hardee, September 18, 1946, RG 331, SCAP, Box 1095, NARA; *United States of America v. Yoshio Tsuneyoshi,* Headquarters U.S. Eighth Army, Yokohama, Japan, May 24, 1949, 5–6, RDCWCT; Olson, *O'Donnell,* 150–54; Tenney, *Hitch,* 66; Knox, *Death,* 155–57.

8. Captain Marion Lawton witnessed Irwin's fate. Chapter 3, note 9; Allen L. Stowell, "Report of Circumstances of Atrocities Committed Against John W. Irwin, Infantry, United States Army," September 4, 1945, Headquarters, Camp Hoten, Mukden, Manchuria, RG331, SCAP, Box 1115, NARA. Colonel Stowell, Signal Corps, of New Jersey, was the signal officer for II Philippine Corps during the Battle of Bataan. He was liberated from a prison camp in Mukden, Manchuria, in August 1945. Stowell, Allen L, RG389, POW-PGM, NARA. Lieutenant Colonel

Garver of Illinois served in the headquarters of the Philippine Department as General Wainwright's adjutant. He died during the Death March on April 14, 1942. One account records that Garver committed suicide by jumping from a bridge, while another reports Garver became delirious and was shot by a Japanese guard. Ashton, *Somebody,* 202; Kary C. Emerson, *Guest of the Emperor* (Sanibel Island, FL: K.C. Emerson, 1977), 12.

9. Original Japanese plan for handling prisoners: Falk, *Bataan,* 45–66.

10. Movement of generals and colonels: Beebe, *Rising,* 92, 99–101; Olson, *O'Donnell,* 59–62; Michno, *Hellships,* 34–35; Wainwright, *General,* 156.

11. Atkinson of Texas served as the American commander of Sub-Group 1 at Camp O'Donnell and Group 1, Camp 1 of Cabanatuan Prison Camp. He died on February 24, 1945, at Fukuoka POW Camp No. 1, Kashii, Kyushu Island, Japan. A Nebraska native, Hunter commanded Group 1 at Camp O'Donnell. He died on October 24, 1944, on *Arisan Maru.* Atkinson, John J. and Hunter, Robert G., RG389, POW-PGM, NARA; Olson, *O'Donnell,* 62.

12. Black market, money, and survival: Bilek, *Uncle,* 74–80; Jacobsen, *Refused,* 99–105; Gordon, *Horyo,* 110–12, 118–19; Olson, *O'Donnell,* 105–16.

13. Hardee's checkbook on May 8, 1942, lists $100.00 payable to Gerken, possible payment for the check cashed in Manila or other services rendered. Checkbook, Philippine Trust Company, DLHP, Box 79, NCA. Technical Sergeant Samuel S. Schulman of New York served in the 19th Bombardment Group and later the Provisional Air Corps Regiment. He was liberated in August 1945 from the Fukuoka POW Camp No. 1, Omuta, Fukuoka, Japan. Schulman, Samuel S., RG389, POW-PGM, NARA.

14. Fall of Corregidor: Morton, *Philippines,* 536–82; Wainwright, *General,* 86–127; Mellnik, *Philippine,* 108–55.

15. Dysentery and death: Hubbard, *Apocalypse,* 96; Kerr, *Surrender,* 61–62; Olson, *O'Donnell,* 155–62. Japanese decision to move prisoners from O'Donnell: Kerr, *Surrender,* 65, 80; Chunn, *Rice,* 37. Bigaa is today known as Balagtas, a municipality in the province of Bulacan, P.I. The Japanese moved Hardee's sister, Lucy Hardee Olsen, her husband, Carl E. Olsen, and their daughters, Roberta and Esten, into the Santo Tomas Internment Camp in Manila on January 8, 1942. Lucy Hardee Olsen, "My War Diary, December 7, 1941 to February 3, 1945" (unpublished manuscript, 1976), 17–19; House Committee on Interstate and Foreign Commerce, *Enemy Property Commission Hearings,* 80th Cong., 1st sess., 1947, 102–4.

16. Prisoner movement to Cabanatuan: Kerr, *Surrender,* 80–81; Dyess, *Story,* 120–21; Bumgarner, *Parade,* 84–85; Edward E. Thomas, *As I Remember: A Barge from Corregidor—A March from Bataan—A Fence at Cabanatuan* (Sonoita, AZ: Edward E. Thomas, 1990), 172; Bilek, *Uncle,* 88–90.

CHAPTER 7 CABANATUAN

1. Cabanatuan prison system and camp description: Heisinger, *Father,* 237–43; Chunn, *Rice,* 16–18, 37–38; Zimmerman, "Diary," 189–90; Caraccilo, *Beyond,* 138–39; Coleman, *Bataan and Beyond,* 91. Jasper E. Brady, Jr., of Washington began the Battle of Bataan commanding the 3rd Battalion, 31st Infantry (U.S.) before taking command of the regiment on March 2, 1942, when Colonel Steel became II Corps chief of staff. He died on *Oryoku Maru* on December 15, 1944. Morton, *Philippines,* 229, 434; Whitman, *Ditch,* 183, 506; Lowe, America's Foreign Legion, Chapter 7, 4; Brady, Jasper E., Jr., RG389, POW-PGM, NARA.

2. 92nd Garage: Mellnik, *Philippine,* 143–61; Joseph A. Petak, *Never Plan Tomorrow: The Saga of the Bataan Death March and Battle of Corregidor Survivors, 1942–1945* (Valencia, CA: Delta Lithograph Co., 1991), 15–29; Glusman, *Conduct,* 203–9.

3. Movement of Corregidor prisoners to Cabanatuan: Petak, *Tomorrow,* 31–35; Mellnik, *Philippine,* 161–64; Kerr, *Surrender,* 74–76. Henryk Sienkiewicz's 1895 novel, *Quo Vadis: A Narrative of the Time of Nero,* is a historical novel set in Rome around AD 64, concerning the relationship between a Christian woman and a pagan Roman officer who will convert.

4. Lieutenant (junior grade) Willis of North Carolina was liberated from the Osaka Main POW Camp, Chikko, Osaka, in August 1945. First Lieutenant Lyon of North Carolina was liberated in August 1945 from the Keijo POW Camp near Seoul, Korea. "News About Alumni in Uniform," *The Alumni Review* (University of North Carolina, Chapel Hill), November 1945, 64; Willis, Meade H., Jr., and Lyon, Julian V., RG389, POW-PGM, NARA.

5. Cabanatuan hospital: Chunn, *Rice,* 37–48; Bumgarner, *Parade,* 87–122; Lawton, *Some,* 44–46; Caraccilo, *Beyond,* 142–45; Thomas, *Remember,* 173–79.

6. This is possibly Lieutenant Oiagi, the camp quartermaster with a reputation of fairness to the prisoners. Chunn, *Rice,* 17. Prisoners crafted names for all the guards. Thomas, *Remember,* 192–93; Chunn, *Rice,* 17; Bilek, *Uncle,* 114–21; Knox, *Death,* 230–33. Cabanatuan black market: Lawton, *Some,* 38–43; Dyess, *Story,* 123.

7. Some prisoners claimed Shigeji Mori had a bicycle repair shop near Cavite Navy Yard by Manila before the war. On November 7, 1947, a U.S. Eighth Army War Crimes Commission sentenced him to life in prison with hard labor for the deaths and atrocities at the Cabanatuan prison camps. Caraccilo, *Beyond,* 286n16; McCoy, Mellnik, Kelley, *Tojo,* 56–57; "Life Term for Japanese: 8th Army Tribunal Convicts Head of Camp O'Donnell," *NYT,* November 22, 1947, 2; *United States of America v. Shigeji Mori,* Headquarters U.S. Eighth Army, Yokohama, Japan, November 22, 1948, RDCWCT; sworn statement by Guy Haines Stubbs, September 15, 1945; perpetuation of testimony of Lester W. Lacy, August 30, 1946;

perpetuation of testimony of Herman H. Archer, June 9, 1945; statement by Charles L. Ashcraft, August 22, 1946, RG 331, SCAP, Box 1080, NARA.

8. Prison camp rumors: Chunn, *Rice,* 106–10; Kerr, *Surrender,* 100–101; Thomas, *Remember,* 217–18; Daws, *Prisoners,* 131–33; McCracken, *Very,* 27–29.

9. Camp commissary: Chunn, *Rice,* 25, 30–31; Thomas, *Remember,* 188–89; Ashton, *Somebody,* 263–64; Zimmerman, "Diary," 205–6.

10. In a letter of August 26, 1942 to his brother-in-law, Hardee acknowledged receiving notes from his sister, Lucy, dated July 13 and 14, and August 9 and 22. Lucy's diary references the August 26 note. She contacted Father Theodore Buttenbruck, a German priest of the Society of the Divine Word in Manila, and Lucy gave him funds and a big carton packed with vitamins, food, soap, toiletries, writing materials, a sewing kit, and other items to take to her brother in Cabanatuan. Unfortunately, the Japanese shipped Hardee to Davao before he received the package. In July 1944, the Japanese arrested, interrogated, and killed Buttenbruck. David L. Hardee to Carl E. Olson, August 26, 1942, DLHP, Box 79, NCA; Olsen, "War Diary, 29–30; Caraccilo, *Beyond,* 149–50; House Committee of the Whole, *Mering Bichara,* 82d Cong., 1st sess., 1951, H. Rep. 1041, 7–27; Thomas, *Remember,* 198–200; Chunn, *Rice,* 89–90.

11. Breakdown of officer-enlisted discipline and relations: Chunn *Rice,* 20–21; Gordon, *Horyo,* 116–19, 125; Hubbard, *Apocalypse,* 95–96; Boyt, *Survivor's Story,* 128–29; Daws, *Prisoners,* 108–10; Ashton, *Somebody,* 302.

12. From June to July 1942, 1,287 Americans died in Cabanatuan, rising to 2,536 deaths by year's end. In 1943, 102 men died, and 2 in 1944. Between O'Donnell and Cabanatuan, the death toll from 1942 to 1944 ranges from 4,204 to 4,271. Chunn, *Rice,* 39–44, 120; Olson, *O'Donnell,* 155–62. Food and sanitation: Bumgarner, *Parade,* 96, 108; Thomas, *Remember,* 193, 202–4; Dyess, *Story,* 126, 129; Caraccilo, *Beyond,* 142, 160–61; Petak, *Tomorrow,* 63–64.

13. *Tenko* meant roll call; *bangō* the count off. Daws, *Prisoners,* 101; Zimmerman, "Diary," 233.

14. The Battle of Midway occurred June 4–7, 1942. Food and medicine impact: Chunn, *Rice,* 28, 43–44; Bumgarner, *Parade,* 96, 107–8, 122; Caraccilo, *Beyond,* 158–59; Zimmerman, "Diary," 207–13.

15. Chief Warrant Officer John M. Curry of Mississippi, assigned to the Adjutant General's Department, died June 28, 1942, at Cabanatuan Prison Camp No. 1. Curry, John M., RG389, POW-PGM, NARA.

16. This incident occurred around June 26, 1942. Chunn, *Rice,* 99–100; Kerr, *Surrender,* 101; Dyess, *Story,* 132; Bumgarner, *Parade,* 101–2; *United States of America v. Shigeji Mori,* Headquarters U.S. Eighth Army, Yokohama, Japan, November 22,

1948, 2–3, RDCWCT. A similar incident happened at Cabanatuan Prison Camp No. 3 on May 31, 1942, when four Americans who attempted escape were executed. Petak, *Tomorrow,* 51–53.

17. In February 1942 the Japanese agreed to pay POWs for work. By August 1942, the Japanese changed the status from "captives" to "prisoners of war," and began paying prisoners in late November-December 1942. As a lieutenant colonel, Hardee received 220 pesos per month, while a private received six pesos. Officer-established welfare funds sought to supplement enlisted pay. Tanaka, *Horrors,* 17; Daws, *Prisoners,* 109–10; Robert W. Kentner, "Kentner's Journal: Bilibid Prison, Manila, P.I. from 12-8-41 to 2-5-45" (Unpublished memoir, transcribed by U.S. Navy Bureau of Medicine and Surgery, Hospital Corps Archives Unit, April 21, 1945), 46; McCracken, *Very,* 65–66; Nordin, *Nothing,* 101–2; Walter Rundell, Jr., "Paying the POW in World War II," *Military Affairs* 22, no. 3 (Autumn 1958): 131–32.

18. Prisoner identification card: Kerr, *Surrender,* 104, 111–12; Mellnik, *Philippine,* 175; Bilek, *Uncle,* 70; Petak, *Tomorrow,* 65–66; Daws, *Prisoners,* 171–72; document marked "Prisoner's Identification Card," Concentration Camp at Cabanatuan, undated, RG407, AGO-POW, Box 12, NARA.

19. Burned rice: Bilek, *Uncle,* 105–6; Mellnik, *Philippine,* 168. Gardens: Thomas, *Remember,* 190, 204–5; Chunn, *Rice,* 32–33, 52; Knox, *Death,* 228–36; Ashton, *Somebody,* 262–63.

CHAPTER 8 MORE PRISON LIFE AT CABANATUAN

1. Imperial Rescript Day: Caraccilo, *Beyond,* 141; Bix, *Hirohito,* 433–36; John Toland, *The Rising Sun: The Decline and Fall of the Japanese Empire, 1936–1945* (New York: Random House, 1970), 227–28; "The Imperial Rescript; Declaring War on USA and Britain," *Philippine Camp News,* 2nd ed., December 1943, 1–2, RG407, AGO-POW, Box 244, NARA. For a complete copy of the rescript, see McCracken, *Very,* 114–16.

2. POW commentary on Japanese training: Dyess, *Story,* 138–40; Glusman, *Conduct,* 269–70; Jacobsen, *Refused,* 157. Japanese military training and discipline: Drea, *Emperor,* 75–90; Tanaka, *Horrors,* 37–40; Norman and Norman, *Tears,* 82–83, 97–99.

3. Cabanatuan library: Chunn, *Rice,* 78–88; Thomas, *Remember,* 197–98; Bumgarner, *Parade,* 114; Jacobs, *Blood,* 72.

4. Amusement programs: Chunn, *Rice,* 63–77; Kerr, *Surrender,* 99–100; Jacobs, *Blood,* 70–72; Dyess, *Story,* 127; Thomas, *Remember,* 221–22. Escape and prisoner conduct: Defense Advisory Committee on Prisoners of War, *POW, the Fight*

Continues After the Battle: The Report of the Secretary of Defense's Advisory Committee on Prisoners of War (Washington, DC: GPO, August 1955); Doyle, *Duty,* 6–7, 149–50; Jack Hawkins, *Never Say Die* (Philadelphia: Dorrance and Co., 1961), 71–81.

5. Japanese brutality and interpretation: Dower, *Mercy,* 41–73; Philip Towle, Margaret Kosuge, and Yoichi Kibata, eds., *Japanese Prisoners of War* (New York: Hambledon and London, 2000), 103–34; Hubbard, *Apocalypse,* 118–19; Harries and Harries, *Soldiers,* 476–84; Tanaka, *Horrors,* 74–78, 197–211. The system of "collective responsibility" for violations of the camp rules originates in exigencies devised by the Imperial Japanese Army in the administration of prisons in Manchuria, and China. Harries and Harries, *Soldiers,* 476–77.

6. Disease and delirious escapees: Chunn, *Rice,* 39–42; Thomas, *Remember,* 173–75, 184–85; Mellnik, *Philippine,* 173; Calvin G. Jackson, *Diary of Col. Calvin G. Jackson, M.D. Kept during World War II, 1941–1945* (Ada, OH: Ohio Northern University Press, 1992), 69. Wearing of signs: Dyess, *Story,* 131–32; Bumgarner, *Parade,* 102, 104; Jacobsen, *Refused,* 169; Levering, *Trek,* 101.

7. Japanese rules: PMG, *Prisoners,* November 19, 1945; Olson, *O'Donnell,* 45, 50; Kerr, *Surrender,* 96–97; Jacobs, *Blood,* 44.

8. Blood brother shooting squads: "Regulations Concerning Concentration Camp," Lieutenant Colonel S. Mori, Commander of Cabanatuan Prisoners of War Concentration Camp, Cabanatuan, May 27, 1942, RG407, AGO-POW, Box 43, NARA; Kerr, *Surrender,* 96–97; Daws, *Prisoners,* 99; Gordon, *Horyo,* 123; Caraccilo, *Beyond,* 151. Exactly which incident Hardee refers to is not known, but this may be an incident at Lumban, Laguna province in June 1942. Chunn, *Rice,* 101–2; Knox, *Death,* 181–84, 227; Daws, *Prisoners,* 156–57.

9. Major Charles F. Harrison, Jr. of Virginia began his career with the cavalry and in 1939 transferred to the Chemical Warfare Department. He was killed in Davao Penal Colony in May 1944 (covered in Chapter 13). Memorials, Charles F. Harrison 1933, West Point Association of Graduates, online.

10. As commander of Camp John Hay at Baguio, Lieutenant Colonel John P. Horan of Texas informed General MacArthur of Japanese movements in the early phase of the invasion of the Philippines. He organized a guerrilla force in January 1942 and on April 8 received authorization to organize the 121st Infantry (PA) as a guerrilla force in North Luzon. On orders of General Wainwright, he surrendered himself but not his forces on May 14, 1942, which continued to operate into 1943. He was liberated from a prison camp in Mukden, Manchuria, in August 1945. Morton, *Philippines,* 135, 574; Lillian E. Herz, "Bataan Anniversary Brings Back Memories to Col. Horan and 16 Men at Ft. Crockett," *Galveston News,* April 6,

1947, 17; Grace Foote, "Japs Looted Prisoners' Gardens, Stole Cows and Money Col. Horan, Captive for More than Three Years, Relates," *Port Arthur* (TX) *News*, October 18, 1945, 2; Bernard Norling, *The Intrepid Guerrillas of North Luzon* (Lexington, KY: University of Kentucky Press, 1999), 83–92; Jackson, *Diary*, 75, 78. The junior officers were navy Ensigns William A. Berry, Richard Tirk, and Philip H. Sanborn, who escaped Cabanatuan on May 29, 1942. The men survived in the jungle with the aid of Filipino guerrillas until being captured by another group of Filipinos and turned over to the Japanese and returned to Cabanatuan. Berry, *Rising*, 87–151, 231–37; McCoy, Mellnik, Kelley, *Tojo*, 33–34, 49, 61–63.

11. The fight for Guadalcanal lasted from August 1942 to February 1943.

12. Fence: Kerr, *Surrender*, 97; Thomas, *Remember*, 186; Chunn, *Rice*, 58–59; PMG, *Prisoners*, November 19, 1945. Biggs was from Illinois, Breitung of Michigan, and Gilbert from New Mexico. The escape attempt took place on the night of September 27, 1942. Jackson, *Diary*, 76; *United States of America v. Shigeji Mori*, November 22, 1948, 2–3, RDCWCT.

13. Regarding the argument: Mellnik, *Philippine*, 173–74; Berry, *Rising*, 139; Chunn, *Rice*, 100; Dyess, *Story*, 132–33; Gordon, *Horyo*, 122; Ashton, *Somebody*, 267; McCoy, Mellnik, Kelley, *Tojo*, 64–65.

14. Beating recollections: Caraccilo, *Beyond*, 151–52; Mellnik, *Philippine*, 174; Berry, *Rising*, 140; Bumgarner, *Parade*, 103; McCracken, *Very*, 30; *United States of America v. Shigeji Mori*, November 22, 1948, 3, RDCWCT; perpetuation of testimony of David L. Hardee, September 18, 1946, RG331, SCAP, Box 1095, NARA.

15. All three had broken noses; Biggs suffered a broken jaw, and Gilbert's arms and ribs were broken. One of the men also suffered a broken leg. Prisoner descriptions: Dyess, *Story*, 134–35; McCoy, Mellnik, Kelley, *Tojo*, 65–66; Grashio, *Freedom*, 66; McCracken, *Very*, 30–31; Chunn, *Rice*, 100; Caraccilo, *Beyond*, 152; *United States of America v. Shigeji Mori*, November 22, 1948, 3, RDCWCT; perpetuation of testimony of David L. Hardee, September 18, 1946, RG331, SCAP, Box 1095, NARA; perpetuation of testimony by Mark H. Wohlfeld, October 23, 1945; perpetuation of testimony of William S. Vaiden, October 8, 1946; perpetuation of testimony of George A. Schatz, Sr., October 30, 1945, RG331, SCAP, Box 1080, NARA.

16. The executions occurred on September 29, 1942. Biggs, despite his injuries, remained defiant to the end. Dyess, *Story*, 135–36; Chunn, *Rice*, 100; Gordon, *Horyo*, 123; Caraccilo, *Beyond*, 152; *United States of America v. Shigeji Mori*, November 22, 1948, 3, RDCWCT; Kerr, *Surrender*, 110–11; Feuer, *Bilibid*, 101–2; perpetuation of testimony of David L. Hardee, September 18, 1946, RG 331, SCAP, Box 1095, NARA.

CHAPTER 9 EN ROUTE TO DAPECOL

1. Food at Cabanatuan: Thomas, *Remember,* 182–83; Chunn, *Rice,* 23, 25–27; Kerr, *Surrender,* 97–99; Dyess, *Story,* 122–23; McCracken, *Very,* 45–46; Bumgarner, *Parade,* 103–7. Lieutenant Colonel Frederick G. Saint of Illinois, Army Corps of Engineers, oversaw the digging of drainage ditches and built proper latrines and septic tanks to improve prison life. Incentive programs to catch flies in exchange for food or cigarettes from the Japanese or American medical personnel further reduced the fly population. Bumgarner, *Parade,* 96, 108; Chunn, *Rice,* 39–42, 59; Ashton, *Somebody,* 258; Knox, *Death,* 223–24; drawing, "Septic Tank Type Latrine, used with complete success in the Prison Camp at Cabanatuan, P.I., designed and constructed by Lieutenant Colonel F. G. Saint (Eng. Corps)," undated, RG407, Records of the Adjutant General's Office, Philippine Archives Collection, POWS/ Civilian Internees, POW Rosters, (AGO-POW), Box 43, NARA.

2. Medicine shipment: Dyess, *Story,* 129; Chunn, *Rice,* 43; Kerr, *Surrender,* 103–4; Bumgarner, *Parade,* 107–8. Cerebral malaria: Bumgarner, *Parade,* 103; Caraccilo, *Beyond,* 143.

3. Japanese use of POW labor: Tanaka, *Horrors,* 16–18, Kerr, *Surrender,* 24–27, 83–89, 104–5; Daws, *Prisoners,* 96–98; Michno, *Hellships,* 130–32; Hisakazu Fujita, "POWs and International Law," in Towle, et al., *Japanese,* 87–102. These men are Walter L. Dencker of California, Arnold D. Amoroso of Massachusetts, Clair M. Conzelman of Connecticut, Albert D. Miller of Ohio, Edwin V. Kerr of Illinois, Memory H. Cain of New Mexico, Oliver B. Witten of New Mexico, John C. Luikart of New Mexico, and Alan R. McCracken of Illinois. Duke may refer to Marine Corps Lieutenant Colonel George D. "Duke" Hamilton of Florida. Only Amoroso, Cain, and McCracken would survive the war to return home. "Alan Reed McCracken," *The Quan,* February 1990, 9; McCoy, Mellnik, Kelley, *Tojo,* 59–60; Lee, *Pacific,* 172; Dencker, Walter L., Arnold D. Amoroso, Clair M. Conzelman, Albert D. Miller, Edwin V. Kerr, Memory H. Cain, Oliver B. Witten, John C. Luikart, Alan R. McCracken, and George D. Hamilton, RG389, POW-PGM, NARA.

4. Shipment of POWs to Manchuria and Japan: Michno, *Hellships,* 47–54; Kerr, *Surrender,* 111–13; Dyess, *Story,* 148.

5. Prison draft for Davao and motivation to leave: Dyess, *Story,* 148; McCoy, Mellnik, Kelley, *Tojo,* 69–72; Lawton, *Some,* 46–47; Kerr, *Surrender,* 116; Caraccilo, *Beyond,* 155; Donald H. Wills with Reyburn W. Myers, *The Sea Was My Last Chance: Memoir of an American Captured on Bataan in 1942 Who Escaped in 1944 and Led the Liberation of Western Mindanao* (Jefferson, NC: McFarland and Co., 1992), 33.

6. Journey timeline: Michno, *Hellships,* 74–75; Dyess, *Story,* 148–53; Kerr, *Surrender,* 117–18; McCracken, *Very,* 35–42; Wills, *Sea,* 33–35.

7. This is probably Colonel Eugene H. Mitchell of Texas, who was liberated from a prison camp in Mukden, Manchuria, in August 1945. Mitchell, Eugene H., RG389, POW-PGM, NARA.

8. *Erie Maru* was a 5,493-ton cargo ship built in 1920 by the Asano Company in Japan. The submarine USS *Sturgeon* sank the ship on January 11, 1944. Michno, *Hellships,* 74, 323n59. Conditions and sleeping aboard *Erie Maru:* Dyess, *Story,* 149–50; Lawton, *Some,* 51; Michno, *Hellships,* 74; Wills, *Sea,* 34; Hawkins, *Never,* 18.

9. The Battle of Santa Cruz took place October 26–27, 1942.

10. Colonel Guy H. Stubbs reported this to be Second Lieutenant Edward J. Fitzgerald of Massachusetts, who, suffering from seasickness, malaria, and dysentery when the ship left Manila, died on October 31, 1942, and was buried in a shallow grave adjacent to the wharf. Dyess, *Story,* 152; Jackson, *Diary,* 82; sworn statement by Guy Haines Stubbs, September 15, 1945, RG331, SCAP, Box 1095, NARA.

11. The ship zigzagged, bore no markings indicating it carried POWs, and left Manila with its lights blacked out. Dyess, *Story,* 150, 152; McCoy, Mellnik, Kelley, *Tojo,* 72–73. These would be the docks for the Lansang Lumber Company. Dyess, *Story,* 153; Heisinger, *Father,* 311. The penal colony was approximately 15 miles from the docks. Kerr, *Surrender,* 118; Mellnik, *Philippine,* 176; Lawton, *Some,* 53.

12. The other death was possibly Chief Warrant Officer Frederic C. Ambrose of Massachusetts, who died on November 4, 1942, and was buried at sea as the ship neared Mindanao. Jackson, *Diary,* 82–83; sworn statement by Guy Haines Stubbs, September 15, 1945, RG 331, SCAP, Box 1095, NARA.

13. Charles Royall Dunnagan was assigned to the headquarters of the Philippine Department. He died on September 7, 1944, on *Shinyo Maru.* Dunnagan, Charles R., RG389, POW-PGM, NARA; North Carolina State College, *Agromeck 1938* (Raleigh, NC: North Carolina State College, 1938), 43. Food aboard ship: Lawton, *Some,* 52; Dyess, *Story,* 150–51; McCoy, Mellnik, Kelley, *Tojo,* 73; McCracken, *Very,* 39; Wills, *Sea,* 34–35.

14. Major Kazuo Maeda, a 53-year-old from Ishi-chi, Mie Prefecture, served as camp commander of Davao Penal Colony from October 15, 1942 to March 1944. He taught middle school gymnastics in civilian life prior to the war. A U.S. Eighth Army Headquarters military commission sentenced him to 30 years imprisonment with hard labor him for mistreatment of prisoners. *United States of America v. Kazuo Maeda,* Headquarters U.S. Eighth Army, Yokohama, Japan, November 8, 1948, 1–5, RDCWCT; interrogation of Kazuo Maeda, July 14, 1947; perpetuation of testimony of Robert J. Endres, September 31, 1946; perpetuation of testimony by Eugene F. Kowalski, August 23, 1946; sworn statement by Alexander Mariano,

September 13, 1945, RG331, SCAP, Box 1079, NARA; Lukacs, *Escape,* 129; Nordin, *Nothing,* 78; Hawkins, *Never,* 32–33.

15. Lieutenant Yoshimasa Hozumi, "The Crown Prince of Swat," was known as a disciplinarian who openly slapped and berated his men. Mellnik, *Philippine,* 188; McCoy, Mellnik, Kelley, *Tojo,* 76; Lukacs, *Escape,* 102–3, 129; Grashio, *Freedom,* 78; Hawkins, *Never,* 13.

16. First Lieutenant Kempei Yuki of Taihoku, Formosa, was a former schoolteacher, a Catholic, and spoke English. At Dapecol he served as the assistant to the commandant and acted as the liaison officer between the prisoners and the camp commander. Kerr, *Surrender,* 129; Heisinger, *Father,* 323; Lawton, *Some,* 66; memorandum to Prosecution Section (Report No. 233) from Executive Officer, War Crimes Branch, United States Army Forces, Pacific, on Davao Penal Colony and Davao City Civilian Internment Camp, March 7, 1946, 10, RG331, SCAP, Box 1128, NARA; testimony of Kempei Yuki, November 23, 1945, RG331, SCAP, Box 1079, NARA; statement of John M. Fowler, October 18, 1945, RG331, SCAP, Box 1087, NARA.

17. Camp Casising, five kilometers southwest of Malaybalay, was a prewar training camp for the Philippine Constabulary, and as a prison camp housed around 1,000 American army personnel who surrendered in May 1942. On October 18, 1942, the Japanese moved these prisoners onto the freighter *Maru 760* at Bugo, arriving at Davao on October 23. Michno, *Hellships,* 73; Nordin, *Nothing,* 57–73; PMG, *Prisoners,* November 19, 1945. Major General William F. Sharp of Maryland was commander of the Visayan-Mindanao Force and later took sole command of all forces on Mindanao. He was liberated from a prison camp in Mukden, Manchuria, in August 1945. Morton, *Philippines,* 69–70, 360, 501–19, 574–82; Beebe, *Rising,* 108, 205; James, *Mukden,* 146. Camp Casising POW supplies: Nordin, *Nothing,* 53, 64, 73; Mellnik, *Philippine,* 180; Grashio, *Freedom,* 82; Sidney Stewart, *Give Us This Day* (New York: W.W. Norton and Co., Inc., 1956), 95–96; Betty B. Jones, *The December Ship: A Story of Lt. Col. Arden R. Boellner's Capture in the Philippines, Imprisonment, and Death on a World War II Japanese Hellship* (Jefferson, NC: McFarland and Co., 1992), 65–77. Lieutenant Colonel Marcus B. Boulware of South Carolina and Lieutenant Colonel Howard R. Perry, Jr., of Illinois both died on *Brazil Maru* on January 23 and 28, 1945, respectively. Lieutenant Colonel Howard J. Edmands of Massachusetts commanded the Cebu Military Police Regiment prior to his surrender in April 1942. He died on *Enoura Maru* on December 27, 1944. Morton, *Philippines,* 503–5; Boulware, Marcus B., Perry, Howard R., and Edmands, Howard J., RG389, POW-PGM, NARA.

18. Davao Penal Colony description: John Hugh McGee, *Rice and Salt: A History of the Defense and Occupation of Mindanao During World War II* (San Antonio, TX: The Naylor Co., 1962), 72–74; Nordin, *Nothing,* 74–75; Lukacs, *Escape,* 122–26; McCracken, *Very,* 42–44. Postwar, the Philippine government rebuilt Davao Penal Colony and it continues to operate today.

CHAPTER 10 LIFE AT DAPECOL

1. Civilian interpreter Mr. Nishimura's moniker "Simon Legree" references the brutal slave dealer in Harriet Beecher Stowe's novel *Uncle Tom's Cabin.* Nordin, *Nothing,* 77–78; McGee, *Salt,* 73; Hawkins, *Never,* 29–30; perpetuation of testimony of David L. Hardee, September 19, 1946, RG331, SCAP, Box 1095, NARA; memorandum to Prosecution Section from Executive Officer, War Crimes Branch, United States Army Forces, Pacific, on Davao Penal Colony, January 9, 1946, 9, RG331, SCAP, Box 1128, NARA; assorted statements and testimonies, RG331, SCAP, Box 1080, NARA.

2. Lieutenant Hiroshi Oura served as guard commander of the camp and was in charge of general affairs. During the movement of prisoners from Dapecol to Manila, he commanded the prison guards and bore primary responsibility for the POW treatment aboard *Yashu Maru* and *Singoto Maru.* Postwar testimony by some Japanese guards implicated him in the killing Major Charles Harrison. McCracken, *Very,* 93; McGee, *Salt,* 87; Gene Dale, John Morrett, and Bert Schwarz, "We Lived to Tell," *Collier's* 115, no. 9 (March 3, 1945): 32; memorandum to Prosecution Section (Report No. 233) from Executive Officer, War Crimes Branch, United States Army Forces, Pacific, on Davao Penal Colony and Davao City Civilian Internment Camp, March 7, 1946, 10, RG331, SCAP, Box 1128, NARA; memorandum to Prosecution Section (Report No. 210) from Executive Officer, War Crimes Branch, United States Army Forces, Pacific, on transportation of prisoners of war under improper conditions from Davao Penal Colony, Mindanao, P.I. to Manila, P.I. from June 6 to June 26, 1944, February 19, 1946, 4, RG331, SCAP, Box 1127, NARA; assorted statements and testimonies, RG331, SCAP, Box 1080, NARA.

3. A judo expert, Sergeant Major Hashimoto was later commissioned as a second lieutenant. Mapes, *Butchers,* 192–93; Dale, Morrett, Schwarz, "We Lived to Tell," *Collier's* 115, no. 9 (March 3, 1945): 32; testimony of Denver R. Rose, James H. Berry, D.J. Olinger, RG331, SCAP, Box 1079, NARA; memorandum to Prosecution Section (Report No. 233) from Executive Officer, War Crimes Branch, United States Army Forces, Pacific, on Davao Penal Colony and Davao City Civilian Internment Camp, March 7, 1946, 8, RG331, SCAP, Box 1128, NARA.

4. Carabao discipline: Dale, Morrett, Schwarz, "We Lived to Tell," *Collier's* 115, no. 9 (March 3, 1945): 32; Stewart, *Give,* 109–11; McCracken, *Very,* 88.

5. Licanan Airfield was built in the district of Bunawan, Barangay San Isidro, Davao, ten miles south of the camp by the Lasang River. "Licanan Airfield," PacificWrecks.com. Airfield detail and *Shinyo Maru:* Michno, *Hellships,* 226–31; Mapes, *Butchers,* 187–216; Knox, *Death,* 293–311; Nordin, *Nothing,* 121–26; U.S. Department of War, Military Intelligence Division Report, *Prisoners of War in the Philippine Islands* (Washington, DC: Military Intelligence Division), September 20, 1944.

6. Hardee recorded that among the officers who were appointed leaders by the Japanese in Dapecol were Lieutenant Colonel Richard G. Hunter as overall American leader, later succeeded by Lieutenant Colonel Russell J. Nelson and then Lieutenant Colonel Kenneth S. Olson. Commander Warner P. Portz, the senior naval officer, served as advisor to the American leader. Lieutenant Colonel Dwight M. Deter, Medical Corps, commanded the hospital, along with Lieutenant Colonel George. T. Colvard as executive officer, until he left for Lasang Airfield. Captain George A. Rader served as hospital adjutant for the camp's entire occupation. Lieutenant Colonel Guy Stubbs served as mess officer. Prominent among the detail leaders and workers in the camp were Majors Van F. Houston and George T. Perkins, Dental Corps; Commander Francis J. Bridget; Lieutenant Colonels John C. Luikart (leader of the basket-making detail), Marcus B. Boulware, Halstead C. Fowler, George D. "Chico" Vanture, Paul S. Beard, Leroy M. Edwards, Howard J. Edmands, Walter L. Dencker, Irving Compton, John H. McGee, Jack W. Sewall, Thomas R. Wilson, Cyril. Q. Marron, Ronald C. "Scottie" Macdonald, Arnold D. Amoroso, Albert D. (Duke) Miller, Clair M. Conzelman, Frank F. Carpenter, Jr., and Chaplain William Dawson. Also prominent were Major Thomas N. Powell, Sr., his son, Captain Thomas N. Powell, Jr., Majors Charles Harrison, Alvin T. Wilson, Ralph E. Rumbold, and Captains Charles R. Dunnagan, Marion R. "Manny" Lawton, and Julian V. Lyon of the Marine Corps.

7. Dapecol library: McCracken, *Very,* 101–2; Wills, *Sea,* 48, 52.

8. "Mactan Dipper" rice rations: McCracken, *Very,* 46; Nordin, *Nothing,* 80. Hat detail: McCracken, *Very,* 50–52, 73; Mellnik, *Philippine,* 181, 203–4.

9. "The Flaming Asshole:" Dyess, *Story,* 162; Grashio, *Freedom,* 90; Zimmerman, "Diary," 121.

10. Del Monte Field was built in a natural meadow amidst the Del Monte Corporation's pineapple plantations from November-December 1941 in northern Mindanao, north of Mangima Canyon off Sayre Highway, for B-17s of the 19th Bombardment Group. Walter D. Edmonds, *They Fought With What They Had: The Story of the Army Air Forces in the Southwest Pacific, 1941–1942* (Boston: Little, Brown, and Co., 1951), 14, 53–57, 68.

11. Major Lawrence F. Prichard of Illinois served with the 45th Infantry (PS) and 43rd Infantry (PS) during the fighting on Bataan. He died on January 9, 1945, on *Enoura Maru.* Prichard, Lawrence F., RG389, POW-PGM, NARA; memorials, "Lawrence F. Prichard 1936," West Point Association of Graduates, online. Christmas 1942: McCracken, *Very,* 53–54; Jackson, *Diary,* 91; Nordin, *Nothing,* 89; Dyess, *Story,* 163–64; Grashio, *Freedom,* 89; Hawkins, *Never,* 52–59.

12. Christmas 1943: Jackson, *Diary,* 145; McCracken, *Very,* 122–25; Hawkins, *Never,* 52–55; Nordin, *Nothing,* 115–16; *United States of America v. Kazuo Maeda,* Headquarters U.S. Eighth Army, Yokohama, Japan, November 8, 1948, 2, 6.

13. Red Cross packages: Kerr, *Surrender,* 125–28, 138–39; McCracken, *Very,* 56–64; McGee, *Salt,* 93; Dyess, *Story,* 160–61; Lawton, *Some,* 69–71; McCoy, Mellnik, Kelley, *Tojo,* 80–83.

14. Japanese camp quartermaster Lieutenant Sumio Shiraji spoke good English and had been a banker in prewar southern Japan. McGee, *Salt,* 88; Sworn statement by Austin J. Montgomery, January 23, 1946, RG331, SCAP, Box 1083, NARA; Lukacs, *Escape,* 131.

15. Tobacco and POWs: McCracken, *Very,* 96, 106; Grashio, *Freedom,* 73–74; Chunn, *Rice,* 88; Daws, *Prisoners,* 114–18.

16. Camp exchange: McGee, *Salt,* 101; McCracken, *Very,* 66; Wills, *Sea,* 44.

17. First Lieutenant Osamu Yoshimura, Imperial Japanese Army Medical Corps, from Kosa, Japan, was in charge of all of Dapecol's medical work and supplies. Some prisoners credited him as the only Japanese guard who helped men to safety in the sinking of *Shinyo Maru.* McGee, *Salt,* 88; Lawton, *Some,* 58; *United States of America v. Kazuo Maeda,* Headquarters U.S. Eighth Army, Yokohama, Japan, November 8, 1948, 11; Heisinger, *Father,* 395; sworn statement by Osamu Yoshimura, February 1, 1946, RG331, SCAP, Box 1095, NARA. Lieutenant Colonel (Dr.) Dwight M. Deter, Medical Corps, of Texas was a surgeon assigned to the headquarters of the Visayan-Mindanao Force. Lawton, *Some,* 55; Deter, Dwight M., RG389, POW-PGM, NARA; "Texan Gets Medal Posthumously for Service on Bataan," *Brownsville* (TX) *Herald,* September 16, 1946, 1. Captain (Dr.) George A. Rader, Medical Corps, of North Carolina, served at Sternberg General Hospital then the 12th Medical Regiment at Fort McKinley. Deter and Rader both died on *Arisan Maru* on October 24, 1944. Andrew Rader U.S. Army Health Clinic, "The Andrew Rader Story," U.S. Army Medical Department online; Lawton, *Some,* 55; Rader, George A., RG389, POW-PGM, NARA.

18. Chaplain (Captain) Frederick B. Howden, Jr., of New Mexico served as the chaplain for the 200th Coast Artillery (AA). At Davao, suffering from dysentery and pellagra brought on by malnutrition, he unselfishly gave his rations to other ill prisoners prior to his death on December 11, 1942. Martin, *Brothers,* 137–40;

Jackson, *Diary,* 89. Lieutenant Colonel Joseph A. Sullivan of New Hampshire was a member of the Quartermaster Corps and died of disease and illness at Dapecol on November 12, 1942. He left behind a wife and three sons, Joseph, Robert, and Donald, in San Francisco. Sullivan, Joseph A., RG389, POW-PGM, NARA; "Lt. Col. Sullivan, Rochester, Dies as Jap Prisoner," *Portsmouth* (NH) *Herald,* July 17, 1943, 1, 8. Dapecol dead: Roger Mansell, "Known to have perished at Davao POW Camp," Center for Research of Allied POWs Under the Japanese online; *United States of America v. Kazuo Maeda,* Headquarters U.S. Eighth Army, Yokohama, Japan, November 8, 1948, 1, 4; sworn statement by Guy Haines Stubbs, September 15, 1945; sworn testimony by Orville T. Shaw, September 11, 1945, RG331, SCAP, Box 1095, NARA.

19. Cabanatuan improvements: Chunn, *Rice,* 28–57; Knox, *Death,* 228–37.

20. Corregidor rations: Morton, *Philippines,* 375–76, 534–35, 543.

CHAPTER 11 A HERNIA SAVED MY LIFE

1. Chickens: Mellnik, *Philippine,* 197–206; Grashio, *Freedom,* 99; McCoy, Mellnik, Kelley, *Tojo,* 84.

2. Coffee grove: McCracken, *Very,* 73–74; Mellnik, *Philippine,* 197–98.

3. NRA meat: McCracken, *Very,* 47; Nordin, *Nothing,* 79–80; Wills, *Sea,* 27, 42; Jackson, *Diary,* 127–134.

4. Escape planning: Mellnik, *Philippine,* 182–223; Lukacs, *Escape,* 133–81; Grashio, *Freedom,* 95–104; McCoy, Mellnik, Kelley, *Tojo,* 78–86; Hawkins, *Never,* 60–71, 81–103.

5. The ten prisoners included Melvyn H. McCoy, Stephen M. Mellnik, William E. Dyess, Austin C. Shoffner, Jack Hawkins, Michael Dobervitch, Sam C. Grashio, Leo A. Boelens, Robert B. Spielman, Paul H. Marshall, and two Filipino convicts who acted as guides through the jungle swamps, Victorio Jumarong and Benigno de la Cruz. Accounts by participants: Dyess, *Story;* Mellnik, *Philippine;* Grashio, *Freedom;* McCoy, Mellnik, Kelley, *Tojo;* Hawkins, *Never.* Japanese reprisal: Lawton, *Some,* 74; Nordin, *Nothing,* 104–5; Mapes, *Butchers,* 180; Grashio, *Freedom,* 114.

6. The Japanese moved the prisoners to the smaller compound around April 11, 1943. McCracken, *Very,* 78; Nordin, *Nothing,* 104; Lawton, *Some,* 74; Jackson, *Diary,* 107. Kangkong is known also as *Ipomoea aquatica,* or Chinese water spinach.

7. Religion at Dapecol: Nordin, *Nothing,* 79, 103–4; McCracken, *Very,* 106; Grashio, *Freedom,* 74–75.

8. Rogers was sent to the island of Cebu to train members of the 33rd Infantry (PA) prior to the American surrender. Captain Griffith M. Berg (also listed as M. Griffith) of Washington served with the 57th Infantry (PS) at Bataan. George T.

Colvard, formerly of the New Mexico National Guard, served as the surgeon for the 200th Coast Artillery (AA). In March 1944, Rogers was placed in charge of a 600 to 650 prisoner contingent sent to Lasang to work on the Licanan Airfield. On September 7, 1944, Rogers, Berg, Colvard, and hundreds of other Americans died on *Shinyo Maru.* Nordin, *Nothing,* 121–22, 126; Mapes, *Butchers,* 189–95; "Lieut. Colonel R.H. 'Bill' Rogers is Reported Prisoner of War of Japanese: Telegram Received Saturday," *Del Rio News-Herald,* May 16, 1943, 1; "Lieut. Col. R.H. Rogers Reported Dead: Lost on Japanese Prison Ship," *Del Rio News-Herald,* February 27, 1945, 1; "Col. Colvard, Lt. Remondini Lost in Action," *Deming* (NM) *Headlight,* March 2, 1945, 1; "Lt. Col George T. Colvard Awarded Bronze Star Medal Posthumously," *Deming Headlight,* March 30, 1945, 1; Rogers, Rufus H.; Berg, M. Griffith; and George T. Colvard, RG389, POW-PGM, NARA.

9. From December 1942 to May 1943, British and Indian forces mounted an offensive into the Arakan coastal area in west Burma, intent on capturing Akyab Island (modern-day Sittwe), but suffered defeat at the hands of the Japanese. Spector, *Eagle,* 346–48; Gerhard L. Weinberg, *A World at Arms: A Global History of World War II* (New York: Cambridge University Press, 1994), 633.

10. Escape versus repercussion: Doyle, *Duty,* 149–61; Lawton, *Some,* 73–74; Knox, *Death,* 269–70; Kerr, *Surrender,* 145–46; Stewart, *Give,* 111–12.

11. Texas native Dyess's story was posthumously published in installments in the *Chicago Daily Tribune* beginning on January 30, 1944, and in the February 7, 1944, issue of *Life* magazine. His account revealed to the American people the fate of the American and Filipino forces on Bataan and Corregidor. The details of Japanese brutality reinvigorated the American war effort in the Pacific. Promoted after his escape, first to major and then to lieutenant colonel, Dyess was preparing to return to combat when he died on December 22, 1943, after his P-38 fighter crashed in California on a training flight. Dyess, *Story,* 26; Lukacs, *Escape,* 277–336; Kerr, *Surrender,* 162–64; Dower, *Mercy,* 50–51; Doyle, *Duty,* 167–68.

12. Hardee's pay: Olsen, "War Diary," 38; "List of Items of Colonel David L. Hardee, Claims Against the Japanese Government to accompany WCC Form 802, January 1950," February 28, 1950, original in possession of Mrs. Mary Hardee Stutz. Havelock, NC.

13. Dapecol barracks and vermin: Nordin, *Nothing,* 75–77, 81; McGee, *Salt,* 105, 111; Lawton, *Some,* 62–63; Dyess, *Story,* 155; Heisinger, *Father,* 314–16; McCracken, *Very,* 42–43, 78; Wills, *Sea,* 36–37, 41–42; testimony of Austin J. Montgomery, January 23, 1946, RG331, SCAP, Box 1128, NARA.

14. At Cabanatuan, the Japanese used prisoners as film extras in the propaganda film, *Down with the Stars and Stripes,* recreating scenes of the American surrender

in the Philippines. Knox, *Death,* 240–42; Jacobsen, *Refused,* 166–67; Bilek, *Uncle,* 117–18.

15. Major George T. Perkins, Medical Corps, of Texas, was liberated from a prison camp in Japan in August 1945. Major Robert V. Nelson of Minnesota served in the Army Dental Corps and died on *Brazil Maru* on January 21, 1945. William D. Miner with Lewis A. Miner, ed., *Surrender on Cebu: A POW's Diary—WWII* (Paducah, KY: Turner Publishing Co., 2001), 101; Perkins, George T. and Robert V. Nelson, RG389, POW-PGM, NARA; "9 South Texans Among Prisoners," *San Antonio Express,* May 4, 1943, 1; "5 Bataan Vets Held in Japan," *San Antonio Light,* July 4, 1945, 10A; "12 from State War Prisoners: Soldiers Held in Jap Camps Listed," *Moorhead Daily News* (MN), July 1, 1943, 9.

16. "Phonies:" Armand Hopkins, "Prisoner of War, 1942–1945, Reminiscences of Armand Hopkins" (unpublished, 1984), 31; McCracken, *Very,* 17. There were instances of civilians, notably Theodore Lewin and Robert W. Levering, being caught up in the prisons and incorporated with the military personnel. Daws, *Prisoners,* 88–89, 310–12; Levering, *Trek.*

CHAPTER 12 MORE LIFE AT DAPECOL

1. Hardee originally included this breakfast menu and other recipes with his memoir. Similar recipes can be found in Dorothy Wagner, *Recipes Out of Bilibid, Collected by Col. H.C. Fowler, U.S.A.* (New York: George W. Stewart, Pub., Inc., 1946).

2. Hunger and mental diversion: McCracken, *Very,* 105–113; McGee, *Salt,* 77; Daws, *Prisoners,* 124–27, 266–67; Caraccilo, *Beyond,* 152–53; Lawton, *Some,* 209, 225–26. *Ladies Home Journal:* McCracken, *Very,* 122–23.

3. Japanese newspapers: Caraccilo, *Beyond,* 165–66; Lawton, *Some,* 79; McCracken, *Very,* 102–13, 129–38. Operation Husky, the invasion of Sicily, took place from July-August 1943.

4. Admiral Isoroku Yamamoto was commander-in-chief of the Imperial Japanese Combined Fleet. He died on April 18, 1943, when American fighters shot down his bomber transport over Bougainville. Donald A. David, *Lightning Strike: The Secret Mission to Kill Admiral Yamamoto and Avenge Pearl Harbor* (New York: St. Martin's Press, 2005); Breuer, *Undercover,* 93–101.

5. The Japanese began to move American prisoners around the Philippines and overseas beginning in August 1942. Kerr, *Surrender,* 107–24; Michno, *Hellships,* 33–86; Wainwright, *General,* 167–75; James, *Mukden,* 45–47. Hardee is referencing the movement of approximately 1,961 prisoners from Cabanatuan in October 1942 to Mukden, Manchuria; Pusan, Korea; and Osaka, Japan, aboard *Tottori Maru;* Michno, *Hellships,* 47–54; Kerr, *Surrender,* 111–13.

6. The landings at Salerno, Calabria, and Taranto took place from September 3–16, 1943.

7. Operation Torch, the invasion of French North Africa, took place from November 8–16, 1942. German Field Marshall Erwin Rommel commanded the *Afrika Korps* from 1941 to 1943, which surrendered to the Allied forces in Tunisia on May 13, 1943.

8. U.S. Pacific strategy: Williamson Murray and Allan R. Millett, *A War to be Won: Fighting the Second World War* (Cambridge, MA: Belknap Press of Harvard University Press, 2000), 338–41; Weinberg, *World,* 636–37, 642–56; Spector, *Eagle,* 225–26; Dan van der Vat, *The Pacific Campaign: The U.S.-Japanese Naval War 1941–1945* (New York: Simon and Schuster, 1991), 282–90. The Battle of Attu, May 11–30, 1943, featured a personnel disparity of over six to one. Stetson Conn, Rose C. Engelman, and Byron Fairchild, *Guarding the United States and Its Outposts* (Washington, DC: CMH, 1962), 279–95. The "Doolittle Raid" led by Lieutenant Colonel James Doolittle took place on April 18, 1942. Weinberg, *World,* 332; Toland, *Rising,* 304–10.

9. Beards and razors: Dyess, *Story,* 132; Nordin, *Nothing,* 81, 105–7. Wilson fought with the 102nd Infantry (PA) on Bataan. He died on January 9, 1945, on *Enoura Maru.* Wilson, Alvin T., RG389, POW-PGM, NARA; Lehigh University, *The Epitome,* vol. 46 (Bethlehem, PA: Lehigh University Junior Class, 1922), 101.

10. Interpreter Shusuke Wada was a married businessman from Shikoku, Japan, and on *Oryoku Maru, Enoura Maru,* and *Brazil Maru* during the movement of prisoners from the Philippines to Japan and Korea. In May 1947, a war crimes tribunal found Wada guilty of the unlawful mistreatment, abuse, and physical and mental suffering of the prisoners and sentenced him to life imprisonment with hard labor. Nordin, *Nothing,* 122; Heisinger, *Father,* 447–50, 488–505; Chunn, *Rice,* 111–19; Micho, *Hellships,* 258–65; Caraccilo, *Beyond,* 220–21; *United States of America v. Junsaburo Toshino et al.,* Headquarters U.S. Eighth Army, Yokohama, Japan, May 4, 1948, 9–14, 26–27, 30–31, 43, RDCWCT; "Doom Two Japs Blamed in 1,300 Hell Ship Deaths," *Chicago Daily Tribune* (*CDT*), May 9, 1947, 3; perpetuation of testimony of David Peace, Jr., August 14, 1946, RG331, SCAP, Box 1083, NARA.

11. Japanese POW cards: Kerr, *Surrender,* 138–39; Ashton, *Somebody,* 298–300; Glusman, *Conduct,* 240.

12. These Red Cross packages and Christmas presents arrived in early November 1943 in Manila. Feuer, *Bilibid,* 148–58; Chunn, *Rice,* 165–66; Jacobsen, *Refused,* 160–62; Jackson, *Diary,* 145.

13. Supply and logistical disparity between American and Japanese fighting men: Richard B. Frank, *Downfall: The End of the Imperial Japanese Empire* (New

York: Random House, 1999), 77–80, 154–56; Allan R. Millett and Peter Maslowski, *For the Common Defense: A Military History of the United States of America*, rev. ed. (New York: Free Press, 1994), 476; Max Hastings, *Retribution: The Battle for Japan, 1944–45* (New York: Alfred A. Knopf, 2007), 53.

14. The third and fourth packages were issued on April 8 and June 8, 1944. McCracken, *Very,* 150–51, 157–58; Nordin, *Nothing,* 132, 143; Jackson, *Diary,* 162, 173.

15. Sergeant John H. McPhee of Michigan served with the 1st General Hospital at Bataan. He was killed on March 30, 1943. Sergeant John H. McPhee, American Battle Monuments Commission, World War II database online. Regarding his death: Lukcas, *Escape,* 180–81; Dyess, *Story,* 158; Jackson, *Diary,* 105; *United States of America v. Kazuo Maeda,* Headquarters U.S. Eighth Army, Yokohama, Japan, November 8, 1948, 9; perpetuation of testimony of David L. Hardee, September 18, 1946, RG331, SCAP, Box 1095, NARA; perpetuation of testimony of Marion W. Taylor, December 26, 1945, RG331, SCAP, Box 1128, NARA. On May 22, 1944, Private First Class Joseph L. Grossman of California apparently forgot a Japanese camp rule to not approach more than one meter from the fence. Nordin, *Nothing,* 137; McCracken, *Very,* 152.

16. One of the two men was Lieutenant Colonel Arnold D. Amoroso of Massachusetts. On his card Amoroso wrote "I am being well treated here, just like a French colony," in reference to the infamous Devil's Island prison in French Guiana. McCracken, *Very,* 66–67; Jackson, *Diary,* 123; *United States of America v. Kazuo Maeda,* Headquarters U.S. Eighth Army, Yokohama, Japan, November 8, 1948, 9.

CHAPTER 13 FINAL DAYS AT DAPECOL

1. Captain Mark M. Wohlfeld of New York served as the executive officer of the 27th Bombardment Group before joining the Provisional Air Corps Regiment. He escaped Dapecol on March 27, 1944, and fought with the Filipino guerrillas until December 1944, when he joined the 1st Cavalry. Doyle, *Duty,* 163–65; Knox, *Death,* 275–82; "Philippines Hero Visits Cruces," *Las Cruces* (NM) *Sun News,* June 2, 1946, 5; "Prisoners in Jap Camp Reunited After 22 Years," *Titusville* (PA) *Herald,* May 5, 1966, 5; "Obituary," *NYT,* May 10, 1978, D16. Second Lieutenant Hadley C. Watson of North Carolina fought with the 57th Infantry (PS) prior to his surrender. After escaping with Wohlfeld he served with Filipino guerrillas on Mindanao until the war's end. Knox, *Death,* 275–82; "Hadley C. Watson," *The Quan,* August 1997, 16. Joining Wohlfeld and Watson were Marvin H. Campbell, Andrew T. Bukovinsky, James D. Haburne, James Edwin McClure, and Baldwin Boone. All but Boone made good their escape. Knox, *Death,* 275–92; Lawton, *Some,* 81–96. The

four men that did not escape and surrendered were Captain Glenn W. Wohler, Warrant Officer Otis A. Carmichael, and Second Lieutenants Elliott David "Mickey" Wright and Carl G. Fansler. McCracken, *Very,* 150; Lawton, *Some,* 86; Knox, *Death,* 277.

2. The Japanese caught and killed Boone of Tennessee after the escape on March 28, 1944. Knox, *Death,* 283; Lawton, *Some,* 96; Jackson, *Diary,* 161; McGee, *Salt,* 123; Boone, Baldwin, RG389, POW-PGM, NARA.

3. The nickname "Pittsburgh" came about as he allegedly lived in prewar Pittsburgh, Pennsylvania. Mapes, *Butchers,* 183; perpetuation of testimony of James L. Sweeney, May 17, 1945; perpetuation of testimony of Walter J. Regehr, June 13, 1945, RG331, SCAP, Box 1083, NARA.

4. Prisoners recovered Boone's body on April 2, 1944, and buried him around the fifth. Nordin, *Nothing,* 132; Jackson, *Diary,* 162. Hardee later received a postcard from Wohlfeld postmarked Tokyo, Japan, with the inscription: "It took me four years and thousands of rounds but I finally got here." Mark Wohlfeld to Dave Hardee, September 25, 1946, folder labeled "Correspondence, 1945–1946, n.d., DLHP, NCA, Box 79.

5. "Toonerville Trolley:" McCracken, *Very,* 42; Mapes, *Butchers,* 178. On October 23, 1943, Privates Robert Lee Pease and Oscar Burton Brown escaped as described by Hardee. Nordin, *Nothing,* 114–15; McCracken, *Very,* 119; Jackson, *Diary,* 135–36; testimony of Austin J. Montgomery, January 23, 1946, RG331, SCAP, Box 1128, NARA.

6. Harrison's attempted escape of May 20, 1944: McCracken, *Very,* 153; Nordin, *Nothing,* 136; Lawton, *Some,* 97; Wills, *Sea,* 48–49; Jackson, *Diary,* 169; perpetuation of testimony of David L. Hardee, September 18, 1946, RG331, SCAP, Box 1095, NARA.

7. Guy Haines Stubbs of Pennsylvania served as antiaircraft liaison officer for USAFFE on Bataan and later as Dapecol camp commander in May 1944. He was liberated from Nagoya POW Camp No. 78, Toyama, Japan, in August 1945. Kerr, *Surrender,* 282; memorials, "Guy H. Stubbs, 1923," West Point Association of Graduates, online; Stubbs, Guy Haines, RG389, POW-PGM, NARA. Death of Harrison: Lawton, *Some,* 99; Jackson, *Diary,* 170; affidavit by Austin J. Montgomery, January 23, 1946; perpetuation of testimony of Charles Edward McKewen, May 14, 1944; sworn statement by Osamu Yoshimura, February 1, 1946, RG331, SCAP, Box 1095, NARA; sworn statement by Osamu Yoshimura April 9, 1946, RG331, SCAP, Box 1080, NARA.

8. Captain James Russell Hutchinson's prison radio: Daws, *Prisoners,* 279–83; Chunn, *Rice,* 106–7; Caracillo, *Beyond,* 162, 190.

9. Juan Acenas detested the Japanese treatment of the Dapecol farms and provided the McCoy-Mellnik escapees with the route out of Dapecol. Postwar, he

became Dapecol's superintendent. Lukacs, *Escape,* 135, 159–60, 349; Mellnik, *Philippine,* 185, 194, 217; Grashio, *Freedom,* 102–3.

10. Filipino agricultural adviser Candido "Pop" Abrina worked as a cashier at the Philippine National Bank in Davao City prior to Dapecol. His assistance to the American prisoners was instrumental in the Mellnik-McCoy escape. Lukacs, *Escape,* 133–35; Mellnik, *Philippine,* 183–85; Grashio, *Freedom,* 98–99.

11. The men left Dapecol for Lasang on March 2, 1944. Nordin, *Nothing,* 121–22; Mapes, *Butchers,* 188–89. Airfield construction: Nordin, *Nothing,* 121–32; Lawton, *Some,* 138–40; Mapes, *Butchers,* 187–96.

12. Hardee owed Gerken over $150, and after his liberation he sent the money to Gerken's mother. Hardee later wrote that "she believed me the most honest of men since no one alive, except myself, knew of the debt. He had saved my life. It was blood money so I had beat the Devil and kept myself squared with the Lord." Checkbook, Philippine Trust Company, DLHP, Box 79, NCA.

13. Hellship losses: Michno, *Hellships,* 281–83, 292–96; Daws, *Prisoners,* 295–97. *Shinyo Maru:* Michno, *Hellships,* 174, 225–30; Knox, *Death,* 293–311; Mapes, *Butchers,* 197–204; Lawton, *Some,* 138–46. Commander Samuel J. Wilson was a millionaire in Manila, but his wife and children were imprisoned in Santo Tomas. On Mindanao, he handled all guerrilla finances for the 10th Military District under Colonel Wendell Fertig but was not involved in the rescue of *Shinyo Maru* survivors. John Keats, *They Fought Alone: A True Story of a Modern American Hero* (Philadelphia: J. B. Lippincott Co., 1963), 6–7, 163, 418–19; Larry S. Schmidt, "American Involvement in the Filipino Resistance Movement on Mindanao During the Japanese Occupation, 1942–1945" (master's thesis, U.S. Army Command and General Staff College, 1982), 92–94.

14. Major (later lieutenant colonel) Iku Takasaki from Kagoshima, Japan, replaced Major Maeda in early April 1944 with orders to close the camp and move the POWs to Manila and Cabanatuan. McCracken, *Very,* 151–52; McGee, *Salt,* 116; Jackson, *Diary,* 161–62; Nordin, *Nothing,* 132; sworn statement by Iku Takasaki, November 13, 1945; interview of Iku Takasaki, November 15–17, 1945, RG331, SCAP, Box 1084, NARA. KGEI radio: Daws, *Prisoners,* 65, 130; Chunn, *Rice,* 106–7; Nordin, *Nothing,* 66; Kerr, *Surrender,* 101; Ashton, *Somebody,* 298. *Bushidō:* Tanaka, *Horrors,* 198–208; Harries and Harries, *Sun,* 24–25; Drea, *Emperor,* 75–90.

15. Shiraji at Santo Tomas: A. V. H. Hartendorp, *The Santo Tomas Story,* ed. Frank H. Golay (New York: McGraw-Hill Book Company, 1964), 312, 327–30, 356–57. Liberation of Santo Tomas: Hartendorp, *Tomas,* 405–13; Rupert Wilkinson, *Surviving a Japanese Internment Camp: Life and Liberation at Santo Tomas, Manila, in World War II* (Jefferson, NC: McFarland and Co., 2014), 143–56.

CHAPTER 14 A HELLSHIP TRIP TO BILIBID

1. Frank Carpenter of California was the assistant supply officer for the Bataan echelon of the USAFFE. He was liberated from Bilibid Prison on February 4, 1944. Mellnik, *Philippine,* 204, 226; Kerr, *Surrender,* 78; Morton, *Fall,* 117, 371; Jackson, *Diary,* 165–66; Carpenter, Frank F., Jr., RG389, POW-PGM, NARA.

2. Movement from Dapecol: McCracken, *Very,* 153–56; Nordin, *Nothing,* 138–43; McGee, *Salt,* 129–31; Lawton, *Some,* 102; Jackson, *Diary,* 172; Wills, *Sea,* 1–2; Glusman, *Conduct,* 350; perpetuation of testimony of Walter J. Hinkle, July 13, 1945; perpetuation of testimony of Elmer Franklin Hannah, October 1–3, 1945; perpetuation of testimony of Franklin Oliver Anders, September 27, 1945; perpetuation of testimony of Ralph H. Miller, May 18, 1945; RG331, SCAP, Box 1127, NARA.

3. *Yashu Maru:* Michno, *Hellships,* 173; McCracken, *Very,* 157; Nordin, *Nothing,* 143; Lawton, *Some,* 102.

4. Red Cross boxes: McCracken, *Very,* 157–58; Nordin, *Nothing,* 143–44; Jackson, *Diary,* 173; perpetuation of testimony of Walter J. Hinkle, July 13, 1945; perpetuation of testimony of Franklin Oliver Anders, September 27, 1945, RG331, SCAP, Box 1127, NARA. *Yashu Maru* and convoy: McCracken, *Very,* 157; Nordin, *Nothing,* 144; Michno, *Hellships,* 174; Wills, *Sea,* 2; Jackson, *Diary,* 173–74; perpetuation of testimony of Franklin Oliver Anders, September 27, 1945, RG331, SCAP, Box 1127, NARA.

5. Lieutenant Colonel John H. McGee of North Dakota jumped overboard just after midnight on June 15, 1944. He knew Zamboanga before the war and linked up with the guerrillas once ashore. McGee, *Salt,* 131–61, 239; Jackson, *Diary,* 174; Lawton, *Some,* 103–4; Wills, *Sea,* 2–3. First Lieutenant Donald H. Wills of Virginia, served with the 26th Cavalry (PS) on Bataan and was the librarian at Dapecol. On the morning of June 15, 1944, Wills jumped overboard. He swam ashore, joined the guerrillas, and fought with them until linking up with American forces on Leyte in April 1945. Wills, *Sea,* 3–12; McCracken, *Very,* 158–59; Nordin, *Nothing;* 144–45; Jackson, *Diary,* 174; assorted testimonials, RG331, SCAP, Box 1127, NARA.

6. Voyage and aftermath of *Oryoku Maru:* Michno, *Hellships,* 258–66; Kerr, *Surrender,* 217–37; Lawton, *Some,* 149–212; Feuer, *Bilibid,* 217–44; Caraccilo, *Beyond,* 191–210; Heisinger, *Father,* 443–542; Ashton, *Somebody,* 221–35; MacArthur, *Sword,* 298–308.

7. Fort San Pedro was built by the Spanish in the 18th century. During the Battle of Bataan it served as the USAFFE headquarters for the Visayan-Mindanao Task Force. Lawton, *Some,* 104; Nordin, *Nothing,* 145; Jackson, *Diary,* 174; McCracken,

Very, 160; perpetuation of testimony of Elmer Franklin Hannah, October 1–3, 1945; perpetuation of testimony of Albert Thomas Greathouse, August 1, 1945, RG331, SCAP, Box 1127, NARA. The Battle of Saipan raged from June 15 to July 9, 1944. The Battle of the Philippine Sea from June 19 to 20, 1944, and destroyed the carrier-based air arm of the Imperial Japanese Navy. Spector, *Eagle,* 301–20; Peattie, *Sunburst,* 187–89; Murray and Millett, *War,* 355–60; Millet and Maslowski, *Common,* 464.

8. *Singoto Maru:* Michno, *Hellships,* 175–76; Nordin, *Nothing,* 145–48; McCracken, *Very,* 161–62; Jackson, *Diary,* 175; perpetuation of testimony of Erwin Meiserick, May 28, 1945; Walter J. Hinkle, July 13, 1945, RG 331, SCAP, Box 1127, NARA.

CHAPTER 15 MANILA AND BILIBID

1. Second Lieutenant Willard E. Weden of Minnesota, Army Signal Corps, died on June 26, 1944. Weden, Willard E., RG389, POW-PGM, NARA; Jackson, *Diary,* 176; Nordin, *Nothing,* 146, 148; Kentner, "Journal," 115; Camp Log for Bilibid Prison, 1942—1944, entry for June 26, 1944, RG 407, AGO-POW, Box 38, NARA. Arrival at Bilibid, June 26, 1944: McCracken, *Very,* 162–63; Feuer, *Bilibid,* 204–5; Camp Log for Bilibid Prison, 1942–1944, entry for June 26, 1944, RG407, AGO-POW, Box 38, NARA. Prisoners to Cabanatuan: Nordin, *Nothing,* 148–53; Michno, *Hellships,* 179–82; Jackson, *Diary,* 177.

2. Commissary: Bumgarner, *Parade,* 138; Ashton, *Somebody,* 273; Feuer, *Bilibid,* 200; Kentner, "Journal," 115–16; Ashton, *Diary,* 223. Welfare fund: Ashton, *Somebody,* 277, 302; McCracken, *Very,* 165; Feuer, *Bilibid,* 120. Mongo, commonly known as mung beans (*Vigna radiata*), are cultivated throughout Southeast Asia.

3. Old Bilibid Prison description: Feuer, *Bilibid,* xvi; Bumgarner, *Parade,* 137; Glusman, *Conduct,* 214–15; Ashton, *Diary,* 209–11.

4. Movement of officers to Japan: Daws, *Prisoners,* 293; McCracken, *Very,* 169–70; Feuer, *Bilibid,* 205–18; Kerr, *Survival,* 197, 202.

5. *Canadian Inventor:* Michno, *Hellships,* 179–82; Kentner, "Journal," 116.

6. Captains Charles P. Samson of Oregon, and Elmer P. Fleming, Jr., of North Carolina, both of the field artillery, were liberated from the Tokyo POW Camp (Shinjuku) in August 1945. Samson, Charles P., and Elmer P. Fleming, Jr., RG389, POW-PGM, NARA. *Noto Maru:* Michno, *Hellships,* 190–93; Kentner, "Journal," 120.

7. *Arisan Maru:* Michno, *Hellships,* 249–58; Kerr, *Surrender,* 204–8; Lawton, *Some,* 113–37; Glusman, *Conduct,* 354–67; Kentner, "Journal," 126–27; Camp Log for Bilibid Prison, 1942–1944, entry for October 11, 1944, RG407, AGO-POW, Box 38, NARA.

8. *Oryoku Maru:* Chapter 14, note 6.

9. Commander Lea B. Sartin was the original American commander of Bilibid, replaced on September 25, 1943 by Commander Thomas H. Hayes, replaced in turn in December 1944 by Major Warren A. Wilson. Feuer, *Bilibid,* 137–38; Glusman, *Conduct,* 216–19, 251–52; Ashton, *Somebody,* 271, 291–92; Kentner, "Journal," 25, 79, 133.

10. Asiatic Fleet: Miller, *Orange,* 60; Morton, *Philippines,* 45–47, 90–92; Samuel Eliot Morison, *The Rising Sun in the Pacific, 1931-April 1942,* vol. 3 of *History of United States Naval Operations in World War II* (Boston: Little, Brown and Co., 1948), 28–29, 151–206.

11. Hart of Michigan served as superintendent of the U.S. Naval Academy prior to becoming the last commander of the Asiatic Fleet, from 1939 to 1942. James A. Leutze, *A Different Kind of Victory: A Biography of Admiral Thomas C. Hart* (Annapolis, MD: Naval Institute Press, 1981).

12. Langdon, assigned to the Canacao Naval Hospital, served in prison hospitals at Cabanatuan and Bilibid, where at the latter he was officer in charge of the sick officers' quarters. He was liberated in August 1945 from the Fukuoka POW Camp No. 1, Kyushu, Japan. Langdon, Benjamin B., RG389, POW-PGM, NARA; Glusman, *Conduct,* 262; Kentner, "Journal," 1, 83, 101.

CHAPTER 16 LIFE AT BILIBID

1. The Pasig River bisects the capital, connecting Laguna de Bay to Manila Bay. Captain Nogi Naraji, MD, served in the Imperial Japanese Army Medical Corps as staff medical officer for the Japanese War Prisoner Headquarters in Manila. Nogi was responsible for medical supply and care at several prisons, notably Bilibid, Cabanatuan, Dapecol, and Santo Tomas. On January 26, 1947, a war crimes commission sentenced Nogi to 25 years hard labor under charges of systematic starvation of American prisoners of war and failure to provide clothing and medical care. Glusman, *Conduct,* 218, 480–81; "Japanese Doctor Sentenced," *NYT,* January 27, 1947, 5; Feuer, *Bilibid,* 49–50, 74–76; Ashton, *Somebody,* 271. Gardens in Bilibid: Ashton, *Somebody,* 274–75, 282; Feuer, *Bilibid,* 164–66, 173–74; Hubbard, *Apocalypse,* 140–42. Prisoner shipments: Michno, *Hellships,* 178–93, 258–62; Kerr, *Surrender,* 195–237; Feuer, *Bilibid,* 201–13; McCracken, *Very,* 169–78; Lawton, *Some,* 149–53.

2. Food reductions: Kerr, *Surrender,* 210, 248–49; Ashton, *Somebody,* 276, 301–2, 317; Feuer, *Bilibid,* 144–45, 174, 202; McCracken, *Very,* 165. Sartin constantly petitioned Nogi for more and better food. Ashton, *Somebody,* 276–77; Glusman, *Conduct,* 224–27; Hubbard, *Apocalypse,* 126, 130.

3. Commissary prices and shortages: McCracken, *Very,* 165; Kentner, "Journal," 115–16, 121–28; Ashton, *Somebody,* 272–78; Hubbard, *Apocalypse,* 136; Feuer, *Bilibid,* 6–7, 162–73, 200–201.

4. Bilibid welfare fund: Ashton, *Somebody,* 277; Feuer, *Bilibid,* 120, 202; Welfare Roster with Contributions and Signatures, Bilibid Prison Hospital, May 1943-September 1944, RG407, AGO-POW, Box 39, NARA.

5. Diet mess: Ashton, *Somebody,* 278; Glusman, *Conduct,* 227.

6. Morphine addiction: Ashton, *Somebody,* 297.

7. Counterfeit pills: Ashton, *Somebody,* 291; Knox, *Death,* 239, Caraccilo, *Beyond,* 185; Hubbard, *Apocalypse,* 137.

8. Medical improvisation: Kerr, *Surrender and Survival,* 62; Ashton, *Somebody,* 262; Lukacs, *Escape,* 97. Medical personnel as prisoners: Bumgarner, *Parade;* Chunn, *Rice,* 37–48; Glusman, *Conduct;* Feuer, *Bilibid;* Ashton, *Somebody;* Knox, *Death,* 168–70, 202–8, 221–22; Daws, *Prisoners,* 86–87, 120–23; Jacobs, *Blood;* Condon-Rall and Cowdrey, *Medical,* 353–83.

9. Indiana native Colonel James W. Duckworth, MD, Medical Corps, commanded General Hospital No. 1 on Bataan. After the surrender, he assumed command of all Army Medical Department personnel in Bataan and moved General Hospital No. 1 to Camp O'Donnell in June 1942 to stem the death toll. Duckworth would later be stationed at Cabanatuan and was acting American commander in January 1945 when members of the U.S. Army 6th Ranger Battalion liberated the prison in a daring raid. Young, *Bataan,* 71–72, 248; PMG, *Prisoners,* November 19, 1945; Caraccilo, *Beyond,* 176–77; Ashton, *Somebody,* 252–53; Olson, *O'Donnell,* 70–87; Hampton Sides, *Ghost Soldiers: The Forgotten Epic Story of World War II's Most Dramatic Mission* (New York: Doubleday, 2001), 233, 277–78; "Medic Asserts 27,000 Died at Camp O'Donnell," *CDT,* February 3, 1945, 2; "Col J. Duckworth, Bataan Veteran," *NYT,* December 27, 1945, 18; Condon-Rall and Cowdrey, *Medical,* 26, 367–69.

10. *Quan* and *quanning:* Chunn, *Rice,* 22; Caraccilo, *Beyond,* 158; Dyess, *Story,* 123–24; Daws, *Prisoners,* 113–14; Nordin, *Nothing,* 109; Kerr, *Surrender,* 99. The *1929 Geneva Convention Relative to the Treatment of Prisoners* states in Part III, Section II, Chapter 2, Article 11 that "Prisoners shall also be afforded the means of preparing for themselves such additional articles of food as they may possess." ICRC, *Convention,* Geneva, July 27, 1929. Lieutenant Commander Charles Shaw, U.S. Coast and Geodetic Survey, 16th Naval District, suffered no ill-effects from his dietary practices. Ashton, *Somebody,* 290; U.S. Department of Commerce, *World War II History of the Department of Commerce, Part 5: U.S. Coast and Geodetic Survey* (Washington, DC: GPO, 1951), 8.

11. Albuquerque references the New Mexican National Guard units, the 200th Coast Artillery (AA) and the 515th Coast Artillery (AA), that fought in the Battle of Bataan. Slogans: McCracken, *Very,* 29, 173; Glusman, *Conduct,* 268; Kerr, *Surrender,* 100.

CHAPTER 17 FINAL DAYS OF IMPRISONMENT

1. Raids of September 21–22, 1944: Kerr, *Surrender,* 200–201; Lawton, *Some,* 107–9; McCracken, *Very,* 171–73; Kentner, "Journal," 123; Ashton, *Somebody,* 321–22; Cannon, *Leyte,* 42–43.

2. Clandestine radios: Ashton, *Somebody,* 222, 298; Lawton, *Some,* 109–11; Feuer, *Bilibid,* 245–46; Caraccilo, *Beyond,* 190–91; Berry, *Rising,* 206–7. Landings at Leyte, Mindoro, and Luzon: Spector, *Eagle,* 426–42, 511–19; Douglas MacArthur, *Reminiscences* (New York: McGraw-Hill Book Co., 1964), 211–38; Murray and Millett, *Won,* 362–73, 493–96; Cannon, *Leyte,* 60–84; Smith, *Triumph,* 44–53; MacArthur, *Campaigns,* vol. 1, 196–224, 242–52; Samuel E. Morison, *Leyte: June 1944-January 1945,* vol. 12 of *History of United States Naval Operations in World War II* (Boston: Little Brown and Co., 1958), 113–338; Samuel E. Morison, *The Liberation of the Philippines: Luzon, Mindanao, the Visayas, 1944–1945,* vol. 13 of *History of United States Naval Operations in World War II* (Boston: Little Brown and Co., 1959), 26–36.

3. Sinking of *Arisan Maru:* Michno, *Hellships,* 249–58; Lawton, *Some,* 113–37; Glusman, *Conduct,* 354–67; Kerr, *Surrender,* 204–9; Calvin Robert Graef and Harry T. Brundidge, "We Prayed to Die," *Cosmopolitan* 118, no. 4 (April 1945): 52–55, 177–80; "U.S. Told 1,800 Americans Died in Japanese Prison Ship Sinking," *NYT,* February 17, 1945, 3; "Survivor Believes Only 5 Saved as Sub Sank Jap Prison Ship," *WP,* February 17, 1945, 1.

4. Major Warren A. Wilson, Medical Corps, of California was assigned to General Hospital No. 2 on Bataan. He became the third and last American senior medical officer at Bilibid Prison on December 13, 1944. Ashton, *Somebody,* 291–92; Kentner, "Journal," 133; Wilson, Warren A., RG389, POW-PGM, NARA.

5. Lieutenant Colonel Thomas M. Tarpley, Jr., of South Carolina was a member of the Adjutant General's department, and served as an aide to General Wainwright during the fighting on Bataan and Corregidor. He was liberated in August 1945 from a prison camp in Mukden, Manchuria. "Seven Spartanburg Officers Known to be in Philippines as Defense of Bataan Ends," *Spartanburg Herald* (SC), April 11, 1942, 4; Tarpley, Thomas M., RG389, POW-PGM, NARA; United States Military Academy, *The Howitzer: The Annual of the United States Corps of Cadets* (Rochester, NY: DuBois Press, 1928), 305. From Ohio, Portz became port director

at Manila Bay in 1940 but was captured while on a special mission to Cebu in early 1942. Commanding the prisoners destined for *Oryoku Maru,* he died ashore from injuries immediately after the sinking on December 15, 1944. "Reburial Set for Hero Who Defied Japs," *WP,* May 18, 1949, B2; "4 From D.C. Held by Japs," *WP,* July 31, 1943, 5; Lawton, *Some,* 169; Heisinger, *Father,* 471; Feuer, *Bilibid,* 218; McCracken, *Very,* 175–76. Messages from departing prisoners: Lawton, *Some,* 152–53; McCracken, *Very,* 176–78. Lawton left a message with Hardee which he posted after his liberation from Bilibid. Today this letter is part of the Manny Lawton Papers, Special Collections Library, Clemson University.

6. Sinking and aftermath of *Oryoku Maru:* Chapter 14, note 6. Hardee's list: "Transport en route to Japan, complied by Lieutenant Colonel D.L. Hardee," RG407, AGO-POW, Box 42, NARA.

7. British prisoners aboard *Hofuko Maru* and aftermath: Ashton, *Diary,* 258–60; Kentner, "Journal," 124–25; Feuer, *Bilibid,* 211–12; MacArthur, *Sword,* 43–147, 297–308; Michno, *Hellships,* 194–249, 242–44; McCracken, *Very,* 170, 173–74.

8. "Luckies" refers to Lucky Strike brand cigarettes.

9. Civilian internees to Bilibid: Wilkinson, *Internment,* 194; Hartendorp, *Tomas,* 144, 387, 414; Frances B. Cogan, *Captured: The Japanese Internment of American Civilians in the Philippines, 1941–1945* (Athens, GA: University of Georgia Press, 2000), 200, 220–22; Kentner, "Journal," 136–37.

10. Air raids: Smith, *Triumph,* 57–59; Kentner, "Journal," 148–49. Major Howard M. Cavender of Washington of the Quartermaster Corps; Major John W. Turner, Jr., of the 515th Coast Artillery Regiment (AA) from California; Major Thomas N. Powell, Jr., of the Cebu Brigade headquarters, from Georgia; Lieutenant Colonel Francis S. Conaty, Quartermaster Corps, of Massachusetts; Major John J. Neiger, II Corps headquarters from Missouri; Major Thompson B. Maury III, of the Provisional Field Artillery Brigade, II Corps of California; and Major John J. Heil, 4th Marine Regiment, headquarters company, 2nd Battalion, from Washington, DC. Lieutenant Colonel Thomas N. Powell, Sr., of the 61st Infantry (PA) of Georgia was Major Powell's father. Aside from Heil, all of these men died on December 15, 1944, aboard *Oryoku Maru.* Heil later died aboard *Brazil Maru* on January 19, 1945. Conaty died on December 13 and Neiger December 14 in the holds of *Oryoku Maru.* Cavender, Howard M., John W. Turner, Thomas N. Powell, Jr., Thomas N. Powell, Sr., Francis S. Conaty, John J. Neiger, Thompson B. Maury III, and John J. Neil, RG389, POW-PGM, NARA.

11. Landings on Luzon: Smith, *Triumph,* 73–87, 104–17, 167–90, 211–17; Murray and Millett, *Won,* 497–98; MacArthur, *Reminiscences,* 239–45; MacArthur, *Campaigns,* vol. 1, 254–71; Morison, *Liberation,* 123–56, 184–93.

CHAPTER 18 LIBERATION

1. Race to Manila: Smith, *Triumph,* 212–36, 249–53; Spector, *Eagle,* 520–24; MacArthur, *Reminiscences,* 246–47; Wilkinson, *Internment,* 143–50. Prisoner perspective: McCracken, *Very,* 182–84; Kentner, "Journal," 154; Olsen, "War Diary," 72–73; Berry, *Rising,* 215.

2. Japanese proclamation: Kentner, "Journal," 154–55; McCracken, *Very,* 183; Berry, *Rising,* 215–16; Cogan, *Captured,* 277–78; Robert Shaplen, "A Reporter at Large: The Freeing of Bilibid," *The New Yorker* 21 (March 3, 1945): 68.

3. Lieutenant Colonel "Pop" Durst of Mississippi served as post quartermaster of Fort Stotsenburg in December 1941 and later as quartermaster at Headquarters, II Corps. Morton, *Philippines,* 179; Caraccilo, *Beyond,* 58, 60–61, 262n27. Lieutenant Colonel "Chick" Fowler of South Carolina, commanded the 71st Field Artillery (PA) during the Battle of Bataan. Morton, *Philippines,* 134–36; Young, *Bataan,* 62, 65; "Col. H.C. Fowler, Bataan Hero, Dies," *NYT,* September 8, 1950, 31.

4. Fowler's ailments included loss of his sight, hearing, and three bullets in his body. "Col Fowler in New List of Liberated," *WP,* February 24, 1945, 5; Wagner, *Recipes,* vii–ix.

5. Liberation of Bilibid: Shaplen, "Freeing of Bilibid," 62–65; Kentner, "Journal," 155; McCracken, *Very,* 183–84; Berry, *Rising,* 216; Cogan, *Captured,* 280–81; Jacobs, *Blood,* 81; Ashton, *Diary,* 308–9; Richard Connaughton, John Pimlott, Duncan Anderson, *The Battle for Manila* (Novato, CA: Presidio Press, 1995), 96–97.

6. Major Orville C. Wendt of Ohio was executive officer of the 2nd Battalion, 148th Infantry when he spoke to the liberated prisoners. Kerr, *Surrender,* 251–52; Kentner, "Journal," 155; Smith, *Triumph,* 254; Russell Brines and Fred Hampson, "Bilibid Prison Guards Flee as Yanks Arrive," *LAT,* February 6, 1945, 1; McCracken, *Very,* 184; "All Manila Won: M'Arthur: 1,350 Prisoners Freed from Ancient Bilibid Jail," *CDT,* February 6, 1945, 1.

7. Valley Forge and Friedrich Wilhelm von Steuben: Robert K. Wright, Jr., *The Continental Army* (Washington, DC: CMH, 1983), 119, 125–26, 138, 140–46; Millett and Maslowski, *Common,* 71–72. Hardee takes his figures and quote directly from Washington's correspondence. George Washington to the President of Congress, December 22, 1777, in John C. Fitzpatrick, ed., *The Writings of George Washington,* vol. X (Washington, DC: GPO, 1931), 192–98.

8. Around 78,100 prisoners, including 11,796 Americans and 66,304 Filipinos surrendered on Bataan. A further 8,700 Americans and 3,300 Filipinos surrendered on Corregidor. Adding the forces on Mindanao, 25,580 Americans were captured in the Philippines. Falk, *Bataan,* 17; Kerr, *Surrender,* 50, 71; Glusman,

Conduct, 161, 203–4; Office of the Adjutant General, *Final Report,* 95. Of the official number of Americans captured in the Philippines between December 7, 1941, to May 10, 1942, 10,650 or 42 percent died in captivity. Postwar, former Japanese POWs continued to suffer from high mortality rates as compared to former European POWs. Condon-Rall and Cowdrey, *Medical,* 383; Bernard M. Cohen and Maurice Z. Cooper, *A Follow-up Study of World War II Prisoners of War* (Washington, DC: Department of Medicine and Surgery, Veterans Administration, 1954), 19, 67–69.

CHAPTER 19 HOMEWARD BOUND

1. Loss of bridges: Smith, *Triumph,* 128–31, 133–35, 232–35. Prisoner perspective: McCracken, *Very,* 185–86; Berry, *Rising,* 220; Cogan, *Captured,* 282.

2. Double rations for freed prisoners: Daws, *Prisoners,* 378–79; Knox, *Death,* 460–82; Cogan, *Captured,* 282; Hartendorp, *Tomas,* 416–17; Berry, *Rising,* 220.

3. Movement out of Bilibid: McCracken, *Very,* 184; Cogan, *Captured,* 282; Berry, *Rising,* 218; Kentner, "Journal," 155; "Yanks Press Mopup as Flames Rage Unchecked," *WP,* February 7, 1945, 1; Lindesay Parrott, "Manila's Business District Burned by Trapped Enemy," *NYT,* February 7, 1945, 1; Shaplen, "Freeing of Bilibid," 70–71; Ashton, *Diary,* 314; Connaughton et al., *Manila,* 97.

4. Captain (Dr.) Charles T. Brown, Medical Corps, of Texas, began the war stationed at Fort McKinley before serving as regimental surgeon of the 14th Engineer Regiment (PS). Ashton, *Somebody,* 295; Brown, *Bars;* "Morale," *The Quan,* August 1968, 3; "4 San Antonians Freed in Manila," *San Antonio Light,* February 19, 1945, 1B; "S.A. Major's Book Includes Prose, Poetry of Bilibid," *San Antonio Light,* March 23, 1947, 15A.

5. 7th Division headquarters: Hartendorp, *Tomas,* 422; Berry, *Rising,* 218–20; Cogan, *Captured,* 282; Kentner, "Journal," 155; Shaplen, "Freeing of Bilibid," 71; Ashton, *Diary,* 314.

6. In April 1943, Lieutenant General Oscar W. Griswold of Nevada became commanding general of the XIV Corps, fighting through New Georgia and Bougainville under General MacArthur, and continuing into the invasion of Luzon and Leyte and the Battle of Manila. "Oscar Griswold, Retired General," *NYT,* October 7, 1959, 43. Lieutenant General Charles P. Hall of Mississippi commanded the 93rd Infantry Division prior to commanding the XI Corps fighting on New Guinea, Morotai, Leyte, and Luzon. He ended the war in Yokohama, Japan, with the occupation force. "Gen. Charles Hall, War Leader, Dies," *NYT,* January 28, 1953, 27. Colonel John Robert Burns from Washington, DC, served as the chemical warfare officer at Fort Mills on Corregidor from 1939 to 1941 before returning to the

U.S. in September 1941. With the commencement of hostilities, he commanded the Chemical Corps Research and Development base in Utah and in 1944 became Chemical Officer for General Walter Krueger's 6th Army. "Brigadier General John Robert Burns, Class of 1926," West Point Association of Graduates, online. Colonel Arthur Richard Walk of Pennsylvania served as chief of staff for the 37th Infantry Division at Guadalcanal, New Georgia, Bougainville, and in the Philippine Campaign. In August 1945 he rose to assistant division commander of the 6th Infantry. "Gen. Walk, Served in Atom Bomb Tests," *NYT*, April 21, 1953, 27.

7. K-ration: Brown, *Dictionary*, 270; Berry, *Rising*, 220.

8. MacArthur visit of February 7, 1945: MacArthur, *Reminiscences*, 248; Frank Robertson, "Manilans Greet M'Arthur With Wild Acclaim," *WP*, February 8, 1945, 1; Ashton, *Diary*, 314. On February 21, 1945, the War Department telegrammed Hardee's wife and officially informed her of his liberation. "Col. Hardee Safe on Luzon After Rescue from Japs," *Durham Sun*, February 21, 1945, 1. Brigadier General Bonner F. Fellers of Illinois was assigned to the American embassy in Egypt in 1940 and unknowingly provided German and Italian spies with information on Allied military movements in North Africa. In 1943, he joined General MacArthur's staff, serving as a military secretary and Chief of Psychological Operations. In the Philippine Campaign, Fellers served as Director of Civil Affairs for the Philippines and later provided liaison between MacArthur's Supreme Commander Allied Powers and the Imperial Household in occupied Japan. John W. Dower, *Embracing Defeat: Japan in the Wake of World War II* (New York: W.W. Norton and Co., 1999), 280–82; Bix, *Hirohito*, 582–85; Diane T. Putney, ed., *ULTRA and the Army Air Forces in World War II* (Washington, DC: Office of Air Force History, 1987), 80.

9. The Olsens were imprisoned in Santo Tomas University from January 1942 to February 3, 1945. Margaret Esten Olsen, age eight, died of tubercular meningitis on September 14, 1944, at Santo Tomas. Olsen, "War Diary," 56–57; Wilkinson, *Internment*, 184.

10. Mary Meehan Harries of Illinois, the daughter of Senator Thomas Meehan, was married to Colonel Herbert Harries who was killed on Corregidor in 1942. "Bluffs Woman Once Prisoner of Japs Dies in New York," *Daily Journal* (Jacksonville, IL), January 31, 1950, 12; "U.S. Officer Buried as Foe's Guns Roar," *NYT*, April 3, 1942, 4.

11. Shelling of Santo Tomas: Wilkinson, *Internment*, 162–63, 166; Cogan, *Captured*, 274–76; Hartendorp, *Tomas*, 417–20.

12. Lieutenant Colonel Perry O. Wilcox of New York served as chaplain of the Headquarters battery for the Harbor Defenses of Manila and Subic Bays. Feuer,

Bilibid, 140, 202, 205; Glusman, *Conduct,* 238, 246; Wilcox, Perry O., RG389, POW-PGM, NARA; Roper, *Brothers,* 269–72.

13. Battle around Intramuros: Smith, *Triumph,* 271–308; Hartendorp, *Tomas,* 422–23; Connaughton et al., *Manila,* 161–71.

14. The story Hardee tells differs from what he and his sister Lucy wrote to his wife. On March 16, 1945, Hardee's sister Lucy Olsen pinned on his colonel's eagles, borrowed from Colonel John R. Mott. David L. Hardee to Elizabeth Hardee, March 16, 1945; Lucy Olsen to Elizabeth Hardee, March 18, 1945, DLHP, Box 79, NCA. Major General James L. Frink, of Iowa, began the war as the U.S. Fourth Army Corps quartermaster and in 1943 assumed command of the U.S. Army Services of Supply, a position he held during MacArthur's Philippines Campaign. "New Policy to Add 30,000 Men to Army," *Gastonia* (NC) *Daily Gazette,* August 7, 1941, 1; "Greensboro Has New Defense Director," *Rocky Mount* (NC) *Evening Telegram,* July 27, 1950, 11A; "38 Iowans Generals in World War II," *Waterloo* (IA) *Daily Courier,* March 1, 1944, 13; Karl C. Dod, *The Corps of Engineers: The War Against Japan* (Washington, DC: CMH, 1966), 534, 650–51.

15. LUBSEC, the Luzon Base Section, was the U.S. Sixth Army's headquarters for the Army Service Command located near Manila Bay. Dod, *Corps,* 591, 600–601; Smith, *Triumph,* 134. Thomas and Carolina Wolff were internees at Santo Tomas and may be who Hardee is referencing. The *calesa,* or *kalesa,* is an inclined cart drawn by a single horse and was introduced by the Spanish in the eighteenth century and used frequently in Manila prior to World War II.

16. Jean Marie Faircloth MacArthur was General MacArthur's second wife, whom he married in 1937. They had one son together, Arthur MacArthur IV. The three left Corregidor in March 1942 and lived in Australia until his return to the Philippines. Manchester, *Caesar,* 162–64, 166–67, 174–77; Enid Nemy, "Jean MacArthur, General's Widow, Dies at 101," *NYT,* January 24, 2000, B8.

17. Escolta Street, running east-west in the district of Binondo, Manila, is one of the oldest streets in the city and is known for its immigrant merchants and stores. By the twentieth century, Escolta Street was the center of Manila's business district and home to many of the city's tallest buildings and the Manila Stock Exchange.

18. Destruction in Manila: MacArthur, *Reminiscences,* 251; Smith, *Triumph,* 271–308; Connaughton et al., *Manila,* 174–76.

19. USAT *Cape Meares* was built and launched by Consolidated Steel Corporation of Wilmington, California in 1943. A standard C1B Maritime Commission designed freighter, she served as a troopship in the Pacific War. Roland W. Charles, *Troopships of World War II* (Washington, DC: Army Transportation Association,

1947), 169. Battle of Corregidor, February 16–26, 1945: Gerard M. Devlin, *Paratrooper! The Saga of U.S. Army and Marine Parachute and Glider Combat Troops During World War II* (New York: St. Martin's Press, 1979), 578–95; MacArthur, *Reminiscences*, 249–50; Smith, *Triumph*, 335–50.

Bibliography

ARCHIVES AND LIBRARIES

Air Force Historical Research Agency, Maxwell AFB, AL
MacArthur Memorial and Archives, Norfolk, VA
National Archives and Records Administration, College Park, MD
State Archives of North Carolina, Raleigh, NC
Research and Documentation Center for War Crimes Trials, Philipp University of Marburg, Germany
Southern Historical Collection, University of North Carolina, Chapel Hill, NC
State Library of North Carolina, Raleigh, NC
U.S. Military Academy Special Collections Library, West Point, NY

NEWSPAPERS, JOURNALS, MAGAZINES

Abilene Reporter-News
Aiken Standard and Review (SC)
The Alumni Review (University of North Carolina, Chapel Hill)
Army and Navy Journal
The Bee (Danville, VA)
Brownsville Herald (TX)
Chicago Daily Tribune
Collier's
Cosmopolitan
Daily Journal (Jacksonville, IL)
Del Rio News-Herald

Deming Headlight (NM)
Durham Herald-Sun (NC)
El Paso Herald-Post
Fayetteville Observer (NC)
Galveston News
Gastonia Daily Gazette (NC)
General Orders—Legion of Valor
Gettysburg Compiler
Gettysburg Times
Greensboro Daily News
Indiana Evening Gazette (PA)
Infantry Journal
Journal of American-East Asian Relations
Journal of Modern History
Laredo Times
Las Cruces Sun News (NM)
Life
Lodi News-Sentinel (CA)
Los Angeles Times
Military Affairs
Moorhead Daily News (MN)
National Geographic
The New Yorker
New York Times
News and Observer (Raleigh, NC)
North Carolina Civil Defense Newsletter
Oil and Fat Industries
Owosso Argus-Press (MI)
Pacific Stars and Stripes
Philippine Camp News
Port Arthur News (TX)
Portsmouth Herald (NH)
Raleigh Times
Reporter-Telegram (Midland, TX)
Rocky Mount Evening Telegram (NC)
San Antonio Express
San Antonio Light

Sandusky Register Star-News (OH)
Spartanburg Herald (SC)
Spirit Lake Beacon (IA)
Star and Sentinel (Gettysburg, PA)
The Quan (Pittsburgh, PA)
Thomasville Times-Enterprise (GA)
Titusville Herald (PA)
Twin City Sentinel (Winston-Salem, NC)
Washington Post
Waterloo Daily Courier (IA)
Wilmington Morning Star (NC)
Winston-Salem Journal (NC)
Zanesville Signal (OH)

UNPUBLISHED SOURCES

Hardee, David L. "War Experience." Unpublished manuscript, 1945.

———. "Memoirs of a Jap Prisoner of War." Unpublished manuscript, 1946.

———. "The Japs Got Me." Unpublished manuscript, 1947.

———. "Memoirs of a Jap Prisoner of War." Unpublished manuscript, n.d., 1962–1966[?].

Hopkins, Armand. "Prisoner of War, 1942–1945, Reminiscences of Armand Hopkins." Unpublished manuscript, 1984.

Lowe, Karl H. *America's Foreign Legion: The 31st Infantry Regiment at War and Peace*. Book manuscript in progress.

Olsen, Lucy Hardee. "My War Diary, December 7, 1941 to February 3, 1945." Unpublished manuscript, 1976.

Schmidt, Larry S. "American Involvement in the Filipino Resistance Movement on Mindanao during the Japanese Occupation, 1942–1945." Master's thesis, U.S. Army Command and General Staff College, 1982.

GOVERNMENT PUBLICATIONS

Cannon, M. Hamlin. *Leyte: The Return to the Philippines*. 1953. Reprint, Washington, DC: United States Army Center of Military History (CMH), 1993.

Casey, Hugh John. *Engineer Memoirs: Major General Hugh J. Casey, U.S. Army*. Washington, DC: Office of History, U.S. Army Corps of Engineers, 1993.

Clear, Warren J. "Close-Up of the Jap Fighting-Man." U.S. Army Command and General Staff School, Fort Leavenworth, KS, October 1942.

———. *Far Eastern Survey Report*. Washington, DC: Government Printing Office (GPO), 1942.

Cohen, Bernard M., and Maurice Z. Cooper. *A Follow-up Study of World War II Prisoners of War*. Washington, DC: Department of Medicine and Surgery, Veterans Administration, 1954.

Condon-Rall, Mary Ellen, and Albert E. Cowdrey. *The Medical Department: Medical Service in the War Against Japan*. Washington, DC: CMH, 1998.

Conn, Stetson, Rose C. Engelman, and Byron Fairchild. *Guarding the United States and Its Outposts*. Washington, DC: CMH, 1962.

Craven, Wesley Frank, and James Lea Cate. *Plans and Early Operations, January 1939 to August 1942*. Vol. 1 of *The Army Air Forces in World War II*. 1949. Reprint, Washington, DC: Office of Air Force History, GPO, 1983.

Defense Advisory Committee on Prisoners of War. *POW, the Fight Continues After the Battle: The Report of the Secretary of Defense's Advisory Committee on Prisoners of War*. Washington, DC: GPO, August 1955.

Dod, Karl C. *The Corps of Engineers: The War Against Japan*. Washington, DC: CMH, 1966.

Emerson, Kary C. "The Operations of the II Philippine Corps on Bataan, 10 January–8 April 1942." Fort Benning, GA: U.S. Army Infantry School, 1949–50.

Finney, Robert T. *History of the Air Corps Tactical School, 1920–1940*. 1955; reprint, Washington, DC: Air Force History and Museums Program, 1998.

Fitzpatrick, John C., ed. *The Writings of George Washington*. Vol. X. Washington, DC: GPO, 1931.

Flores, Manuel T. "An Analytical Study of the Defense of Bataan." Fort Leavenworth, KS: Command and General Staff College, 31 May 1949.

International Committee of the Red Cross. *Convention Relative to the Treatment of Prisoners of War*. Geneva: July 27, 1929.

Kentner, Robert W. "Kentner's Journal: Bilibid Prison, Manila, P.I. from 12–8–41 to 2–5–45." Unpublished memoir, transcribed by U.S. Navy Bureau of Medicine and Surgery, Hospital Corps Archives Unit, April 21, 1945.

MacArthur, Douglas. *The Campaigns of MacArthur in the Pacific*. Vol. 1 of *Reports of General MacArthur*. 1966. Reprint, Washington, DC: CMH, 1994.

Maurer, Maurer, ed. *Air Force Combat Units of World War II*. 1961. Reprint, Washington, DC: Office of Air Force History, 1983.

Mead, Everett V. "The Operations and Movements of the 31st Infantry Regiment (Philippine Division), 7 December 1941–9 April 1942." Fort Benning, GA: U.S. Army Infantry School, 1947–48.

Mendelson, Sheldon H. "Operations of the Provisional Air Corps Regiment in the Defense of Bataan Peninsula, P.I., 8 January–10 April 1942." Fort Benning, GA: U.S. Army Infantry School, 1946–47.

Morton, Louis. *Strategy and Command: The First Two Years*. 1962. Reprint, Washington, DC: CMH, 2000.

———. *The Fall of the Philippines*. 1953. Reprint, Washington, DC: CMH, 1989.

Putney, Diane T., ed. *ULTRA and the Army Air Forces in World War II*. Washington, DC: Office of Air Force History, 1987.

Smith, Robert Ross. *The Approach to the Philippines*. 1953. Reprint, Washington, DC: CMH, 1996.

———. *Triumph in the Philippines*. 1963. Reprint, Washington, DC: CMH, 1993.

U.S. Congress. House Committee on Interstate and Foreign Commerce. *Enemy Property Commission Hearings*. 80th Cong., 1st sess., March 20, 21, and April 21, 1947.

———. Committee of the Whole. *Mering Bichara*. 82d Cong., 1st sess., 1951. H. Rep. 1041.

———. House War Claims Commission. *Report of the War Claims Commission*. 81st Cong., 2d sess., 1950. H. Doc. 580.

———. House War Claims Commission. *War Claims Arising Out of World War II*. 83d Cong., 1st sess., 1953. H. Doc. 67.

U.S. Congress. Senate Committee on the Judiciary. *War Claims Commission: Hearings before Subcommittee of Committee on the Judiciary*. 80th Cong., 2d sess., February 17, 19, March 9, and May 11, 1948.

U.S. Army Forces, Pacific. General Headquarters. Military Intelligence Section. General Staff. *Intelligence Activities in the Philippines during the Japanese Occupation*. Tokyo: General Headquarters, Far East Command, 1948.

U.S. Department of the Army. Office of the Adjutant General. *Army Battle Casualties and Nonbattle Deaths in World War II: Final Report, 7 December 1941–31 December 1946*. Washington, DC: Department of the Army, 1953.

———. 31st Infantry Regiment. "History of the 31st Infantry Regiment." Carlisle, PA: U.S. Army Military History Institute, 1958.

U.S. Department of Commerce. *World War II History of the Department of Commerce, Part 5: U.S. Coast and Geodetic Survey*. Washington, DC: GPO, 1951.

U.S. Department of the Navy. Naval History and Heritage Command. *Dictionary of American Naval Fighting Ships*. Online.

U.S. Department of State. *Foreign Relations of the United States: Diplomatic Papers, 1942*. Vol. 1. Washington, DC: GPO, 1960.

U.S. Department of War. Military Intelligence Division Report. *Prisoners of War in the Philippine Islands*. Washington, DC: Military Intelligence Division, September 20, 1944.

———. Office of the Provost Marshal General. *American Prisoners of War in the Philippines*. Washington, DC: Office of the Provost Marshal General, November 19, 1945.

U.S. Surgeon-General's Office. *Annual Report of the Surgeon General, U.S. Army to the Secretary of War for the Fiscal Year ended June 30, 1921*. Washington, DC: GPO, 1921.

Wright, Robert K., Jr. *The Continental Army*. Washington, DC: CMH, 1983.

Zimmerman, Leslie F. "Diary of Lieutenant Colonel Leslie F. Zimmerman, POW in Philippines, World War II." Unpublished memoir, transcribed by U.S. Air Force Historical Research Agency, December 1989.

MEMOIRS

Alexander, Irvin. *Surviving Bataan and Beyond: Colonel Irvin Alexander's Odyssey as a Japanese Prisoner of War*. Edited by Dominic J. Caraccilo. Mechanicsburg, PA: Stackpole Books, 1999.

Ashton, Paul L. *Bataan Diary*. Santa Barbara: Ashton Publications, 1984.

———. *"And Somebody Gives a Damn!"* Santa Barbara: Ashton Publications, 1990.

Beebe, Lewis. *Prisoner of the Rising Sun: The Lost Diary of Brig. Gen. Lewis Beebe*. Edited by John M. Beebe. College Station: Texas A&M University Press, 2006.

Berry, William A., and James Edwin Alexander. *Prisoner of the Rising Sun*. Norman: University of Oklahoma Press, 1993.

Bilek, Tony, with Gene O'Connell. *No Uncle Sam: The Forgotten of Bataan*. Kent, OH: Kent State University Press, 2003.

Boyt, Gene, with David L. Burch. *Bataan: A Survivor's Story*. Norman: University of Oklahoma Press, 2004.

Brougher, William E. *The Long Dark Road*. N.p., 1946.

Brown, Charles. *Bars from Bilibid Prison*. San Antonio: The Naylor Co., 1947.

Bumgarner, John R. *Parade of the Dead: A U.S. Army Physician's Memoir of Imprisonment by the Japanese, 1942–1945*. Jefferson, NC: McFarland and Co., 1995.

Chunn, Calvin Ellsworth, ed. *Of Rice and Men: The Story of Americans Under the Rising Sun*. Tulsa: Veterans' Publishing Co., 1946.

Coleman, John S., Jr. *Bataan and Beyond: Memories of an American POW*. College Station: Texas A&M University Press, 1978.

Dyess, William E. *The Dyess Story: The Eye-Witness Account of the Death March from Bataan and the Narrative of Experiences in Japanese Prison Camps and of Eventual Escape*. Edited by Charles Leavelle. New York: G.P. Putnam's Sons, 1944.

Emerson, Kary C. *Guest of the Emperor*. Sanibel Island, FL: K.C. Emerson, 1977.

Fujita, Frank. *Foo: A Japanese-American Prisoner of the Rising Sun: The Secret Prison Diary of Frank "Foo" Fujita*. Denton: University of North Texas Press, 1993.

Gause, Damon. *The War Journal of Major Damon "Rocky" Gause*. New York: Hyperion, 1999.

Gordon, Richard M., with Benjamin S. Llamzon. *Horyo: Memoirs of an American POW*. Edited by Benjamin S. Llamzon. St. Paul, MN: Paragon House, 1999.

Grashio, Samuel C., and Bernard Norling. *Return to Freedom: The War Memoirs of Col. Samuel C. Grashio USAF (Ret.)*. Tulsa: MCN Press, 1982.

Hawkins, Jack. *Never Say Die*. Philadelphia: Dorrance and Co., 1961.

Hayes, Thomas. *Bilibid Diary: The Secret Notebooks of Commander Thomas Hayes: POW, the Philippines, 1942–45*. Edited by A.B. Feuer. Hamden, CT: Archon Book, 1987.

Hubbard, Preston John. *Apocalypse Undone: My Survival of Japanese Imprisonment During World War II*. Nashville: Vanderbilt University Press, 1990.

Jackson, Calvin G. *Diary of Col. Calvin G. Jackson, M.D. Kept during World War II, 1941–1945*. Ada: Ohio Northern University Press, 1992.

Jacobs, Eugene C. *Blood Brothers: A Medic's Sketch Book*. New York: Carlton Press, 1985.

Jacobsen, Gene S. *We Refused to Die: My Time as a Prisoner of War in Bataan and Japan, 1942–1945*. Salt Lake City: University of Utah Press, 2004.

James, D. Clayton, ed. *South to Bataan, North to Mukden: The Prison Diary of Brigadier General W.E. Brougher*. Athens: University of Georgia Press, 1971.

Lawton, Manny. *Some Survived: An Eyewitness Account of the Bataan Death March and the Men Who Lived Through It*. Chapel Hill: Algonquin Books, 2004.

Levering, Robert W. *Horror Trek: A True Story of Bataan, the Death March and Three and One-Half Years in Japanese Prison Camps*. Dayton, OH: Horstman Printing Co., 1948.

MacArthur, Douglas. *Reminiscences*. New York: McGraw-Hill, 1964.

Mapes, Victor L., with Scott A. Mills. *The Butchers, The Baker: The World War II Memoir of a United States Army Air Corps Soldier Captured by the Japanese in the Philippines*. Jefferson, NC: McFarland and Co., 2000.

McCoy, Melvin H., Stephen M. Mellnik, and Welbourn Kelley. *Ten Escape from Tojo*. New York: Farrar and Rinehart, 1944.

McCracken, Alan. *Very Soon Now, Joe*. New York: Hobson Book Press, 1947.

McGee, John Hugh. *Rice and Salt: A History of the Defense and Occupation of Mindanao During World War II*. San Antonio: The Naylor Co., 1962.

Mellnik, Stephen. *Philippine Diary, 1939–1945*. New York: Van Nostrand Reinhold Co., 1969.

Miner, William D., with Lewis A. Miner. *Surrender on Cebu: A POW's Diary—WWII*. Paducah, KY: Turner Publishing Co., 2001.

Nordin, Carl S. *We Were Next to Nothing: An American POW's Account of Japanese Prison Camps and Deliverance in World War II*. Jefferson, NC: McFarland and Co., 1997.

Petak, Joseph A. *Never Plan Tomorrow: The Saga of the Bataan Death March and Battle of Corregidor Survivors, 1942–1945*. Fullerton, CA: Aquataur, 1994.

Quezon, Manuel Luis. *The Good Fight*. New York: D. Appleton-Century Co., 1946.

Reynolds, Robert. *Of Rice and Men*. Philadelphia: Dorrance and Co., 1947.

Romulo, Carlos P. *I Saw the Fall of the Philippines*. New York: Doubleday, Doran and Co., 1944.

Sakai, Saburo, with Martin Caidin, and Fred Saito. *Samurai!* New York: E. P. Dutton, 1957.

Stewart, Sidney. *Give Us This Day*. New York: W. W. Norton and Co., 1956.

Tenney, Lester I. *My Hitch in Hell: The Bataan Death March*. Washington, DC: Brassey's, 1995.

Thomas, Edward E. *As I Remember: A Barge from Corregidor—A March from Bataan—A Fence at Cabanatuan*. Sonoita, AZ: Edward E. Thomas, 1990.

Wainwright, Jonathan M. *General Wainwright's Story: The Account of Four Years of Humiliating Defeat, Surrender, and Captivity*. Edited by Robert Considine. Garden City, NY: Doubleday and Co., 1946.

Wills, Donald H., with Reyburn W. Myers. *The Sea Was My Last Chance: Memoir of an American Captured on Bataan in 1942 Who Escaped in 1944 and Led the Liberation of Western Mindanao*. Jefferson, NC: McFarland and Co., 1992.

BOOKS

Anderson, Gerald R. *Subic Bay from Magellan to Pinatubo: The History of the U.S. Naval Station, Subic Bay*. 3rd ed. S.I.: CreateSpace, 2006.

Bartsch, William H. *December 8, 1941: MacArthur's Pearl Harbor*. College Station: Texas A&M University Press, 2003.

———. *Doomed at the Start: American Pursuit Pilots in the Philippines, 1941–1942*. College Station: Texas A&M University Press, 1995.

Bianculli, David. *Dangerously Funny: The Uncensored Story of The Smothers Brothers Comedy Hour*. New York: Simon and Schuster, 2009.

Bix, Herbert P. *Hirohito and the Making of Modern Japan*. New York: HarperCollins, 2000.

Blair, Clay, Jr. *Silent Victory: The U.S. Submarine War Against Japan*. Annapolis, MD: Naval Institute Press, 1975.

Breuer, William B. *MacArthur's Undercover War: Spies, Saboteurs, Guerrillas and Secret Missions*. Edison, NJ: Castle Books, 2005.

Brown, Jerold E., ed., *Historical Dictionary of the U.S. Army*. Westport, CT: Greenwood Press, 2001.

Burton, John. *Fortnight of Infamy: The Collapse of Allied Airpower West of Pearl Harbor*. Annapolis, MD: Naval Institute Press, 2006.

Butow, Robert J.C. *Tojo and the Coming of the War*. Stanford: Stanford University Press, 1961.

Butterweck, Joseph S., and George A. Muzzey. *A Handbook for Teachers: An Integrating Course for Classroom Teachers in Secondary Schools*. New York: E.P. Dutton and Co., 1939.

Charles, Roland W. *Troopships of World War II*. Washington, DC: Army Transportation Association, 1947.

Coates, Austin. *Rizal: Philippine Nationalist and Martyr*. New York: Oxford University Press, 1968.

Cogan, Frances B. *Captured: The Japanese Internment of American Civilians in the Philippines, 1941–1945*. Athens: University of Georgia Press, 2000.

Connaughton, Richard. *MacArthur and Defeat in the Philippines*. New York: The Overlook Press, 2001.

Connaughton, Richard, John Pimlott, and Duncan Anderson. *The Battle for Manila*. Novato, CA: Presidio Press, 1995.

Cook, Haruko Taya, and Theodore F. Cook. *Japan at War: An Oral History*. New York: The New Press, 1992.

Crager, Kelly E. *Hell Under the Rising Sun: Texan POWs and the Building of the Burma-Thailand Death Railway*. College Station: Texas A&M University Press, 2008.

David, Donald A. *Lightning Strike: The Secret Mission to Kill Admiral Yamamoto and Avenge Pearl Harbor*. New York: St. Martin's Press, 2005.

Daws, Gavan. *Prisoners of the Japanese: POWs of World War II in the Pacific*. New York: William Morrow and Co., 1994.

Devlin, Gerard M. *Paratrooper! The Saga of U.S. Army and Marine Parachute and Glider Combat Troops During World War II*. New York: St. Martin's Press, 1979.

Doll, John G. *The Battling Bastards of Bataan: A Chronology of the First Days of World War II in the Philippines*. 6th ed. Bennington, VT: Merriman Press, 2008.

Dower, John W. *War Without Mercy: Race and Power in the Pacific War*. New York: Pantheon Books, 1986.

———. *Embracing Defeat: Japan in the Wake of World War II*. New York: W.W. Norton and Co., 1999.

Doyle, Robert C. *A Prisoner's Duty: Great Escapes in U.S. Military History*. Annapolis, MD: Naval Institute Press, 1997.

———. *Voices from Captivity: Interpreting the American POW Narrative*. Lawrence: University of Kansas Press, 1994.

Drea, Edward J. *In the Service of the Emperor: Essays on the Imperial Japanese Army*. Lincoln: University of Nebraska Press, 1998.

Edmonds, Walter D. *They Fought With What They Had: The Story of the Army Air Forces in the Southwest Pacific, 1941–1942*. Boston: Little, Brown and Co., 1951.

Evans, David C. and Mark R. Peattie. *Kaigun: Strategy, Tactics, and Technology in the Imperial Japanese Navy, 1887–1941*. Annapolis, MD: Naval Institute Press, 1997.

Falk, Stanley L. *Bataan: The March of Death*. New York: W.W. Norton & Co., 1962.

Frank, Richard B. *Downfall: The End of the Imperial Japanese Empire*. New York: Random House, 1999.

———. *Guadalcanal: The Definitive Account of the Landmark Battle*. New York: Penguin Books, 1992.

Glusman, John A. *Conduct Under Fire: Four American Doctors and Their Fight for Life as Prisoners of the Japanese, 1941–1945*. New York: Penguin Group, 2005.

Gordon, Andrew. *A Modern History of Japan: From Tokugawa Times to the Present*. 2nd ed. New York: Oxford University Press, 2009.

Grover, David Hubert. *U.S. Army Ships and Watercraft of World War II*. Annapolis, MD: Naval Institute Press, 1987.

Hardee, David L. *The Eastern North Carolina Hardy-Hardee Family in the South and Southwest*. Raleigh: David L. Hardee, 1966.

Harries, Meirion, and Susie Harries. *Soldiers of the Sun: The Rise and Fall of the Imperial Japanese Army*. New York: Random House, 1991.

Hartendorp, A.V.H. *The Santo Tomas Story*. Edited by Frank H. Golay. New York: McGraw-Hill, 1964.

Hastings, Max. *Retribution: The Battle for Japan, 1944–45*. New York: Alfred A. Knopf, 2007.

Heisinger, Duane. *Father Found*. Longwood, FL: Xulon Press, 2003.

Henson, Maria Rosa. *Comfort Woman: A Filipina's Story of Prostitution and Slavery Under the Japanese Military*. New York: Rowman and Littlefield Publishers, 1999.

Hicks, George. *The Comfort Women: Japan's Brutal Regime of Enforced Prostitution in the Second World War*. New York: W.W. Norton and Co., 1995.

Holmes, Linda Goetz. *Unjust Enrichment: American POWs Under the Rising Sun*. Old Saybrook, CT: Konecky and Konecky, 2001.

Hubbard, Charles M., and Collis H. Davis, Jr. *Corregidor in Peace and War*. Columbia: University of Missouri Press, 2006.

Hunt, Michael H. *Ideology and U.S. Foreign Policy*. New Haven, CT: Yale University Press, 1987.

Ienaga, Saburō. *The Pacific War: World War II and the Japanese, 1931–1945*. New York: Pantheon Books, 1978.

Ind, Allison. *Bataan: The Judgement Seat: The Saga of the Philippine Command of the United States Army Air Force, May 1941 to May 1942*. New York: Macmillan Co., 1944.

Jansen, Marius B. *The Making of Modern Japan*. Cambridge, MA: Belknap Press of Harvard University Press, 2000.

Jones, Betty B. *The December Ship: A Story of Lt. Col. Arden R. Boellner's Capture in the Philippines, Imprisonment, and Death on a World War II Japanese Hellship*. Jefferson, NC: McFarland and Co., 1992.

Jordan, Donald A. *China's Trial by Fire: The Shanghai War of 1932*. Ann Arbor: University of Michigan Press, 2004.

Keats, John. *They Fought Alone: A True Story of a Modern American Hero*. Philadelphia: J.B. Lippincott Co., 1963.

Kelly, Carol Adele, ed. *Voices of My Comrades: America's Reserve Officers Remember World War II*. New York: Fordham University Press, 2007.

Kennedy, David M. *Freedom from Fear: The American People in Depression and War, 1929–1945*. New York: Oxford University Press, 1999.

Kerr, E. Bartlett. *Surrender and Survival: The Experience of American POWs in the Pacific, 1941–1945*. New York: William Morrow and Co., 1985.

Knox, Donald. *Death March: The Survivors of Bataan*. New York: Harcourt Brace Jovanovich, 1981.

LaFeber, Walter. *The New Empire: An Interpretation of American Expansion, 1860–1898*. Ithaca, NY: Cornell University Press, 1963.

Lee, Clark. *They Call It Pacific: An Eye-Witness Story of Our War Against Japan from Bataan to the Solomons*. New York: Viking Press, 1943.

Leffler, Hugh T. *History of North Carolina: Family and Personal History*. Vol. 3. New York: Lewis Historical Publishing Co., 1956.

Lehigh University. *The Epitome*. Vol. 46. Bethlehem, PA: Lehigh University Junior Class, 1922.

Leuchtenburg, William E. *Franklin D. Roosevelt and the New Deal, 1932–1940*. New York: Harper and Row, Publishers, 1963.

Leutze, James A. *A Different Kind of Victory: A Biography of Admiral Thomas C. Hart*. Annapolis, MD: Naval Institute Press, 1981.

Levine, Alan J. *Captivity, Flight, and Survival in World War II*. Westport, CT: Praeger, 2000.

Lukacs, John D. *Escape from Davao: The Forgotten Story of the Most Daring Prison Break of the Pacific War*. New York: Simon and Schuster, 2010.

Lundstrom, John B. *The First Team and the Guadalcanal Campaign: Naval Fighter Combat from August to November 1942*. Annapolis, MD: Naval Institute Press, 1994.

MacArthur, Brian. *Surviving the Sword: Prisoners of the Japanese in the Far East, 1942–45*. New York: Random House, 2005.

Manchester, William. *American Caesar: Douglas MacArthur, 1880–1964*. Boston: Little, Brown and Co., 1978.

Martin, Adrian R., and Larry W. Stephenson. *Operation Plum: The Ill-fated 27th Bombardment Group and the Fight for the Western Pacific*. College Station: Texas A&M University Press, 2008.

Masuda, Hiroshi. *MacArthur in Asia: The General and His Staff in the Philippines, Japan, and Korea*. Translated by Reiko Yamamoto. Ithaca, NY: Cornell University Press, 2009.

Michno, Gregory F. *Death on the Hellships: Prisoners at Sea in the Pacific War*. Annapolis, MD: Naval Institute Press, 2001.

Miller, Edward S. *War Plan Orange: The U.S. Strategy to Defeat Japan, 1897–1945*. Annapolis, MD: Naval Institute Press, 1991.

Millett, Allan R., and Peter Maslowski. *For the Common Defense: A Military History of the United States of America*. New York: The Free Press, 1994.

Morison, Samuel Eliot. *Leyte: June 1944–January 1945*. Vol. 12 of *History of United States Naval Operations in World War II*. Boston: Little, Brown and Co., 1958.

———. *The Liberation of the Philippines: Luzon, Mindanao, the Visayas, 1944–1945*. Vol. 13 of *History of United States Naval Operations in World War II*. Boston: Little, Brown and Co., 1959.

———. *The Rising Sun in the Pacific, 1931–April 1942*. Vol. 3 of *History of United States Naval Operations in World War II*. Boston: Little, Brown and Co., 1948.

———. *The Two-Ocean War: A Short History of the United States Navy in the Second World War*. Boston: Little, Brown and Co., 1963.

Murray, Williamson, and Allan R. Millett. *A War to Be Won: Fighting the Second World War*. Cambridge, MA: Belknap Press of Harvard University Press, 2000.

Norling, Bernard. *The Intrepid Guerrillas of North Luzon*. Lexington: University of Kentucky Press, 1999.

Norman, Elizabeth M. *We Band of Angels: The Untold Story of American Nurses Trapped on Bataan by the Japanese*. New York: Random House, 1999.

Norman, Michael, and Elizabeth M. Norman. *Tears in the Darkness: The Story of the Bataan Death March and its Aftermath*. New York: Picador, 2009.

North Carolina State College. *Agromeck 1938*. Raleigh: North Carolina State College, 1938.

Olson, John E. *O'Donnell: Andersonville of the Pacific*. Lake Quivira, KS: John E. Olson, 1985.

Paret, Peter, ed. *Makers of Modern Strategy from Machiavelli to the Nuclear Age*. Princeton, NJ: Princeton University Press, 1986.

Parkinson, James W., and Lee Benson. *Soldier Slaves: Abandoned by the White House, Courts, and Congress*. Annapolis, MD: Naval Institute Press, 2006.

Peattie, Mark R. *Sunburst: The Rise of Japanese Naval Air Power, 1909–1941*. Annapolis, MD: Naval Institute Press, 2001.

Pleasants, Julian M. *Buncombe Bob: The Life and Times of Robert Rice Reynolds*. Chapel Hill: University of North Carolina Press, 2000.

Powell, William S. ed. *North Carolina Lives: The Tar Heel Who's Who*. Hopkinsville, KY: Historical Record Association, 1962.

Rees, Laurence. *Horror in the East: Japan and the Atrocities of World War II*. Cambridge, MA: Da Capo Press, 2002.

Rogers, Paul P. *The Bitter Years: MacArthur and Sutherland*. New York: Praeger, 1990.

Roper, Richard S. *Brothers of Paul: Activities of Prisoner of War Chaplains in the Philippines During WWII*. Odenton, MD: Revere Printing, 2003.

Sarnecky, Mary T. *A History of the U.S. Army Nurse Corps*. Philadelphia: University of Pennsylvania Press, 1999.

Schaefer, Chris. *Bataan Diary: An American Family in World War II, 1941–1945*. Houston: Riverview Publishing, 2004.

Sides, Hampton. *Ghost Soldiers: The Forgotten Epic Story of World War II's Most Dramatic Mission*. New York: Doubleday, 2001.

Sienkiewicz, Henryk. *Quo Vadis: A Narrative of the Time of Nero*. Translated by Jeremiah Curtin. Boston: Little, Brown and Co., 1896.

Sloan, Bill. *Undefeated: America's Heroic Fight for Bataan and Corregidor*. New York: Simon and Schuster, 2012.

Smethurst, Richard J. *A Social Basis for Prewar Japanese Militarism: The Army and the Rural Community*. Berkeley: University of California Press, 1974.

Smith, George W. *MacArthur's Escape: John "Wild Man" Buckeley and the Rescue of an American Hero*. St. Paul, MN: Zenith Press, 2005.

Spector, Ronald H. *Eagle Against the Sun: The American War with Japan*. New York: The Free Press, 1985.

Steinberg, David Joel. *Philippine Collaboration in World War II*. Ann Arbor: University of Michigan Press, 1967.

Stetz, Margaret, and Bonnie B.C. Oh, eds. *Legacies of the Comfort Women of World War II*. Armonk: M.E. Sharpe, 2001.

Stoler, Mark A. *Allies and Adversaries: The Joint Chiefs of Staff, The Grand Alliance, and U.S. Strategy in World War II*. Chapel Hill: University of North Carolina Press, 2000.

Tanaka, Yuki. *Hidden Horrors: Japanese War Crimes in World War II*. Boulder, CO: Westview Press, 1996.

———. *Japan's Comfort Women: Sexual Slavery and Prostitution During World War II and the U.S. Occupation*. New York: Routledge, 2002.

Toland, John. *But Not in Shame: The Six Months After Pearl Harbor*. New York: Random House, 1961.

———. *The Rising Sun: The Decline and Fall of the Japanese Empire, 1936–1945*. New York: Random House, 1970.

Towle, Philip, Margaret Kosuge, and Yoichi Kibata, eds. *Japanese Prisoners of War*. New York: Hambledon and London, 2000.

United States Military Academy, Class of 1928. *The Howitzer: The Annual of the United States Corps of Cadets*. Rochester, NY: DuBois Press, 1928.

Van der vat, Dan. *The Pacific Campaign: The U.S.-Japanese Naval War, 1941–1945*. New York: Simon and Schuster, 1991.

Vance, Jonathan F., ed. *Encyclopedia of Prisoners of War and Internment*. Denver, CO: ABC-CLIO, 2000.

Wagner, Dorothy. *Recipes Out of Bilibid, Collected by Col. H.C. Fowler, U.S.A.* New York: George W. Stewart, 1946.

Waterford, Van. *Prisoners of the Japanese in World War II: Statistical History, Personal Narratives and Memorials Concerning POWs in Camps and on Hellships, Civilian Internees, Asian Slave Laborers and Others Captured in the Pacific Theater*. Jefferson, NC: McFarland and Co., 1994.

Weigley, Russell F. *The American Way of War: A History of United States Military Strategy and Policy*. Bloomington: Indiana University Press, 1977.

Weinberg, Gerhard L. *A World at Arms: A Global History of World War II.* New York: Cambridge University Press, 1994.

Whitman, John W. *Bataan: Our Last Ditch: The Bataan Campaign, 1942.* New York: Hippocrene Books, 1990.

Wilkinson, Rupert. *Surviving a Japanese Internment Camp: Life and Liberation at Santo Tomás, Manila, in World War II.* Jefferson, NC: McFarland and Co., 2014.

Williford, Glen M. *Racing the Sunrise: Reinforcing America's Pacific Outposts, 1941–1942.* Annapolis, MD: Naval Institute Press, 2010.

Young, Donald J. *The Battle of Bataan: A Complete History*. 2d ed. Jefferson, NC: McFarland and Co., 2009.

Zaide, Gregorio F. and Sonia M. Zaide. *Jose Rizal: Life, Works and Writings of a Genius, Writer, Scientist and National Hero*. Quezon City, Philippines: All-Nations Publishing Co., 1999.

Zephaniah, John Holwell. *A Genuine Narrative of the Deplorable Deaths of the English Gentlemen, and Others, who were Suffocated in the Black-Hole in Fort-William, at Calcutta, in the Kingdom of Bengal; in the Night succeeding the 20th Day of June, 1756*. London: A Millar, 1758.

Index

Page numbers in italics refer to illustrations.